CLARENDON LAW SERIES

Edited by

H. L. A. HART

CLARENDON LAW SERIES

———

CONSTITUTIONAL THEORY

BY

GEOFFREY MARSHALL

Fellow of The Queen's College, Oxford

OXFORD
AT THE CLARENDON PRESS
1971

Oxford University Press, Ely House, London W. 1

GLASGOW NEW YORK TORONTO MELBOURNE WELLINGTON
CAPE TOWN SALISBURY IBADAN NAIROBI DAR ES SALAAM LUSAKA ADDIS ABABA
BOMBAY CALCUTTA MADRAS KARACHI LAHORE DACCA
KUALA LUMPUR SINGAPORE HONG KONG TOKYO

PRINTED IN GREAT BRITAIN
AT THE UNIVERSITY PRESS, OXFORD
BY VIVIAN RIDLER
PRINTER TO THE UNIVERSITY

'You are then, to conceive the constitution in the formal sense as the nucleus of a set of ideas. Surrounding this and overlapping it to a greater or less extent is constitutional law.... . Outside this finally, but interpenetrating it and underlying it is constitutional theory, which may be defined as the sum total of ideas of some historical standing as to what the constitution is or ought to be. Some of these ideas do actually appear more or less clearly in the written instrument itself . . . others tend toward solidification in the less fluid mass of constitutional law; and still others remain in a more or less rarified or gaseous state, the raw materials, nevertheless, from which national policy is wrought.'

EDWARD S. CORWIN

American Constitutional History (1964)

PREFACE

I HAVE tried in this book to sketch out some of the basic questions that face students of constitutional government, whether they start from the political scientist's or the lawyer's viewpoint. On all these topics there is a great deal more to be said and most of them need a book to themselves. Issues such as sovereignty and constitutional amendment border on questions about the nature of law and legal systems that are properly the concern of jurisprudence and political philosophy. Other topics such as executive immunities and public order merge rapidly into detailed and difficult questions of English, American, and Commonwealth constitutional law. Despite its appearance in august legal company in the Clarendon series, this is a political scientist's and not a lawyer's book and I have been very conscious that it involves expeditions into areas where one must tread carefully, hoping for the best and seeking forgiveness for error.

Part of Chapter VII originally appeared in the Yearbook of the American Society for Political and Legal Philosophy, *Nomos IX. Equality* (1967), ed. J. R. Pennock and J. W. Chapman, and is reproduced with grateful acknowledgements to the editors and to the Atherton Press, Inc. of New York.

GEOFFREY MARSHALL

January 1971

CONTENTS

INTRODUCTION

A BOOK about 'constitutional theory' needs some apology. It is not a phrase that is very much used in England and I am not sure that it can be very easily defined. Thirty-odd years ago in the early editions of *The Law and the Constitution* Sir Ivor Jennings spoke of the need for 'a five-volume treatise on constitutional law, which would set out in the first thousand pages the general principles of public law and which would discuss and analyse at length the ideas expressed in the similar works of the great continental authorities and in the books on political science in English'. Not surprisingly nobody has managed to write it; and for constitutional lawyers the books on political science in English must have proved something of a disappointment too.

'Constitutional theory' might perhaps be an apt description of the contents of those first thousand pages of Sir Ivor's imaginary treatise. Much of it would be difficult to distinguish from political theory of a traditional kind. Possibly its scope could be roughly defined as a collection of general ideas about the legislative, executive, and judicial branches of government. Various sorts of generality may be in issue. One general concern is with conceptual or comparative questions about the structure and working of government—for example the uses and implications of ideas such as 'constitution', 'state', 'sovereignty', 'separation of powers', or 'judicial review'. Another sort of generality may be to do with either conceptual or critical questions about the ends or purposes of constitutional government, such as freedom, equality, public order, and the protection of civil rights.

In Britain and the United States the professed aims of government are in principle similar, whilst the organization of the three branches of government designed to further them are characteristically different. As it happens, much of the world's constitution-making has reflected the competing claims of the English concentration of powers and the American separation of powers—one featuring a theory of legislative sovereignty with its ideological roots in Hobbes; the other a doctrine of equal and semi-autonomous authorities, in part derived from the Lockian philosophy of restricted governmental power and natural law. Along with these differences go different roles for the judiciary and different methods of protection for the rights and freedoms of citizens.

Accordingly, Chapters I–IV of what follows deal mainly with the powers and relationships of the three branches of government under the English constitutional system in which the legislature is held to be a supreme or sovereign organ to which the executive and judicial branches are subordinate, and which is not (as matters now stand) subject to any substantive limitations on the ambit of its powers; the freedom and equality of citizens being maintained by legislative restraint and by the impact of political and constitutional conventions.

In Chapters V–VIII civil rights and freedoms are more fully considered, and some comparisons attempted with their protection under the system typified by the American separation of powers. Here citizens' rights are not finally determined by legislative majorities, but in part set out in a formal declaration of rights, and enforced by judicial review of legislative and administrative action. A final chapter considers what many in Anglo-American society have come to think one of the fundamental political and moral rights—the right, when need arises, to disobey oppressive laws and to embark upon civil disobedience.

The use of phrases such as 'constitutionalism', 'due process', 'equality before the law', 'judicial independence', and 'civil liberties', testifies to an overlap both of concepts and purposes between the two systems of government. What these ideas and purposes amount to within each system cannot be fully understood without some appreciation of the manner in which they are conceived and applied outside it. For Englishmen and Americans, at any rate, a glance at these principles is one way of approaching the study of constitutional law properly so-called. It is also possible to believe that constitutional theory has always been, and still is, an important part of political science, since theorizing about government is itself a characteristic piece of political behaviour.

I

THE LAW AND THE CONSTITUTION

We may begin by asking the question: 'What is constitutional law and what part does it play in our constitution?' In fact, as Maitland remarked in *The Constitutional History of England*, 'constitutional law' is scarcely a technical phrase in the law at all. 'I am not aware', he added, 'that it has ever been used in the statute book or that any judge has set himself to define it.'[1] For all that, a procession of writers have thought that the concept needed to be explored and delimited. The difficulties they have seen have been partly practical and partly theoretical. One motive for seeking a definition of constitutional law has been simply to settle conventional questions of usage within the legal system for purposes of exposition—to mark, for example, the boundaries of constitutional and administrative, or public and private law. Another point to the question 'What is constitutional law?' has been to establish or refute the existence of a clear distinction between rules of strict law on the one hand and rules established by political practice or constitutional convention on the other. Much of the criticism and defence of A. V. Dicey's discussion of the topic in his *Introduction to the Study of the Law of the Constitution* was inspired by this motive. But the dispute has merged at times into a more general question about the eligibility of constitutional law to count as positive law in the sense given to that term by Austinian jurisprudence. The points made in John Austin's *Province of Jurisprudence Determined* themselves illustrate this theoretical concern well enough.

1. AUSTIN'S VIEW

'I mean by the expression "constitutional law", Austin said, 'the positive morality or the compound of positive morality and positive law which fixes the constitution or structure of the supreme government—which determines the character of the

---

[1] *The Constitutional History of England* (1908), p. 527.

person or the respective characters of the persons in whom for the time being the sovereignty shall reside.'[1] Since Austin held that laws were commands issued by sovereign bodies, it was for him a necessary implication that constitutional laws which defined the sovereign body could not be positive laws pure and simple. He did believe them to be in part compounded of positive law, however, on the ground that when sovereignty was placed not in a monarch but in a collective body, the particular elements or persons making up the collegiate or collective sovereign might have commands aimed at them and be legally subject to the rules which allotted them their places in the governmental structure. Considered collectively, he suggested the parts and members of the sovereign British Parliament are not subject to positive law. But in their private capacities and as constituent parts of the sovereign, they are so subject. The members of either House of Parliament, he thought, are subject to law, and if, as forming a 'limb of Parliament', they exceeded their constitutional powers—if the King or the Commons pretended to give legal effect to their own proclamations—positive law would render their action illegal. 'The members of a sovereign body, even as members of the body, may be legally bound by laws of which the body is the author . . . a law set by the body to any of its own members is properly a positive law or a law strictly so called although it be imposed upon the obliged party as a member of the body which sets it.'[2]

It is not entirely clear what situation this description is meant to cover. One such situation might be a 'law set by the sovereign body to its members' and to everyone else as well. Members of the legislature are citizens and subject to the law of the land. Another possibility is a statute or sovereign command which regulates the behaviour of members not as citizens at large but as members of the legislature—for example a statute requiring them to take a medical examination or providing pensions for retired or defeated members of the House. This situation merges into a much more important type of rule which governs and defines the participation of legislators in the legislative process itself and in the issuing of sovereign commands. Here it is difficult to see how these rules can be treated as if they were

[1] *The Province of Jurisprudence Determined*, ed. H. L. A. Hart (1954), pp. 258–9.
[2] Ibid., p. 263.

commands of the sovereign body to its own parts. The sovereign body does not prescribe these rules to itself. Rather are they a pre-condition of there being a sovereign body to prescribe anything. It is these rules that 'fix the constitution or structure of the supreme government'. If they are rules of 'positive constitutional morality' they do not become any sort of mixture of law and morality, because in certain other senses members of the supreme legislature can be subject with other citizens to particular laws. So although Austin perhaps gives a mixture of *reasons* for considering constitutional law to be law or morality, his description of it as a mixture or 'compound of positive law and positive morality' is not a happy one.

Austin's discussion could serve as an introduction to a number of questions about constitutional law, both jurisprudential and practical. Even if we reject his imperative theory of law as command, the status as law of at least some of the basic rules which define the activity of the supreme rule-issuing organs of the State will remain problematical. What Professor H. L. A. Hart has called the 'rule of recognition',[1] which defines the conditions under which the rules of a particular system of positive laws are acknowledged to be valid laws, cannot itself be called valid in the same sense as are the rules that derive their validity from it. Such rules—defining for example in Great Britain the legislative competence of the Queen in Parliament, or in the United States the processes by which specified majorities in the Federal Congress and the component states may make and amend existing law—are obviously an important element in constitutional law. But they are obviously not the whole of constitutional law. The practical query which arises from Austin's characterization of constitutional law is whether his delimitation of the field is not too constricting. May it not conveniently include more than the determination of the character of the sovereign and the mode in which its powers are shared and its elements arranged? This was a question that Maitland took up in the concluding section of his *Constitutional History*.

2. MAITLAND'S CRITICISM

A part of Maitland's discussion is in effect a criticism of Austin's notion of the English Sovereign. It was, he thought,

[1] *The Concept of Law* (1961), chap. vi.

an inconvenient consequence of Austin's belief (that the purpose of constitutional law was to define the Sovereign) that all
the law as to the qualifications of members of the House of
Commons would need to be excluded from the ambit of constitutional law, since Austin placed sovereignty not in King,
Lords, and Commons, but in the King, Lords, and the electorate. This, Maitland went on, was in practice inconvenient
and merely served to exclude 'a very great part of what is
ordinarily called constitutional law'. He added: 'Most certainly
any student set to study constitutional law would be ill-advised
if he were to trust that his examiners would not go beyond
Austin's definition. To take one instance, the question whether
the King has power to tax without the consent of Parliament
would be very generally treated as a grave and typical question
of constitutional law, but it does not fall within Austin's
definition.'[1]

The preferences of the Cambridge law examiners may not
in themselves constitute more than a persuasive argument. But
it would not be difficult to add examples to Maitland's list.
All the laws which relate to the liberties of the subject, to
Ministers' powers, and to the duties of the police are usually
thought of as having constitutional importance, but they are not
directly connected with the definition of the Sovereign. We can
agree with Maitland that no easy logical limit can be set to the
labour of the constitutional lawyer. It is perhaps less true now
than in the nineteenth century that parliamentary suffrage is
incomprehensible without a knowledge of the differences between various forms of land tenure—so that 'our whole constitutional law seems at times to be an appendix to the law of
real property'[2]. Nevertheless, any branch of the law, whether
it deals prima facie with finance or crime or local government,
may throw up constitutional questions. Like policy, they are
bred in the interstices of administration. A tax demand, a by-
law, or a trade union regulation can give rise to them as easily
as a statute.

All of these matters Austin would have allotted to the sphere
of administrative law. Constitutional law for him determined
who should bear the sovereignty, whilst administrative law

---

[1] *Constitutional History of England*, pp. 531–2.
[2] Ibid., p. 538.

defined the way in which the powers of sovereignty were to be exercised, either directly by the Sovereign or by those to whom they had been delegated. Of course nothing of fundamental importance hangs upon the fixing of boundaries between constitutional and administrative law. But Austin's demarcation seems at the least inconvenient and places a greater weight on the distinction between 'structure' and 'powers' than the distinction can easily bear when the sovereign legislator is not a monarch or a single ruling-person. This is particularly evident with the structure and powers of a legislative body. Consider, for example, the questions of composition and powers posed by those provisions of the Parliament Acts of 1911 and 1949 that set out the circumstances in which the Lords veto may be overridden by the Commons. Are they a matter of constitutional law, regulating the 'structure' of the sovereign authority, or do they deal with the exercise of 'powers' delegated to the Commons and the Crown?

Of the various motives for raising the question 'What is constitutional law?', Austin's discussion largely exemplifies what one might call the philosophical or jurisprudential motive. Maitland's concern is more with the internal compartmental convenience of the working and teaching lawyer. A third motive, also involving a form of demarcation dispute, appears in the debate brought on by Dicey's attempt to set off the sphere of constitutional law from that of constitutional convention. In effect, this was an essay in regulating not so much the internal business of the law as its frontier with political science, political sociology, and political theory. One might dub it the 'professional motive'.

3. DICEY'S DOCTRINE AND ITS CRITICS

Dicey's attempt to define the business of the constitutional lawyer, so as to distinguish it clearly from that of the historian and political scientist, has not, on the whole, been warmly received. Shortly put, Dicey's thesis was that constitutional law consists only in those rules affecting the structure and powers of government which are enforceable in courts of law. The exclusion of what he described as 'conventional rules' has been strongly criticized by a number of writers, amongst them Sir

Ivor Jennings and Dr. A. L. Goodhart. More recently, it has been claimed that the sharp distinction made by Dicey between legal and conventional rules should be abandoned.[1] The distinction itself, it is added, is a 'dogmatic' one and 'the product of an outmoded jurisprudence'.[2] There is, it seems to be felt, something amiss with Dicey's distinction, which must, on this account, be a less clear one than he supposed.

Prima facie this seems surprising. Fairly clear instances that exemplify the distinction do not seem hard to find. We might consider, for example, the activities of the Crown's servants in Parliament. Some of these are plainly governed by rules of law. The maximum number of office-holders and their maximum tenure of office in the legislature are determined by statute. So are parts of the legislative procedure and, in part, the relationship of one legislative chamber with the other. Other facets of these relationships are not determined by statutory or common law rules at all. But it is, on the whole, clear enough which are and which are not, and there is, on the face of it, nothing particularly dogmatic or Austinian about the distinction between these different situations. It is true that the characterization of constitutional law as including only common law and statutory rules enforceable in the courts may arguably fail to accommodate some marginal cases (for example the rules relating to internal Parliamentary procedure, or to Parliamentary privilege, or to the duties of the Speaker) which at least in part derive from statute but are not in fact enforced in courts of law. Nevertheless, it is a matter of law not convention that this is so. The law simply gives conclusive effect to certain parliamentary transactions. These instances do not in themselves suggest that the distinction between law and convention is vague or unclear, any more than do the provisions in statutes conferring conclusive powers of determination in certain spheres on Ministers and effectively ousting judicial review. All such provisions, like the rules of Parliamentary privilege, are subject to judicial interpretation and the law effectively determines what rule-making decisions can be made in these spheres. And certainly decisions made by the Speaker or by Ministers are backed by legal sanctions if disobedience to them should occur.

[1] Geoffrey Wilson, *Cases and Materials on Constitutional and Administrative Law* (1966), p. v.   [2] Loc. cit.

Again, it may be true that Dicey's suggestion about the connection between obedience to convention and obedience to law is unsound. (He argued that conventions were obeyed because breach of them led eventually to breaches of law.) But that mistake has nothing to do with any blurring of the boundary line between convention and law. One might indeed wonder why the distinction between law and non-law in the constitutional field should be any mistier than it is outside it. Courts very frequently decide what is and what is not law without being accused either of dogmatism or Austinian fallacies.

Much of the criticism levelled at Dicey seems, in fact, to have concentrated either on deficiencies in his analysis of the reasons for obedience to conventions which are unconnected with the law–convention distinction itself, or on issues such as the marginal vagueness of the word 'court'. We might perhaps concede that rules enforced by administrative tribunals, or rules of privilege enforced by the High Court of Parliament or one of its elements, are not rules enforced by 'courts of law'. In that event some parts of administrative law and the law and custom of Parliament may be put in a special category. But this hardly strikes at the root of Dicey's distinction between rules of law and rules of political morality or conventions.

It is worth noting that Dicey himself, perhaps confusingly, did remark that 'constitutional law' customarily does include conventional rules and that it is the phrase 'law of the constitution' to which he attaches his stricter definition. He also admitted that it was legitimate for a constitutional lawyer to demonstrate the connection between the habits and conventions of political life and the rules of constitutional law. Indeed, he himself set an example; but possibly he spoke a little over-dramatically when he suggested that political conventions were not the lawyer's real concern and that they 'need trouble no lawyer or the class of any professor of law'.[1]

Attacks on the 'separation of law and politics'—like attacks on the 'separation of law and morals'—have often failed to distinguish between different sorts of connection between the one and the other. There are, of course, many similarities, connections, and intersections between legal and conventional rules of constitutional behaviour. They often cover in different ways

[1] *Law of the Constitution,* 10th edn. (1959), p. 31.

the same subject-matter. One, on occasion, may nullify the other or be thought more important. There is, for example, both a legal and a conventional rule about the Crown's assent to legislation. The conventional rule is more important than the legal rule, but it in no way follows from this that they are indistinct or indistinguishable from each other. Again, it may be the case that legal and conventional rules are obeyed for the same kinds of reasons, or that positive law presupposes the existence of conventions; or that its form is influenced by existing conventions; or that conventions are treated as appropriate objects of judicial notice; or that the purpose of some laws is difficult to understand without knowledge of relevant associated conventions. But none of these assertions entails the conclusion (suggested, for example, by Sir Ivor Jennings) that conventions 'are rules whose nature does not differ fundamentally from that of the positive law of England'.[1] A large part of Sir Ivor's supporting argument against Dicey's 'separation of law and convention' is directed towards indicating the existence of various types of connection between the two. It is urged, for example, that 'without the conventions, the legislation and even the case law are quite unintelligible'. The two cannot be separated because conventions 'are not politics save in the sense that all law and all government are politics'.[2] But might not these propositions perhaps mislead us as much as Dicey's, and even possibly more so? One reason for not lumping together law and convention is that conventions differ very greatly amongst themselves. On one flank they slide into precepts and usages having little prescriptive force, which are very different from laws and which are frequently broken or ignored without penalty and almost without comment. (The principle that the Foreign Secretary should be a member of the House of Commons might be offered as an example.) No one really knows where the boundaries of convention lie and though there are some few conventions that are as firm, clear, and compulsive as laws, there are not very many of them. (The rights of Ministers to exercise the various legal prerogatives of the Crown are the main examples.) Even conventions that are well established in principle, such as the rules about collective and indivi-

---

[1] *The Law and the Constitution*, 5th edn. (1959), p. 74.
[2] Loc. cit. Cf. Jennings, *Cabinet Government*, 3rd edn., chap. 1.

dual ministerial responsibility, or about Cabinet secrecy, are vague in application. Their meaning is open to continuous argument. The arguments are hardly ever conclusively resolved, and the processes by which they are carried on are not in the least like litigation.

The assertion that the law of the constitution standing alone is unintelligible also contains an element of exaggeration. Not all of the law affecting matters of State is incomprehensible as it stands. Most of the contents of the section on constitutional law in Halisbury's *Laws of England* consist of what Dicey would have called 'the law of the constitution' and much of it is intelligible, though no one obviously would consult it as a complete guide to the governance of England.

At one point Sir Ivor Jennings remarks: 'It is a singular constitutional law which mentions the Cabinet because it is referred to in the Ministers of the Crown Act, 1937, but cannot say what it does. . . . It is a constitutional law which says very little about the constitution. It is not a system at all but a mass of disconnected rules depending upon historical accidents.'[1] But what follows from this? That English constitutional law (perhaps unfortunately) is not as rationally organized as it might have been, may suggest the need for codification or further enactments. But it does not provide an argument for the agglomeration of what is now law and what is now convention. English constitutional law may well be a singular constitutional law and if it tells us little about the constitution, we need hardly be surprised. On any account the constitution or system of government of a country is a wider concept than the law of the constitution. That was precisely Dicey's starting-point.

Others have criticized Dicey on the apparent ground that his principle deflates the importance and interest of constitutional law. His emphasis on the enforcement of legal rules in the courts, Dr. A. L. Goodhart has written, 'implies that the most interesting and probably the most important parts of the British system of Government fall outside the field of constitutional law'. But need anyone be depressed by that? Dr. Goodhart went on to propose that constitutional law should be held to consist in 'those rules of conduct governing the exercise of official (or State) power which are recognised as obligatory by the

[1] *The Law and the Constitution*, pp. 70–1.

legislative, executive or judicial organs of the State'.[1] The disadvantage of such a formulation is its evident imprecision. It is not known which rules are regarded as obligatory, or in what form many of the allegedly obligatory rules should be stated. A continuous process of sociological inquiry would be necessary to determine what feelings or beliefs about obligation existed, and this is not an obviously appropriate task for a constitutional lawyer.

The difficulty is acknowledged by Professor J. D. B. Mitchell. For conventions to be regarded as being of the same nature as law, he writes, 'it is necessary that conventions should be distinguished from mere practices'.[2] But it is doubtful if there is any area in which this can be done. Though past practices and usages can be cited, it would be almost impossible, for example, to state exactly the agreed conventional rule which now governs the right of a Prime Minister or Cabinet to require a dissolution of Parliament. It is equally difficult to separate binding convention from debatable practice when questions arise about the accountability of Ministers to the House of Commons. Often —as with the doctrine of the Mandate—different principles or supposed conventions conflict. Sometimes—as with the rights of the Parliamentary Opposition—some single vague principle is widely acknowledged, but on a plane which is so general that few issues which actually arise are ever settled by it. There seems little to be gained by insisting that the rules of political behaviour that are observed in these matters are fundamentally of the same nature as rules of law.

To defend Dicey's delimitation of the sphere of constitutional law is not of course to deny that its study is best carried on (as Dicey's was) in conjunction with what he called 'the facts of constitutional government'. Naturally enough, a simple diet of judicial decisions, statutes, and delegated legislation is inadequate nourishment for a constitutional lawyer. Like the historian and political theorist he needs often to straddle but not, for that reason, to blur, the boundary line between law and politics.

[1] 75 L.Q.R. 112.
[2] *Constitutional Law*, 2nd edn. (1968), p. 39.

II

THE STATE, THE CROWN, AND
THE EXECUTIVE

IN most systems of government the executive power and the
State—in at least one of its senses—are synonymous. In the
English system it seems a moot question whether there is any
such notion of the State, or whether it remains 'a person whose
personality our law does not formally or explicitly recognise'.[1]
Certainly neither legal nor political theorists have shown much
inclination to handle the term or the ideas it represents. Plura-
lists such as Harold Laski and G. D. H. Cole did, perhaps, make
some use of the notion of the State in attacking its sovereignty
or pre-eminence and in supporting group interests such as
those of trade unions or churches. But more recently political
philosophers at least have paid little attention to these issues
and have sometimes given the State fairly summary treatment,
or discussed it mainly as a potential source of unnecessary onto-
logical puzzlement. In his *Vocabulary of Politics*, for example,
T. D. Weldon set out to show that questions asked about 'the
State' were often unprofitable or misleading. 'The confident
and uncritical way in which "the State" is used by modern
writers suggests [he wrote] that "state" is the same sort of word
as "water", "mountain" or "sun".'[2] One interesting feature of
Weldon's discussion was that when he came to illustrate the
way in which sentences about states are normally used, the
sense that he gave to the term 'state' was plainly not that which
has been most troublesome in constitutional and political theory.
Weldon's interest here was in the State as an international
entity. His argument was that whether something was or was
not a state was a question to be resolved by a simple and
unmysterious procedure. Moreover, there was, he suggested,
nothing unique, extraordinary, or problematical about the association of people in states as compared with their association

---

[1] F. W. Maitland, 'The Crown as Corporation', *Selected Essays*, ed. Hazeltine,
Lapsley, and Winfield (1936), p. 104.   [2] *The Vocabulary of Politics*, pp. 46–50.

in churches, trade unions, or cricket clubs. He concluded that more or less everyone knows how to use the word 'state' in ordinary speech. It has, allegedly, on the one hand a vague but convenient ordinary use and on the other hand a precise technical or legal use, and the two should not, he thought, be confused.

It is by no means clear, though, that most people do know exactly how to use the term 'state' in their ordinary or political conversation. Nor is there a single precise technical use. Both the ordinary and the technical senses which appear in Weldon's examples seem to relate to the word 'state' used to mean, roughly speaking, an independent political community amongst other communities—the nation state as a unit in international relations and international law. International lawyers do indeed have tests for distinguishing states in this sense from things which are not states. But this is to ignore the ordinary and technical senses of the term 'state' in its domestic context, where it also has both unclear and overlapping uses. Here there are some questions that are not dispelled or resolved by reminding oneself that the State is not an object or a real essence. For example, we[1] imprison those who act for purposes contrary to the interests of 'the State'.[2] So its nature, characteristics, and interests must be of some practical as well as theoretical importance to us.

I. SENSES OF 'STATE'

The sense given to what is referred to as 'the State' when the term is used by citizens or moralists is at least roughly that which it is given by lawyers. It refers to some or all of the legal administrative or legislative institutions operating in a community. A work with the title 'The State and the Individual' might consist exclusively of moral judgments but the choice of the word 'state' would suggest that it dealt with the impact on the individual of legal and constitutional rules or institutions. If it dealt with non-legal sanctions or pressures most people would admit that its title was inept and that it might more

---

[1] One of the synonyms for the term under discussion.

[2] Official Secrets Act, 1911, s. 1; see *Chandler* v. *Director of Public Prosecutions*, [1964] A.C. 763.

properly be called 'Society and the Individual' or 'The Social (or General, or Collective, or Public) Interest and the Individual'.

Yet, paradoxically, although 'state' is in common use in political theory and jurisprudence, its technical status in the actual fabric of English law is notoriously uncertain. The Crown is known to the law. The Crown's servants and advisers in Parliament assembled are known to the law. But the State, on the face of it, seems to be missing. 'We cannot', Maitland said, 'get on without the State or the Nation or the Commonwealth or the Public or some similar entity and yet that is what we are professing to do.'[1]

Perhaps this explains in part why little seems to have been written in English about the development of 'the State' in this sense as a governmental term of art.[2] Just as 'constitution' came to its modern unattached use from an earlier occurrence in such phrases as 'constitution of government', 'state' seems to emerge in an uncertain way at an uncertain point in time from expressions such as 'state of the realm' and is used in a range of senses covering the ideas of 'status', 'condition', 'pomp', 'rank', and 'order'. The Act of Supremacy of 1558 was enacted 'for restoring to the Crown the ancient jurisdiction over the State ecclesiastical and spiritual'. The sense is that of 'order' or 'estate'. Professor G. N. Clark in a paper on 'The Birth of the Dutch Republic' quotes an anonymous author writing about 1626 as alleging that 'the word "State" was learned by our neighbourhood and commerce with the Low Countrys, as if we were, or affected to be governed by States. This the Queen saw and hated.'[3]

The difficulty is to separate three senses of the term 'state'. In the first place it is used, as for example by Blackstone in Book One, chapters 12 and 13 of the *Commentaries*, to contrast 'The Civil State' with the 'Military and Maritime States'. The civil state, estate, order, or condition consists of 'the nobility and commonalty'. Secondly, it may be used as a simple synonym for

---

[1] 'The Crown as Corporation', *Selected Essays* (1936), p. 112.

[2] F. M. Powicke, 'Reflections on the Medieval State', *Transactions of the Royal Historical Society*, 4th series, vol. xix, p. 1, and H. C. Dowdall's article, 'The Word State' (1923), 39 *Law Quarterly Review*, show how difficult it is to be certain of the sense borne at various times by the Latin 'status'.

[3] *Proceedings of the British Academy* (1946), vol. 32, pp. 189, 213.

the nation or people considered as a unit. Thirdly, it may appear in a much more modern sense as standing for either the whole or a part of the machinery of government.[1] Nugent's translation (in 1752) of Burlamaqui's *Principles of Politic Law* contains the first sense, quickly followed by the second and perhaps by even a hint of the third. The civil *state*, it is said, is 'of all human *states* the most perfect and consequently the natural *state* of man'. In a later chapter (entitled 'the essential constitution of states') the State is defined as 'a society by which a multitude of people unite together' and it is then said to be 'considered as a body or as a moral person of which the sovereign is the chief or head'.[2] When Maitland wrote that 'There is wonderfully little of the state in Blackstone's commentaries',[3] it cannot have escaped his eye that in the general way in which it has the sense of 'nation' or 'community' as a whole the word occurs naturally enough. Municipal law is defined as a rule of civil conduct 'prescribed by the supreme power in a state'.[4] A state is 'a collective body composed of a multitude of individuals, united for their safety and convenience and intending to act together as one man'.[5] The State to which Burke refers so freely is a unity or partnership of a similar kind, with an odour of sanctity attached. But neither Burke's nor Blackstone's 'state' seems to be unambiguously thought of as the legal personality of the executive government, or as the collective name for all agencies of governmental power standing over and against the members of the community in their private capacity. The 'supreme executive power of this Kingdom' Blackstone knew to be 'vested by our laws in a single person, the king or queen'. Though Dicey and others emphasized the modifying effect of convention on the law, Maitland was the first to set out the legal and constitutional inconsistencies of this pristine English theory.[6] Executive powers, he pointed out, were frequently

---

[1] With some of the earlier references given in the *O.E.D.* it is not easy to discriminate amongst these possibilities: e.g. 'Gouernance of the commynalty and polytyke state' and 'authoryte upon the hole state' (1538).

[2] Op. cit., p. 25.

[3] *The Crown as Corporation*, p. 113.

[4] *Commentaries on the Laws of England*, 16th edn., bk. 1, p. 46.

[5] Ibid., p. 51.

[6] A bold suggestion was put forward some years ago by Professor D. M. Walker (admittedly a Scotsman) that the British State might in law be considered to be 'a corporation aggregate consisting of all those persons connected with . . . Great

conferred directly on Secretaries of State, or on Ministries or boards. Consequently the theory that executive power is in the King 'is not even true to law. To a very large extent England is now ruled by statutory powers which are not, in any sense, not even as strict matters of law, the powers of the king.'[1]

2. THE KING AND THE CROWN

Maitland described with some suspicion the pressing into service of the notion of the Crown ('a convenient cover for ignorance') to supply the deficiencies of the King as a receptacle for executive authority. 'In the thirteenth century, this golden circlet is beginning to be useful. We first hear talk of it when crimes are committed not only against the King's Peace but also against "his crown and dignity".'[2] But the Crown, Maitland wrote, is strictly 'a chattel, lying in the Tower and partaking of the nature of an heirloom'.[3] 'In fully half the cases in which Sir William Anson writes "Crown" Blackstone would have written "King".'[4] Blackstone's handling of the Crown did not, however, lack ambiguity. To write that the Crown is hereditary and 'descends to the next heir on the death or demise of the last proprietor'[5] fits well enough the notion of a chattel or piece of property, but the assertion that the Crown of England, unlike other regal governments, is not elective is more appropriate, grammatically at least, to the idea of an office. Blackstone certainly speaks of the *King*'s prerogatives but he bisects the King into his two capacities, the personal and political.[6] Against the King in his political capacity time does not run. There is no folly or infirmity in him. He is incapable of either doing or thinking wrong. He is, so the Elizabethan lawyers insisted, both immortal and invisible. This politic sovereign was far removed, Maitland suggested, from the medieval king, who 'was every inch a king but just for that reason he was every inch a man

---

Britain and Northern Ireland by ties of nationality and domicile' with 'a managerial body called the government' ('The Legal Theory of the State' (1955), 65 *Juridical Review* 255 at 288).

[1] '*Constitutional*' *History of England*, p. 415.

[2] Pollock and Maitland, 'The King and the Crown', *The History of English Law* (ed. Milsom, 1968), vol. 1, p. 525.

[3] *The Crown as Corporation*, p. 116.   [4] Loc. cit.

[5] 1 Comm. 191.   [6] Ibid., pp. 105–6.

and you did not talk nonsense about him'. The Athanasian nonsense of the King's two bodies[1] scouted by Maitland is of course distinguishable from the earlier medieval distinctions between the Crown and the King's person,[2] and the surviving notion of treating the Crown as the name of a legally continuing office or corporation sole. This artificial person, at least, seems metaphysically more innocuous and indeed useful. It certainly cannot now be maintained that the Crown 'is not . . . among the persons known to our law unless it is merely another name for the king'.[3] The King in Parliament has, for example, enacted that 'the Crown shall be subject to all those liabilities in tort to which, if *it* were a private person of full age and capacity, it would be subject'.[4] Claims may be enforced, it is added, 'without the fiat of His Majesty'. Clearly it is not the heirloom in the Tower against which proceedings lie under the Act of 1947. And though Maitland doubted whether the Crown could give garden parties, the supposition is no harder to entertain of the Crown than of the Royal Academy or the University of Oxford. Certainly the Foreign Office gives cocktail parties.[5] And though it may remain true that the crown 'by that name never sues, never prosecutes never issues writs or letters-patent', the Crown is said to employ servants,[6] to own estates,[7] and to possess colonies.

Nevertheless, there remain a number of oddities about this development. The Crown lives an uneasy life alongside the King. We are certain that the Sovereign in person marries or abdicates. We are fairly certain that it is Her Majesty who

[1] Which of them owned the Duchy of Lancaster caused some debate. In the *Case of the Duchy of Lancaster* (1 Plowden 213) it was said: 'The King has in him two bodies . . . his body politic is a body that cannot be seen or handled consisting of policy and government and constituted for the direction of the people and the management of the public weal.' The theological analogies and origins of this doctrine of a natural and political (or 'mystical') body are suggested in E. H. Kantorowicz, *The King's Two Bodies: A Study in Medieval Theology* (Princeton, 1957).

[2] Pollock and Maitland, op. cit. Also R. S. Hoyt, *The Royal Demesne in English Constitutional History* (entries in index under 'crown and king, growth of distinction between') and Jollife, *Constitutional History of Medieval England*, pp. 127–8 and 205–6.

[3] Maitland, p. 116. Sir Frederick Pollock thought that 'In England we now say that the Crown is a corporation sole', though he added: 'This is an innovation made in an age of pedantry and seems to be of no real use' (*First Book of Jurisprudence*, pp. 121–2).

[4] Crown Proceedings Act, 1947, s. 1.

[5] Or is it the Government Hospitality Office?

[6] Crown Proceedings Act, 1947, s. 2.   [7] Crown Estates Acts, 1956 and 1961.

assents to legislation and creates peers. There can be little doubt that it is the Queen who dies, though this event is accompanied by what Parliament has called a demise of the Crown. In the earlier statutes passed under this title in 1727 and 1830 the person, the office, and the property are bundled together, since the Acts speak also of the 'demise of his Majesty'. The Act of 1901, however, was passed to ensure that the holding of any office under the Crown 'shall not be affected . . . by the demise of the Crown'. Some sort of continuing artificial office or person seems to be necessary for many purposes. The King's Peace must not die with him, and there is a need for something to which a money claim may adhere when the royal debtor dies.[1] Whether this is because the Crown is, as Maitland preferred, a corporation aggregate with the King at its head, or whether it is the 'parsonified' corporation sole may never need to be resolved, but it certainly appears to be a corporation of some kind.[2] Between the King and the Corporation there can be transactions, as witness the statute 2 Ed. VII c. 37, in which a part of the Isle of Wight was conveyed from one to the other. His Majesty having signified his generous pleasure that on the occasion of his coronation the property in question should become 'part of the public property of the sovereign', it was enacted by the King's most Excellent Majesty (in Parliament) that the estate 'shall by virtue of the Act become vested in His Majesty in right of the Crown'.[3]

Again, it was the Crown, and not King George the Fifth which the Statute of Westminster in 1931 described as 'the symbol of the free association of the members of the British Commonwealth of Nations'. But it does not seem to be to the Crown, or at least not to the Crown alone, that allegiance is due and against which treason can be committed. Coke's report of the decision in *Calvin*'s case[4] records that allegiance is due to the natural person of the King and 'not due to the politic capacity only, that is to his Crown or Kingdom distinct from his natural capacity' (though it is added that the natural person is ever accompanied by the politic capacity). The Treason

---

[1] *In re Mason*, [1928] 1 Ch. 385.

[2] Ibid., p. 401, 'It must I think be taken as established law that the Crown is a corporation', *per* Romer J.

[3] The Osborne Estate Act, 1902. [4] (1608), 7 Co. Rep. 1a.

Statute of 1351 and the British Nationality Act of 1948 speak of 'our Lord the King' and of 'His Majesty'. The oath of allegiance in the latter statute is to 'His Majesty and his heirs and successors according to law'.[1] Treason may be committed by levying war against the King in his Realm or adhering to the King's enemies. Can a corporation have enemies?

The development of independent member states within the Commonwealth, retaining in some cases a common allegiance raised difficult problems of legal unity and indivisibility. But the difficulty must obviously be described as one about the possibilities of dividing up the Crown. The question could hardly be respectfully posed as one about the Queen. Of course, Her Majesty may have a number of jobs, as a man may hold a number of directorships (and nobody raises questions about the indivisibility of company directors). But the Crown is more than a similar-sounding title for a number of disparate organizations. It has provided a working legal personality for Commonwealth and colonial governments, though the process has raised awkward conceptual queries.[2] It once taxed the imagination of Commonwealth lawyers to describe what was happening when the King in Council disallowed an Act passed by the King in a colonial Parliament.[3] Nowadays we can imagine a number of more impossible things than that. Parts, pieces, or segments of the Crown can send diplomatic representatives to each other, and, in some federal Commonwealth countries, fight legal

---

[1] Allegiance has curious characteristics. It is not, for example, created or brought into operation by the process of swearing it, as far as British subjects are concerned. A nineteenth-century humorist once wrote that allegiance had 'something of the nature of portable gas, for it is movable and only lighted up in the bosoms of aliens during their residence in this country, after which it may be turned off or otherwise extinguished'. Not always easily, however, as the outcome of *Joyce* v. *Director of Public Prosecutions*, [1946] A.C. 347 reveals.

[2] For example: 'What is to happen to the royal prerogative in a Dominion if the King goes mad?'—a question raised according to Harold Laski at the 1930 Imperial Conference (*Holmes–Laski Letters*, vol. 2, p. 1286).

[3] And in 1904 Professor W. Harrison Moore wondered whether, if the government of New Zealand were to establish shops in Great Britain to sell New Zealand mutton, they might (as Crown property) enjoy immunity from rates and be carried on under the protection of the prerogative (1904 *Law Quarterly Review* 351, 357 ff.). The problem is not entirely imaginary. Cf. *Reference re Powers of Ottawa and Rockcliffe Park to levy Rates on Foreign Legations and High Commissioners' Residences*, [1943] S.C.R. 208. Land held in Canada on behalf of the Crown in Right of Great Britain has been held exempt from taxation (*Jennings* v. *The Township of Whitby*, [1943] O.W.N. 170). Cf. *Mellinger* v. *New Brunswick Development Corporation* (*The Times* 16.2.71).

THE KING AND THE CROWN

way can be made by the use of the convenient phrase 'The
Crown in right of . . .'. This is made to work; but what does it
mean?

Whatever the theory, the term 'Crown' seems to be preferred
in modern statutes and judicial usage when the Queen's servants are obviously or primarily involved. So it is the prerogatives of the Crown which the Cabinet by convention exercise.
The privilege of withholding documents in the course of judicial
proceedings is described as Crown privilege. It is the Crown
which (in the absence of express enactment) statutes are presumed not to bind. The distinctions between the Queen, the
Crown, and the Queen-in-Parliament are of some relevance
here, since the original justification for this particular immunity
was closely tied to the idea of Blackstone's executive king. When
'the king gives his assent he does not mean to prejudice himself
or to bar himself of his liberty and privileges but he assents that
it shall be law among his subjects'.[1] But in considering whether
'subjects', in the sense of those subject to law, should include
the Crown's servants, officers, and agents, there is no reason
whatever to impute to the Queen-in-Parliament any such
monarchical reluctance to contemplate governmental agencies
being bound by statutes enacted for the general welfare. The
assumption that the legislator cannot mean to prejudice 'himself' obviously offers no satisfactory basis for bringing a Minister,
or the Post Office, or a Regional Hospital Board under the
shield of royal immunity. There must be better reasons for
holding that a government locomotive may exceed a speed
limit;[2] or that a hospital chimney may emit fumes despite the
provisions of the Clean Air Act;[3] or that the Postmaster General

---

[1] *Willion* v. *Berkley*, 1 Plowden 240. The report adds: 'Inasmuch as the Act is
made by the subjects who it is to be presumed would not restrain the King and
also by the King himself who cannot be presumed to mean to restrain himself . . .
the King should be exempted out of the general words of restraint unless here expressly named and restrained.' The theory was not entirely coherent, since there
was also authority for holding that the presumption in favour of the Crown did not
apply where statutes were made 'for the public good'. Since 'every statute must be
supposed to be for the public good' (*Province of Bombay* v. *Municipal Corporation of
Bombay*, [1947] A.C. 58, at p. 63) much might have been made of this useful
exception. But the opportunity seems to have been declined.

[2] *Cooper* v. *Hawkins*, [1904] 2 K.B. 164.

[3] *Nottingham No. 1 Area Regional Management Committee* v. *Owen*, [1958] 1 Q.B. 50.

may authorize tendering arrangements for the supply of tele-
phonic equipment which would otherwise be caught by the
provisions of the Restrictive Trade Practices Act.[1] None of
these consequences provides an argument against the usefulness
of the Crown as a legal concept, or against the usefulness of
executive immunities as such. What they suggest is that the
justification and extent of such exemptions for executive agencies
must involve a theory of public functions and that such a theory
is hindered rather than helped by the notion of the Crown's
exercise of authority being that of a physical person. The most
far-reaching of the implications flowing from this concept—that
the King could not be made subject to process as of right in his
own courts—was of course nullified for most purposes when the
Crown Proceedings Act was passed.[2] But given that some
procedural and substantive immunities are to be retained by
selected public or state officers there remains a serious question
about the proper criterion for deciding which organs of central
and local administration should share the privileged position of
the Crown's servants and officers.[3] The attempt to distinguish
between Crown functions and services of a 'non-governmental'
or 'quasi-governmental' kind carried on under public authority
has produced differences of status which are difficult to justify
on principles of utility or efficiency.

A number of distinctions between the forms assumed by
official activity were made, for example, in *Tamlin* v. *Hannaford*,[4]

---

[1] *In re Telephone Apparatus Manufacturers' Application*, [1963] 1 W.L.R. 463.

[2] Whilst the old rule remained, a plausible conservative argument might be
fashioned from the possibility that nationalization would place all the basic industries in a privileged legal position. In 1935 Mr. A. P. Herbert suggested that if the
monarchy were permitted to survive under a Labour Government with the law as
it then was, 'the citizen will have no effective remedy in tort or contract against
any industry. Have the "Planners" ever considered this point?' (*Uncommon Law*, pp.
295–6). Nationalization as it turned out did not make the publicly owned industries
Crown agencies.

[3] For relatively recent instances of statutes held not to bind the Crown, see
Attorney General v. *Hancock*, [1940] 1 K.B. 427 and *Ministry of Agriculture Fisheries
and Food* v. *Jenkins*, [1963] 2 All E.R. 147. In Commonwealth federal monarchies
problems arise as to whether the Crown in right of one jurisdiction is bound by
legislation enacted in another. See, for example, *In re Silver Brothers Ltd: Attorney
General for Quebec* v. *Attorney General for Canada*, [1932] A.C. 514. (There Lord
Dunedin said: 'It is true that there is only one Crown, but . . . there is a distinction
made between the revenues and property in the Province and the revenues and
property in the Dominion. There are two separate statutory purses.')

[4] [1950] 1 K.B. 18.

when the Transport Commission, as then constituted, was held to possess none of the immunities or privileges of the Crown, though it was added that 'It is of course a *public authority* and its purposes no doubt are *public purposes*, but it is not a government department nor do its powers fall within *the province of govern-ment*'. It is not the case that Crown functions are confined within government departments. Regional Hospital Boards which fall under the shield of the Crown are not government departments. But how is it to be decided whether their activities fall within 'the province of government'? Since this phrase has been seriously used by a number of judges it might be expected to have a fairly precise meaning, but it is not easy to see what the meaning is. In one sense any activity authorized or regulated by statute might be said to be within the province of government. Or one might confine the meaning to that which is actually carried out by government. But 'government' in the technical sense of ministerial department is too narrow, and 'government' in the more general sense of 'administration of the country' is too vague. For some purposes a wider sense may be reasonable and may well have been in mind when the test of 'falling within the province of government' was used in earlier decisions on exemption from rating of premises occupied for public or Crown purposes. Lord Westbury L.C., in *Mersey Docks and Harbour Board* v. *Cameron*,[1] for example, spoke of such services as those 'required and created by the government of the country and . . . therefore to be deemed part of the use and service of the Crown'. It may be noted that tests of this kind led to the inclusion of premises occupied by the police in the category sharing Crown immunity,[2] though for other purposes police services are not those of the Crown and police officers are not Crown servants. In *Pfizer* v. *Ministry of Health*,[3] however, the Court of Appeal accepted the relevance of the rating exemption cases and the 'province of government test', but took advantage of its gener-ality to assert that it could well cover the supplying of medical services. The point at issue was whether the drug tetracycline, when used to treat patients in National Health Service Hospitals,

[1] (1864), 11 H.L. Cas. 443 at 445. On this occasion Blackburn J. spoke of public services as being of the kind that 'fall within the province of government' (ibid. 505).
[2] *Coomber* v. *Justices of Berkshire* (1883), 9 App. Cas. 61.
[3] [1963] 3 W.L.R. 999.

was used 'for the services of the Crown'. Under the Patents Act, 1949, such a use might be made of any patented invention. The plaintiffs, the registered legal owners of the letters patent, were seeking a declaration that the Minister of Health was not empowered to authorize use of the drug under the provisions of the 1949 Act.

Willmer L.J. took a broad view of the functions of government in several senses. In Victorian times, he suggested, the treatment of patients in hospital beds would have been regarded as something quite foreign to such functions. But since then there had been a revolution in political thought. Oddly, perhaps, revolution and privilege went hand in hand. For since the supplying of facilities to the public was, according to modern conceptions, a function of government, they might be considered 'as such, part of the services of the Crown'.[1]

In the House of Lords, this conclusion was upheld on narrower grounds[2] and 'Crown services' was given a more restricted interpretation than that arrived at in the rating exemption cases. The National Health Service Act certainly indicates that Hospital Boards and Management Committees act on behalf of the Minister. In this respect there are differences between some of the nationalized undertakings and others. But these differences reflect in part the needs of parliamentary accountability as conceived when the relevant statutes were passed. They do not necessarily furnish us with a rational criterion for deciding the extent and distribution of governmental or 'sovereign' immunity within the province of governmental activity. Consideration of 'the twentieth-century revolution in political thought' may be a possible way of ruling out anachronistic tests, but like the 'province of government' test it is too blunt an instrument to distinguish between the medical facilities provided by the National Health Service and the transport facilities provided by nationalized railways.

3. THE CROWN AND THE PUBLIC

It might perhaps be argued that the Crown as we now understand it should simply be re-christened 'the State' and that the difference between them is now a mere historical technicality.

---

[1] Willmer L.J., [1963] 3 W.L.R. 999 at 1006.   [2] [1965] A.C. 512.

Nevertheless, this solution would have disadvantages. As matters stand, 'state', 'crown', 'government', and 'public' do have different uses, and represent distinctions which it may be useful not to obscure under a single head.

One illustration may be seen in the matter of criminal prosecution. In Britain this has certain, possibly unique, features which stem partly from plurality in the public official personality and exemplify the oddity of our 'State' theory. The term 'public' makes frequent appearances here and it easily lends itself to ambiguity. Maitland, for example, used the phrase 'public prosecution' not as a synonym for 'State prosecution' but to point a contrast with it. Our law, he wrote, has left the prosecution of criminals very much in the hands of the public. 'To speak of the English system as one of *private* prosecutions is misleading. It is we who have *public* prosecutions, for any member of the public may prosecute; abroad they have state prosecutions or official prosecutions.'[1] That the term 'public' can be understood as meaning either 'official' or 'unofficial' shows us that there are at least two 'publics'—one which is 'the people' simply considered, and another which for official purposes takes the people's name (sometimes, they may think, in vain). It is often enough insisted that our prosecution is essentially 'private' or 'in theory private'. In principle anybody (if Scotland is left out of account) may prosecute, and when an information is laid by a police officer, he acts it is said, not by reason of his office but as a private citizen interested in the maintenance of law and order.[2] Perhaps this is one of the harmless official myths of the English way of life and nothing much hangs upon its truth. But it tends to confuse a meaningful distinction between official (or public) and unofficial (or private) action which in some contexts may be important. The theory of private prosecution can hardly, given the modern statute book, stand up with the assurance it might have assumed in the mid nineteenth century. What has it to say for example about prosecutions which follow from offences created by statute, such as obstructing the police,[3] where the police, however interested they may be *qua* citizens in the maintenance of law

[1] *Justice and Police* (1885), p. 141.
[2] Devlin, *The Criminal Prosecution* (1960), p. 17.
[3] Prevention of Crimes Acts, 1871 and 1885. Police Act, 1964, s. 51.

and order, are acting in ways not open to private citizens? Again, under a number of statutes (for example those dealing with Public Order, Official Secrets, and Prevention of Corruption) prosecutions may be brought only by leave of the Attorney-General or, in other cases, of the Director of Public Prosecutions. These are essentially official or 'State prosecutions', as are those proceedings directly initiated on behalf of the Attorney-General. In what capacity are the Law Officers acting in these cases? As representing the Crown or State? In a sense of course. But this again conceals some distinctions. Ministers and their departments also represent the Crown or State. There is a traditional but vague theory to the effect that the Attorney-General is in himself a separate embodiment of justice, or public policy, or Crown policy, detached from such other manifestations of it as are embodied in government or ministerial policy. The theory deserves to be treated with scepticism, but it warns us against too easy an equation of public policy and governmental interest.

The Crown, indeed, plays several roles in the legal process. Maitland's expression was that in criminal proceedings an issue is joined 'between our lady the Queen of the one part and the accused of the other part'.[1] It may seem odd and a little unfair that our sovereign lady is not only a party in litigation but that the courts are her courts and the judges who determine the cause are her own judges. But we see that the principal service rendered by the judges is to the Queen-in-Parliament and not to that Crown element which is a party to the case. Between that element and other parts of the governmental machinery interesting relations may subsist. On an application for *certiorari* (*Rex* v. *Minister of Health; Ex parte Davis*,[2] for example) the Crown appears at the instigation of a subject in the Queen's courts in formal opposition to a Minister of the Crown. A republican translation would be that 'the State seeks justice from the State on behalf of the citizen' (though it might also be suggested that in a utilitarian republic citizens would apply for their own legal remedies and that the prerogative orders would not be amongst them).

Like the Crown, the Public is a complex thing which takes on more than one sort of duty. For one purpose it is simply the

---

[1] *Justice and Police*, p. 140.   [2] [1929] 1 K.B. 619.

Crown. Public prosecutions are undoubtedly Crown prosecutions. But public ownership need not be Crown ownership or ownership in the name of the Crown. Public authority may be wielded by bodies acting on behalf of a Minister but not themselves government or public departments. Official or public status for other purposes may even be given to bodies or persons who are not public or governmental in being either ministerial departments or acting as agents of Ministers. The police, though not agents or servants of the Crown, are persons holding office under Her Majesty.[1] Then there were public authorities within the meaning of the Public Authorities Protection Act, 1893. For this purpose a public authority was defined as a body with public or statutory duties to perform and which carried them out for the benefit of the public.[2] A local authority might be a public authority. Indeed anybody, whatever his status, acting in pursuance or execution of an Act of Parliament might for these purposes be so classified.[3] The Public Bodies (Admission to Meetings) Act, 1960, contains no general definition but refers to 'certain bodies exercising public functions' and lists a collection of local authorities, executive boards, and committees.

Here we see a number of different and overlapping criteria, according to which bodies may for various ends be regarded as in one way or another 'public' and invested with some official right or immunity. One criterion is association or identification with the Crown. A second is the exercise of 'governmental' or national responsibilities. A third is the carrying out of 'statutory' duties or the existence of statutory regulation of the function in question or the expenditure of money raised by rates or taxes. The differences between these criteria show themselves most plainly in what each of them is implicitly contrasted with—i.e. 'non-ministerial', 'non-national', 'non-official'; or 'independent', 'local', and 'private'.

[1] *Lewis* v. *Cattle*, [1938] 2 K.B. 454.
[2] Cf. the Public Bodies (Corrupt Practices) Act, 1889, which refers to bodies having power to act under local government legislation or to administer money raised by rates in pursuance of any public general Act.
[3] A private company has also been held to be a public company since incorporated under a public Act (for purposes of the Larceny Act, 1916) (*R.* v. *Davies*, [1955] 1 Q.B. 71).

4. THE 'STATE' IN THE STATUTES

Despite its ambivalence, the notion of the 'public' does much of the work of providing a receptacle for State authority in England. As a term of art it may have first emerged, Maitland suggested, in connection with financial matters and the National Debt. By the terms of 26 Geo. III c. 62, he pointed out, it was 'the Publick' which stood indebted to the East India Company in a sum of 4 million pounds and more.

The Public seems now even more firmly entrenched in usage. There are Public Accounts and Public Order, a Public Trustee, Public Records, Public Works and Buildings, Public Inquiries, and Public Corporations. Here the various publics are delicately intermingled (as they are in 'public mischief'). In not all cases would a substitution of the adjective 'state' or 'official' be appropriate. Public lavatories and libraries may be provided for from rates and taxes but they are not State institutions. The sense here is obviously that of 'open to the general public'. Some instances are unclear or ambiguous. 'Public Records' (and perhaps with a further contrast implied—'non-confidential') has something of each sense. So has 'Public Inquiry'.

In the sense that Parliament has adopted the relevant terms in legislation it is no longer so obviously true that 'We cannot get along without the State or the Nation or the Commonwealth or the Public . . . and yet that is what we are professing to do'. The Nation as well as the Public is by implication now rather ostentatiously present. It might be thought that the relatively recent political use of phrases such as 'national ownership' and 'nationalization' might have helped the adjectival term on to the statute book. But National Health and the National Coal Board were antedated by many earlier and less controversial enterprises such as National Savings, National Parks, and the National Gallery. The Nation, in addition, is possessed of a Debt and an Anthem. Insurance and military service are national, as was, until recently, assistance to the destitute (though that once used to be public). Sometimes, but on no very clear principle, Her Majesty lends her name. Two of the armed services are Royal[1] and so is the Mail.[2] Customs, Inland

---

[1] Cf. D. M. Walker, op. cit. (p. 16 n. 6 above).

[2] Though some entirely non-official bodies are Royal too—e.g. the Royal Opera House Company.

Revenue, the Stationery Office, the Opposition, and the Secret Service are 'Her Majesty's'.

On the other hand, Broadcasting, Railways, the Air Corporations, and the State Museum and Library are neither 'Royal', nor 'National', nor 'Public', but 'British'. The State Information Office is 'Central' and there is a 'Civic' Trust. The foreigner might well be puzzled by all this. Why, he might wonder, should there be National coal rather than British coal? What distinction might there be between public policy and national policy?[1] Why should there not be a Director of State Prosecutions?

What, in fact, about the State? That, as a legal term of art, is more elusive, though it is not, as sometimes suggested, completely unknown to the law of England. There are many quasi-official references to it. We speak in a general way of State Education and also of State Papers and State Secrets.[2] A series of reports records the proceedings in State Trials. Judges sometimes refer in their decisions, perhaps loosely, to military or civil servants of the Crown as 'State officials'.[3] There are certainly Secretaries and Ministers of State and they have on occasion been able to maintain in the courts that they were engaged in an 'Act of State'. In some phrases, however (such as 'State funeral' or 'State apartments'), the adjective or noun, 'State', is as much connected with the notion of pomp or rank as with the State considered as the official personality of government. And part of the essence of an 'Act of State' is that it is not a defence which is available to Government as against the rights of the general body of British subjects. It is more appropriately thought of as an act of the nation as a whole, outside the realm.

---

[1] National policy is what Ministers of the Crown making non-party-political broadcasts may appeal for the co-operation of the general public in pursuing. It may not (as at a critical stage during the Suez crisis of 1956) exist at all. Government policy, if the government is competent, always exists. There is evidence in the law reports of the existence of public policy in a theoretically frozen but occasionally malleable state.

[2] The Privy Councillors' Report on Security of 1956 (Cmd. 9715) speaks of 'tilting the balance in favour of offering greater protection to the security of the State'.

[3] e.g. *Bombay and Persian Steam Navigation Co.* v. *Maclay*, [1920] 3 K.B. 402 at 406 *per* Rowlatt J. 'If an official of the State does something which if done by anyone else would be a tort . . .'.

Sometimes, too, a common adoption of the term is not reflected by the statute book. Although State Land registration is often described by that name, the Land Registration Act, 1925, refers only to a register of title 'kept at His Majesty's Land Registry'. Nor do the Education Acts speak of 'state education' as distinct from 'a statutory system of education'.[1] However, regulations made by the Minister under s. 100 (1) (c) of the Education Act of 1944 did create 'State Scholarships' —though they were, according to the Act, to be awarded by the Minister and not, it would seem, by the State.

In 1963 the House of Lords in *Chandler* v. *D.P.P.* found it difficult to construe the meaning of 'State' as it occurs in s. 1 of the Official Secrets Act of 1911, which forbids a number of acts when undertaken for a purpose 'prejudicial to the safety or interests of the State'. Lord Reid thought that in this context 'the State' must mean 'the organized community'. It did not mean 'the government', or 'the executive', or 'the majority of the people'.[2] Lord Pearce denied that the interests of the State could mean 'the interests of the amorphous populace without regard to the guiding policies of those in authority'. Lord Devlin thought that a proper interpretation would be 'the organs of government of a national community'. Though there are many organs of government, it meant in the context of the Act, he concluded, 'the Crown', whose definition of its interests, though not in principle irrebuttable, must normally be regarded as conclusive.

One patent and notorious intervention by 'the State' in the lives of Englishmen (and some Scotsmen) occurred initially during and after the First World War. In 1917 Committees were appointed 'to consider the financial aspects of Control and Purchase of the Liquor Trade *by the State*'.[3] The result was the Licensing Act of 1921, which wound up the Liquor Control Board established under the Defence Regulations and provided for the continuance of sale and control through the agency of '*State* Management Districts' in Carlisle, Gretna, Enfield, and Cromarty Firth. So it may well be the case that the only

---

[1] Though there are State Registered Nurses, and s. 7 of the Truck Amendment Act, 1887, speaks of a 'State inspected school'. There is also a reference in the 1924 National Insurance Act (s. 72) to the 'state business' carried on by approved societies.

[2] [1964] A.C. 763 at 790.   [3] 1917–18, Cd. 8619 (italics added).

function which in Britain has been clearly conferred on 'the State' by that name is the management of a certain number of licensed premises.[1]

5. 'STATE', 'GOVERNMENT', AND 'SOVEREIGN'

The variety of nomenclature for State agencies in Britain is, it must be conceded, chaotic, but the distinctions which are represented may well have a positive value. With 'the Crown', 'the public', 'ministers', 'the nation', 'Parliament', and 'the executive', any proposition may be asserted which it is possible to advance in a sentence containing the word 'State', and often with some gain in clarity. It may be true that little harm arises in general conversation from using 'State' as a label for executive, legislative, and judicial institutions, when nothing turns upon the difference between them, or when the context simply demands an uncomplicated distinction between political and private life. But any detailed argument about political institutions requires an awareness of the differences between forms of governmental activity, and the term 'State' in certain contexts can be dangerously misleading. Something of this may be observed in any encyclopedia or dictionary definition of the concept 'State'. The *Encyclopædia Britannica*, for example, asserts that 'the State' may be understood as 'the abstract idea of government in general or the governing authority as opposed to the governed'. The second alternative is the one which principally concerns us. But here the sense of 'governing authority' is either general enough to be replaced by 'the national (or general, or public) interest', or it is precise enough in intention to be better replaced by the relevant technical words (ministers, Cabinet, Parliament, etc.). Its force will depend upon which particular elements of governmental authority—judicial, legislative, or executive—is being opposed to, or contrasted with, individual initiatives or interests. The opposition between *all* political institutions, or unspecified authority and the individual's interest, is not a subject which needs to be pursued very far except by anarchists or social psychologists.

[1] Until 1971, when their intended disposal was announced, there were 173 establishments in Carlisle, 15 in Gretna, and 18 in the Cromarty Firth. Here the term 'public house' enjoyed a pleasing ambiguity.

Indeed, the term 'State' masks a number of necessary distinctions between activities that are in different senses 'official'. This may well have helped to generate confusion in arguments about the subjection of governments to legal liability, and also in some traditional discussions of the doctrine of sovereignty.[1] An example may be taken from Sir William Anson's chapter, 'The Place of Constitutional Law in Jurisprudence'.[2] Public Law, the author remarks, deals with 'rights which *the State* asserts to itself against the citizens and rights which it permits to be exercised against itself'. The meaning of 'itself' here is clearly crucial. In the following paragraphs Anson goes on to define the State as 'the Sovereign body . . . by which rights are *created* and *maintained*, by which the acts or forbearances necessary to their maintenance are habitually enforced'. But this is to use the word 'state' to designate both the body which creates and amends law, and the executive agencies which enforce it. The claim which has sometimes been expressed by saying that 'the State' cannot be subject to the law except by its own consent, rests upon the notion that the State or Sovereign as legislator creates law and is not 'subject to it'. From this assumption the State, considered as the *government or executive* which maintains and enforces law, ought not, except by confusion of thought, to gain any privilege. Yet the legal doctrine of sovereign immunity from suit has sometimes seemed to involve a running together of the two notions. The entry under 'State' in Jowitt's *Dictionary of English Law*[3] begins by defining the State as 'in its internal relations that part of the sovereign government of a state which is trusted with the executive power'. Since it represents 'the whole state', this body is frequently termed 'the State'. It is then suggested that 'As the State has the power of enforcing the law it cannot be subject to legal duties for otherwise it would have to enforce the law against itself'. There is nothing in the notion of *enforcement* which makes it absurd or impossible for a body to be subject to enforcement procedures if it, like other persons, is subject to rules made by others. It is only if the executive is equated with, or held in some sense to represent, the sovereign rule-making authority that there is any plausibility

[1] See below, pp. 37–40.
[2] *Law and Custom of the Constitution*, 3rd edn., pt. i, chap. 1.
[3] 1959 edn.

in the proposition that 'the State' is beyond the law, except when subjected by its own volition. But why should law-enforcing or governmental agencies have imputed to them this 'sovereign' characteristic, or be thought in Jowitt's words to 'represent' 'the whole state'? A similar argument remained in the eleventh edition of Salmond's *Jurisprudence*.[1] A subject may, it was said, institute proceedings against 'the State'. But the duties which 'the State' recognizes are fulfilled 'of its own free will and unconstrained good pleasure'. For 'the strength of the law is none other than the strength of the state and cannot be turned or used against the state whose strength it is'. In England the existence of the Crown meant that governmental immunity never really needed to be defended by this form of double-counting in which 'State' and 'Government' are used first in a narrow, and then in a much broader sense. The notion of a King's immunity in his own courts rests perhaps more on feudal propriety than on logical necessity. But when the procedural immunity of the Crown attached itself, in the emancipated North American colonies, to authorities that had expelled the Crown in exchange for 'the State', a form of govern-mental immunity found itself supported by arguments about the alleged logical implications of 'State' authority. In 1850 (in *Hill* v. *U.S.*)[2] it was said that 'a sovereign *or a government repre-senting the sovereign* cannot *ex delicto* be amenable to its own creatures or agents employed under its own authority for the fulfilment of its own legitimate ends'. Mr. Justice Holmes compared the claim that the United States might be bound by law without its assent to the raising of one's fist against the sky —an assertedly impotent gesture against the source of energy which permitted the fist to be raised. Since judges were not 'mouthpieces of the infinite' but simply 'directors of a force that comes from the source that gives them their authority',[3] they could not be expected to turn the force against that source. Here, both the legislative source and the privileged executive object is 'the United States'. This merging of sovereign legisla-tive organ and privileged governmental agency can be seen even more clearly in Holmes's dictum that 'a sovereign is

[1] Ed. Glanville Williams (1953), p. 282.
[2] (1850), 50 U.S. 386, 389 (italics added).
[3] *Holmes–Laski Letters*, ed. M. de Wolfe Howe (1953), vol. 2, p. 822.

exempt from suit . . . on the logical and practical ground that
there can be no legal right as against the authority that makes
the law on which the right depends'.[1]

In England, sovereign immunity, whatever its rationale, was
softened by the ability of subjects to pursue claims against
officials and by the practice of the Crown authorizing and consenting to the bringing of a petition of right in appropriate
cases. In the United States

by a magnificent irony this body of doctrine . . . lost one half of its
efficacy. . . . Because the King had been abolished, the courts concluded that where in the past the procedure had been by petition of
right there was now no one authorised to consent to suit! If there was
any successor to the King qua sovereign it was the legislature. It has
taken the state and federal legislatures many years to authorise
suit.[2]

At least a part of the reason for the seductive logic of sovereign
immunity as expressed by Holmes seems to lie in the temptation
that the notion of 'the State' offers to a merging of the ideas of
totality and legislative sovereignty on the one hand, and executive government on the other. In Europe theorists such as
Duguit in *Law and the Modern State* took it as axiomatic that 'the
nation sovereignly organised can do no wrong and escapes
liability'.[3] Krabbe in *The Modern Idea of the State* describes the
State as 'an original source of legal values' which is sovereign
and 'subject to nothing'.[4] To subject official agencies to legal
liability it then becomes necessary to dissect the State into
sovereign and non-sovereign elements, or to find some term for
'the complex public interests' which may be subjected to law
by being 'excluded from the concept of the state'.[4] Thus for
republicans the struggle to subject the executive to law begins
with a conceptual struggle to separate and clarify what the
term 'State' confuses.

[1] *Kawananakoa* v. *Polyblank* (1907), 205, U.S. 349, 353.
[2] Louis L. Jaffe, 'Suits against Governments and Officers: Sovereign Immunity',
77 *Harvard Law Review* 1 and 209 at p. 2. Cf. K. C. Davis, *Administrative Law
Treatise*, vol. iii, p. 436.
[3] Trans. Laski (1921), at p. 200.
[4] Trans. Sabine and Shepard (1930), at p. 232.

III

LEGISLATIVE POWER AND SOVEREIGNTY

SOVEREIGN legislative power, according to traditional doctrine, is 'illimitable, perpetual, and indivisible'. The attribu-
tion to the Queen-in-Parliament of these characteristics has
striking consequences. It means, amongst other things, that
'Parliament can legislate for all persons and all places. If it
enacts that smoking in the streets of Paris is an offence, then it
is an offence.'[1]

Prima facie this is an odd doctrine. In fact sovereign legislative
power, as expounded by Hobbes, Austin, and Dicey, has never
enjoyed universal acceptance or acclaim. It has been attacked
by Whigs, democrats, political philosophers, and academic
lawyers (though the categories are not exclusive). If, as Sir
Ivor Jennings has suggested, theoretical persons of the latter
kind were responsible for importing the sovereignty doctrine
into the common law in the first place,[2] they have certainly
done their best to make amends ever since. Some have assailed
its historical roots. Others have wanted flatly to disown it as
dangerous (without always saying in the clearest way what it
was that ought to be disowned). Others, again, have tried to
disarm and reformulate the theory from within.

I. INDIVISIBILITY AND ILLIMITABILITY OF SOVEREIGNTY

Such reformulation has sometimes aimed at attacking one
attribute of sovereignty by denying another—for example
denying its 'indivisibility' in order to reduce the impact of its
'illimitability'. Dicey's division of Parliamentary sovereignty
into 'legal' and 'political' of course brought this about in some
degree, but his sovereign legislative power remained, as it were,
all of a piece. A priori, however, many types of divisibility of

[1] Sir Ivor Jennings, *The Law and the Constitution*, 5th edn., p. 170.
[2] Ibid., p. 160. But Cambridge academics have been absolved. R. F. V. Heuston,
Essays in Constitutional Law (1961), p. 1 ('The doctrine of parliamentary sovereignty
is almost entirely the work of Oxford men').

legal authority are conceivable. Bertrand de Jouvenel illustrates one sort of division or 'duality' of sovereignty in describing the functionally differentiated sovereigns of Tonga. In Tonga 'a monarch called the Tuitonga was revered. On his appearance all prostrated themselves and kissed his feet. If he took part in a gathering, which he did not do very often, no one dared to sit beside him. If he spoke all listened attentively and when he had finished, cried out as one man "How true!" '[1] For all that, however, this particular sovereign did not rule. His life was spent in meditation, prayer, and ritual, and the reins of government were in the hands of a second monarch, the Tui haatakatana. We can, in other words (as Bentham in his discussion of sovereignty admitted),[2] conceive of a constitution in which authority inheres in different persons or institutions for different purposes. Though there will in most constitutional systems be an amending process and some 'collection' of persons, possibly complex, in whom sovereign authority to alter any legal rule inheres, there is no logical necessity for any such single sovereign amending body to exist at all and, if it does exist, no necessity for its authority to extend to all parts of the constitution. In Germany and India,[3] for example, some constitutional provisions are held to be unamendable.

It is a fact, nevertheless, that constitutions unamendable in all or some respects are non-standard cases and a sovereign entity whether (as in Britain) a simple legislative majority, or a complex specially convened majority can be discovered and labelled 'sovereign' in almost all systems. It is the 'illimitability' of this body which has worried some political theorists, and made them wish to resolve or dissolve what has been described as the 'problem' or 'dilemma' of sovereignty. 'How', it has been asked, for example, 'can a supreme legal authority be legally subject to its own rules?' In 1950 in a well-known article, 'The Theory of Sovereignty Restated',[4] Mr. W. J. Rees proposed

---

[1] *Sovereignty* (1957), p. 98.

[2] *Fragment on Government*, ed. W. Harrison (1948), pp. 98–9. See also H. L. A. Hart, 'Bentham on Sovereignty' (1967), *Irish Jurist* 327.

[3] *Golak Nath* v. *State of Punjab*. A.I.R. 1967, S.C. 1643. Other examples of constitutions containing basic provisions declared to be immune from amendment are the Cyprus Constitution of 1960 and the Greek constitution of 1952.

[4] *Mind*, vol. lix (1950), p. 495. Reprinted in *Philosophy, Politics and Society*, ed. Laslett, p. 56.

a number of reformulations designed to meet this and other difficulties. The argument begins with the assertion that the concept of sovereignty is inapplicable (or perhaps inconvenient) in the face of three phenomena of the modern world—political democracy, federalism, and public law as represented in welfare legislation. On the last point Rees quotes a passage from Duguit's *Law and the Modern State*, in which it is suggested that State intervention in economic life under a system of public law cannot proceed on the basis of sovereign command. There can be no legal binding of a sovereign authority to provide such welfare legislation. Hence, it is urged, sovereign power cannot be permitted to exist. Political theorists have all found it logically necessary, Rees continues, 'either to deny the existence of legal duties on the part of the government so as to be able to maintain its legal sovereignty, as with Austin, or else to deny its legal sovereignty in order to assert its legal duties as with Duguit'.[1] The conceptual source of this difficulty can be exposed and the dilemma removed, Rees argues, if a distinction is made between 'legal' and 'coercive' sovereignty. The question as to how the Sovereign can be subject to its own rules can be answered by saying that rules prescribed by the legal Sovereign to itself may be enforced against itself by the coercive Sovereign (being that power or powers in the State which wields effective force). The legal Sovereign (presumably Parliament) is thus subject to rules in virtue of their *enforcement* by the coercive Sovereign and not in virtue of their *prescription*, 'in which case it is still no less sovereign legally'.[2] It is to be observed, however, that 'subjection' to law is here being used in two different ways. If the legal Sovereign makes rules, and they are validly made, they prescribe for, and legally subject, anyone to whom they are addressed, including the agents of the coercive Sovereign. If, on the other hand, those who have laid down the laws are unwillingly compelled to obey them by the coercive forces of the State they are 'subjected' in a different sense, which has nothing in common with legal 'subjection'. Even on an imperative theory of law according to which issuing a law is, or is analogous to, issuing a command, there is a conceptual gulf between the coercive orders of the police or the commander-in-chief, and legislative commands to subjects. 'Coercive Sovereign' in any

---

[1] Op. cit., ed. Laslett, p. 79.   [2] Loc. cit.

event is an unclear concept. Does it mean any preponderant body of force or only the official and legally authorized forces? If there are no criteria for legitimately exercised force there may well be many potential locations for it and no possibility of identifying a coercive Sovereign or distinguishing it from a private army or a gang of criminals. If one puts aside such notions as a Congo or Algerian situation and makes the assumption that normal chains of command and notions of legitimacy prevail, coercive sovereignty must be located presumably in the leaders of those who are to exercise force in the last resort. But where does this lead? If one assumes that policemen and soldiers obey their superiors, the coercive Sovereign will turn out to be, say, the Secretary of State for War. There is a certain oddity in the image of a Cabinet meeting at which the Secretary of State for War issues the commands of the coercive Sovereign to the Prime Minister and the Foreign Secretary. He could hardly, consistently with his oath of allegiance, issue them to the Crown, or without a breach of privilege, to Parliament. How, moreover, would one describe the situation if the legal or legislative Sovereign were legally to exempt itself or to forbid the coercive Sovereign to enforce any measures against itself? *Ex hypothesi* the coercive Sovereign, though not subject physically or coercively, is prescriptively subject to, and bound by, the legal Sovereign's rules and cannot therefore in its official or legal capacity properly be conceived of as enforcing anything in defiance of those rules. A situation of disobedience or anarchy can hardly be recommended as a form of constitutional guarantee. Yet without disobedience or anarchy, coercion of the presciptive Sovereign, even if it can be imagined, can always be legally forbidden by the exercise of prescriptive sovereignty. In other words, if we are concerned with the physical sense of subjection there is no problem or paradox about 'subjecting' sovereigns. If, on the other hand, we are concerned with the formal or legal sense of 'subjection' the solution suggested here seems one that would not remove the difficulty.

The uncertainty about 'subjection' is part of a wider uncertainty. It springs from the suggestion, already noted, that political theorists have found it necessary 'either to deny the existence of legal duties on the part of the government, so as to be able to maintain its legal sovereignty, as with Austin, or else to deny its legal sovereignty in order to assert its legal duties as with Duguit'. Austin, however, surely did not deny the existence of legal duties on the part of the *Government*, at least not on the part of what we should call the Government. Whether one locates sovereignty with the Queen, the Lords, and the electors, as did Austin, or with the Queen-in-Parliament alone, as did Dicey, the 'Government' is in no sense sovereign, but, except as exempted by common law or statute, is as much subject to law and regulation as private individuals. There is, therefore, no substance in the notion that legislative sovereignty stands in the way of the Government's being bound by Parliament to provide welfare services for the public, or that the sovereignty doctrine is in any way hostile to the Welfare State. Certainly the Government may have legal privileges. Some of them were removed in Britain in 1947 by the Crown Proceedings Act, which subjected the 'Sovereign' (in the sense of Crown or Government) to normal processes of law, but this was itself an illustration that the agencies which provide welfare services may be placed under duties as stringent as Parliament and the electorate conceive necessary. As we have already seen (in discussing executive power and the State) legislative sovereignty is not in any way inconsistent with the idea or existence of either political democracy or governmental accountability, unless we first of all locate sovereignty in 'the State' and then equate 'State' with 'Government'. What legislative sovereignty—at least in some senses—may perhaps be hostile to, or incompatible with, is a *guarantee* that welfare services or public law—or anything else for that matter—will never be tampered with or abolished. That is a genuine problem about the plenary powers of a legislative body or sovereign in a state, but it is not made clearer by talking about the sovereignty of the State, the powers of the State, or allegiance to the State, where 'State' may more appropriately be translated by 'Government', 'Crown', or 'Executive'.

Harold Laski's criticism of 'sovereignty' provides an example in which sovereignty seems to be associated sometimes with 'government' and sometimes with legislative power. In one of his letters to Mr. Justice Holmes Laski wrote: 'I don't want the King in Parliament to be able to suspend Habeas Corpus. I want it to pay if its agents in the admiralty invade a patent granted by the Board of Trade. I don't want the captain of a man of war to be able to evade paying damages if its captain has handled it carelessly.'[1] The last two complaints clearly do not involve the problem of limiting sovereignty in the sense that the first does. Indeed, they require for their remedying an exercise of legislative sovereignty aimed at giving citizens legal rights against governmental officers (the Crown, the 'Sovereign'). Sometimes the target that Laski called 'sovereignty' was the immunity of the Crown: sometimes it seemed to be unjust legislation or unqualified allegiance.[2] Sometimes again it appeared as absolute power and at other times it became the 'Austinian' theory of unlimited legal authority. *The Sovereignty of the State*, an essay first published in 1917,[3] seems open to this criticism. Even in context it is not easy to see what is meant by the expression used in the title or when it refers to legal and when to other forms of power. ('If the state be admitted limitless power' . . . 'The monistic theory of the state, making it sovereign and therefore absolute' . . . 'In the monist theory of the state there seems no guarantee that man will have any being at all.') One who was not impressed by this mode of expression was Sir Frederick Pollock. Laski's Austinianism he thought was 'a figment'.[4]

Pollock himself published in 1890 a volume of lectures, one chapter of which dealt with 'Sovereignty and Legislation'. Like Bryce and Dicey he made a distinction between political and legal supremacy.[5] But unlike Dicey he went on (though without elaborating its implications) directly to a point upon which many recent arguments have turned—namely that supreme

---

[1] *Holmes–Laski Letters*, ed. Mark de Wolfe Howe, vol. 2, p. 832.

[2] 'The individual should refuse submission to the powers that be where he is sincerely convinced that he can do no other . . . Now this is frankly . . . a denial of the sovereignty of the state' ('On the Study of Politics', reprinted in *The Danger of Being a Gentleman* (1940), p. 45).

[3] In *Studies in the Problem of Sovereignty*, pp. 12–25.

[4] *Pollock–Holmes Letters*, vol. 2, p. 25.

[5] Pollock thought, incidentally, that the clear distinctions in English jurisprudence between legal power and political and moral influence had been much aided by the 'single strong and conspicuous part' played by positive law in all public life for centuries. In the German states this was not so, and in the United States, 'in spite of English tradition and communications the bent of modern American publicists appears to be decidedly toward the Continental habit of thought. They believe in the Common Law like English judges of the seventeenth century and in the Law of Nature like German Philosophers' (*History of the Science of Politics*, p. 117).

legal power is in one sense limited by the rules which prescribe how it shall be exercised. Even if no constitutional rule places a limit or boundary to what can be done by sovereign legal authority, the organs which are to exercise it must be delimited and defined by rules. 'Parliament', he says, 'is the supreme power in England.' But what is Parliament? Who is the wielder of sovereign power? The enacting clause of a statute reveals the Sovereign to be made up of three distinct entities. 'They might have been and as a matter of history were near being four.'[1] It is, he adds, part of the positive law of the land that they must all agree if a law is to be made.

There are two points involved here. In the first place Pollock's proposition shows that the relation between the 'illimitability' and 'indivisibility' of sovereignty is more complex than may seem when the Sovereign's authority is pictured as the sovereign 'will' of some single entity or person. An artificial legislative body may be composed of a number of elements— estates of the realm, chambers, human persons, or specified majorities of human persons—which may combine together, and possibly in different ways for different purposes. From this argument a completely fresh analysis of the nature of legal sovereignty may be drawn. Some of its implications may have immediate and practical consequences. The question 'What is Parliament?', for example, became the crucial one in South Africa in 1952, when the claim of a simple majority of legislators to exercise sovereign power was rejected by the Supreme Court.[2]

The second conclusion which can be drawn out of Pollock's brief remark is that the procedure by which law is made, or the elements and majorities which must combine to enact it, may conceivably themselves be altered.[3] If this is possible, special procedures or enhanced majorities for legislation of particular constitutional importance may enable the construction of protections or 'entrenchments' which were previously thought incompatible with the theory of legislative sovereignty, or only possible in systems based upon a separation of powers

[1] *History of the Science of Politics* (1890), p. 107.
[2] *Harris* v. *Minister of the Interior* (1952), (2) S.A. 429 (A.D).
[3] One of the first clear statements of the implications of this is in the appendix on Sovereignty in Sir John Salmond's *Jurisprudence*, 1st edn., 1902—especially at p. 478, 3rd edn.

or a notion of fundamental law, superior in its authority to that of the legislature. As Dicey described sovereignty, such constitutional barriers did indeed appear to be impossible. But Dicey simply implied, without examining, the proposition that authority in a 'sovereign' Parliament must be exercised at all times by a simple majority of legislators, who, since they are unrestricted in their powers, can always repeal any constitutional protections or restrictions on power enacted into law by their predecessors. To do Dicey justice, the Sovereign described in the *Law of the Constitution* is the British Parliament (though he did sometimes speak in terms of sovereigns in general). But even in relation to the British Parliament he did not fully examine the possibility that Parliament as at present constituted might conceivably bind the future or circumscribe the freedom of future legislators, not by laying down blanket prohibitions or attempting to enact a fundamental Bill of Rights, but by using their authority to provide different forms and procedures for legislation. A referendum or a joint sitting, for example, might be prescribed before certain things could be done. Or a two-thirds majority. Or a seventy-five per cent or eighty per cent majority. If it is also provided that any repeal of such provisions should not be by simple majority, the courts may be able to protect the arrangements laid down by declaring in suitable proceedings that any purported repeal by simple majority of a protected provision is *ultra vires* as being not, in the sense required by law, an 'Act of Parliament'. In this finding they would not be in any way derogating from parliamentary sovereignty but protecting Parliament's authority from usurpation by those not entitled for the purpose in hand to exercise it. Thus, for the English lawyer or political theorist, sovereignty may be purged of its dangerous absolutism. He can believe both in an ultimate Sovereign and in the possibility of restraint imposed by law upon the way in which legal power is used. He can believe in the possibility even of a modified Bill of Fundamental Rights grafted into the British constitution—or, to be more accurate, in a relatively fundamental set of provisions in which selected civil liberties are protected from attack in the future by, so to speak, taking out legislative insurance in the present, in the shape of requirements of special procedures or majorities. This would be to do rather more than is done in

Canada's Bill of Rights, which declares certain rights and freedoms to be fundamental, but leaves them open to attack by any future legislation which specifically declares itself to apply, notwithstanding the Bill of Rights.

At least one experiment in entrenchment has been made by a sovereign Parliament. In 1956 the legislature of New Zealand enacted that a number of provisions relating to elections and the parliamentary franchise should not be repealed or amended unless the amending statute were passed by a majority of seventy-five per cent of all the members of the House of Representatives or by a majority of votes cast at a poll of the electors. The Act of 1956 was not itself protected by a similar explicit requirement, though that step was considered.

2. SOVEREIGNTY AND ENTRENCHMENT

Such in outline is what has been called the 'new view'[1] of Parliamentary sovereignty. On this view a sovereign legislature may validly reformulate what shall count as legislation for particular purposes. Unfortunately for the science of politics the 'new view' is far from being a unanimous view. There is no case decided in an English court which can be cited as clearly supporting it. There are cases which, though they may be explained away as irrelevant, appear to tell against it, as do the uncompromising but ambiguous statements of Coke, Blackstone, and Dicey that Parliament cannot 'bind' its successors. The 'new view' may claim to be supported by the authority of Sir Ivor Jennings. On the other hand, it has been roughly treated by Professor H. W. R. Wade.[2] If an inquiring foreigner

[1] Arguments in its favour are to be found in Sir Ivor Jennings, *The Law and the Constitution*, 5th edn., chap. 4 and App. III; R. F. V. Heuston, *Essays in Constitutional Law* (1961), chap. 1; D. V. Cowen, *Parliamentary Sovereignty and the Entrenched Sections of the South Africa Act* (1951); G. Marshall, *Parliamentary Sovereignty and the Commonwealth* (1957), chaps. 2–4; cf. E. C. S. Wade, Introduction to 10th edn. of Dicey's *Introduction to the Study of the Law of the Constitution*, pp. xxxiv–xcvi.

[2] In 'The Legal Basis of Sovereignty' (1955), *Cambridge Law Journal* 172. It is here argued that the ability of Parliament in its present form to legislate both as to substance and as to the manner and form of legislation is a unique rule which is beyond the reach of statute and unchangeable by Parliament. The obedience of the courts to statute is the source of the authority of statute. It is a political fact and until changed by political decision reflects the continuous sovereignty of Parliament, a position which Parliament at any given time has no legal means of changing. Professor Wade's is the most detailed recent examination and defence of what may for convenience be called 'Dicey's theory'.

were at the present time to consult the major textbooks[1] expecting to find some clear and settled view on the first principle of English government, he would probably emerge in a state of confusion. Until fairly recently he would have found Blackstone's and Dicey's remarks, and a handful of dicta about implicit repeal and the conclusiveness of the Parliamentary Roll. Today he would also see discussed some Commonwealth decisions whose implications are uncertain, and a number of speculative conclusions put forward with varying degrees of diffidence.

Disagreement about what is implied by sovereignty springs from more than one source. The problem is complicated by its containing a factual uncertainty about the English legal system wrapped up in a theoretical problem about legal systems in general.

This may be clearer if one considers the various forms of doubt which have been expressed about the new thesis. Professor H. W. R. Wade for example has followed up his earlier vigorous attack by saying (about the view that Parliament may bind its successors as to the manner and form of law-making):
'Granted that this position is *possible* the question is whether it is *probable* in the light of the authorities.'[2] The *possibility* mentioned here is perhaps ambiguous. It could be understood to be simply the possibility of interpreting existing authority in England in favour of the theory under debate. It might, on the other hand, be taken as a reference to the logical possibility of such a theory in any system embodying a sovereign authority. Professor Wade's view is probably that the placing of procedural limitations upon its own actions by a sovereign authority is possible in both these senses, but that such a theory cannot plausibly be inferred from the decisions of English courts. Others, however, have argued that there is an *a priori* impossibility about the notion of sovereign self-limitation, either as to the substance of power or as to making law about the Sovereign's own structure or method of operation. Dicey and Austin, of course, regarded the first kind of limitation—i.e. on the substance of

---

[1] There is an extended account of the legislative supremacy of Parliament in O. Hood Phillips, *Constitutional and Administrative Law*, 4th edn., 1967, chap. 3, but Professor Hood Phillips is not a supporter of revisionist views. Cf. Professor J. D. B. Mitchell, *Constitutional Law*, 2nd edn., chap. 4.

[2] *Law, Opinion and Administration* (O.U.P., 1962), p. 5 (italics added).

power—as a simple contradiction in terms: and so it is. With the second kind of limitation the answer is less easy. In Great Britain it is undoubtedly the law that (in Sir Ivor Jennings's formulation) 'Parliament shall do as it pleases'. This prescription, of course, needs to be elaborated and refined somewhat, and one important uncertainty is whether it should be formulated so as to include the proposition that a simple majority of the legislature may make any law, including a law about the way in which law is to be made, only altering such law, in the manner already laid down. It is clear enough, though perhaps paradoxical, that a legislative authority which exercises 'sovereign' power in terms of a rule of this kind can, by the use of its power, cut down its own freedom to legislate in any particular manner. An alternative basic rule (and one which according to the traditional theory is the one we actually have) would be that legislation by a simple majority of legislators, assented to by the Crown and passed through both Houses, will always make valid law notwithstanding any previous attempt to alter the law about what shall constitute legislation.[1] The contrast between these two notions of sovereignty and the two basic constitutional norms which correspond to them has been marked by Professor H. L. A. Hart by the use of the terms *continuing* and *self-embracing* sovereignty.[2] If sovereign power is thought of as legal omnipotence, both rules assume an odd character. On the one hand, continuing omnipotence can only be guaranteed by making it subject to a paradoxical restriction, limiting its ability to affect its own competence. On the other hand, self-embracing omnipotence may embrace itself in such a way as to bring its omnipotence to an end. There is an analogy with two sorts of divine omnipotence. One might conceive 'on the one hand a God who at every moment of His existence enjoys the same powers, and so is incapable of cutting down those powers, and, on the other a God whose powers include the power to destroy for the future his omnipotence'.[3] However, there is no special necessity to think of sovereign legislative bodies as collective persons at all. If each type of

---

[1] Once the concept of legislation about the manner and form of law-making is admitted for any purpose, the notion of 'implicit repeal' of course becomes question-begging—as indeed does the very word 'legislation', since what is in issue is whether the subsequent operations *are* legislation.

[2] In *The Concept of Law* (1961), p. 146.   [3] Loc. cit.

'sovereignty' is set out in a 'basic norm', or in what Professor
Hart, more euphoniously for the English ear, calls a 'rule of
recognition', we have simply two alternative rules to choose
between, and there is no presumption that the legislative persons who exercise power under them should themselves be
thought of as sovereign, or omnipotent, or absolved from
limitations.

'Self-embracing sovereignty' as a possible rule of recognition
seems, however, to be rejected by some legal theorists on the
ground that a basic constitutional rule cannot contain the conditions relating to its own amendment. In his work *On Law and
Justice*, first translated into English in 1958, the Danish jurist
Alf Ross, for example, argues that the manner in which any
statute or legal norm may be amended must be set out in a
higher norm or rule of law. Consequently it is impossible for
the highest legal norm, or rule of recognition itself, to make any
legal statement about the way in which it may be amended.
The rules for its amendment exist as a 'presupposed ideology'
and if they are altered this is simply a 'social psychological
fact outside the province of legal procedure'.[1] Ross illustrates
this point by taking the rules contained in Article V of the
United States Constitution which provides for amendment of
the constitution, not excluding Article V itself. These embody,
Ross holds, the 'highest ideological presupposition' of the
American legal system and, he maintains, *they cannot be amended*.
Everyone assumes, he writes, that Article V could in fact be
amended by the amendment procedure laid down in that
article itself. But if this took place, he argues, it would be an 'a-
legal fact' and not the creation of law. Using the legal procedure
in this way would, in other words, merely be a way of disguising
a revolutionary act. Politicians are, it is suggested, dominated
by ideas which cannot be expressed rationally, and one of them
is the belief in the 'magical force'[2] of the procedure of Article V.
No norm, it is argued, can determine the conditions for its own
amendment, since 'a reflexivity of this kind is a logical impossibility and is generally recognised as such by logicians'. If

[1] *On Law and Justice*, p. 81.

[2] This phrase should be read with the reservation that it has been a hold-all
form of denunciation used by Scandinavian realists in much the same circumstances as others have used words like 'metaphysical' and 'positivist'. It does not
substantially affect Ross's argument here.

therefore Article V were 'amended' by a procedure in conformity with its own rules it would not be possible to regard the new 'Article V' as 'derived' from the old one. Any such derivation[1] presupposes the validity of the superior norm and thereby the continued 'existence' of it. Since a constitution, like a statute, is unable to state the conditions for its own amendment, Article V cannot logically itself be part of the American constitution at all but must stand on a higher plane.

If these arguments are accepted they appear to throw doubt upon whether 'self-embracing sovereignty', as a legal rule under which law may be used to transform the mode of law-making, is a possibility in any legal system at all. But Ross's argument raises a number of queries. He uses the example of an amendment of the American constitution purporting, with the assent of three-quarters of the states (as required by Article V), to provide that for the future a four-fifths majority of the states should be necessary for constitutional amendment. Such amendment by four-fifths, cannot, he argues, be legally derived from amendment by three-quarters. If, however, such a derivation cannot be made without presupposing the continued validity and existence of the original three-quarters rule it seems equally unclear how the three-quarters constitution amendment rule was derived from the constituent and amending power of the People, as assembled in a Convention or constituent assembly. Would the constitution be violated if an attempt to amend it were made by ignoring its amendment provisions altogether and appealing to the people as constituent power on the ground that the superior norm permitting them to act still exists? If so, can anybody appeal to the people or convene a fresh constituent assembly? May the executive do so? Or any private person? Or should not such a decision be made by majorities sufficient under the existing constitution for its amendment? Is it not possible for a constituent assembly to enact a constitution which can thereafter be amended only by the amendment procedures set out in it? Ross implies that the power of the original assembly or constituent body remains in existence.

---

[1] Is it clear here what meaning is given to 'derive from'? Obviously not a merely historical sense. Compare the ways in which it has been suggested that Commonwealth constitutions which originated in British statutes, but are now independent, have a different 'derivation' and an 'autochthonous' status.

This also appears to have been the view of President De Gaulle in 1962 in seeking to amend the French constitution by popular mandate without regard to the established amendment procedures.[1]

Ross sometimes puts his point in terms of the impossibility of a law providing for its own 'transformation' or including itself or the procedure for law-making which it lays down as one of the things which can be amended under its authority, since this would involve 'reflexivity' or self-reference of a kind which is 'forbidden by logic'. Whether rules about legislation may involve self-reference in the sense under discussion does not seem to be a question to which formal logic offers any simple answer.[2] But not all self-reference involves 'transformation' and it is possible to devise for such a rule as 'X shall have unlimited power, including the power to alter this rule' a substitute that does not involve 'transformation'. We might say 'X shall have unlimited power *until* he declares that his power is limited to Y and thereafter his power shall be limited to Y'. Such a 'phased' rule seems to allow for a rule of recognition that embodies 'self-embracing' sovereigns without being open to suggested difficulties about laws providing for their own transformation.

Of course it is true that any rule of recognition, whatever its form, does in a sense embody 'ideology', and it is (amongst other things) a political fact, or something for which historical or extra-legal explanations can be given. So much indeed was said by Sir John Salmond. The source of the rule that Acts of Parliament have the force of law he wrote, is 'historical only, not legal. It is the law because it is the law and for no other reason that it is possible to take notice of.'[3] To cast this fact into a statement that the basic rule of a system of laws is (only) a political or ideological rule emphasizes in an emphatic way the difference between the most general rule and the rules taking their validity or legality from it. These inferior rules are

---

[1] Questions of this kind have arisen in relation to the amendment of American state constitutions. See Thomas Cooley, *Constitutional Limitations*, 2nd edn., p. 598, and W. W. Willoughby, *The Fundamental Concepts of Public Law* (1924), pp. 94–6.

[2] This point is discussed by H. L. A. Hart, 'Self-Referring Laws', *Festskrift till Karl Olivecrona* (1964), p. 307; and by Ross, 'On Self-Reference and a Puzzle in Constitutional Law', *Mind*, 1969, p. 1.

[3] *Jurisprudence*, 3rd edn., p. 125.

all backed by the authority of more general rules in a way that
the authority-giving rule of recognition itself cannot be. But it
is also useful to be able to apply the term 'legal rule' to all the
rules, including the most general, in a legal system—to distinguish them as rules from the rules of, say, social, political, religious, or sporting systems. So it is a legal rule (though a rather
special one) for those operating the English legal system that the
courts apply Acts of Parliament. That principle is constantly
being applied and if challenged would be held to be part of the
law of England. Similarly it may be felt to be one of the rules
of a game (though a rather special one) that its procedures may
be altered by the governing body,[1] though the statements that
this rule exists and that all the other rules exist can also be
political and factual or sociological statements. It is this that
gives rise to the contrast between 'internal' and 'external'
statements about the ultimate rule of recognition discussed by
Professor Hart in *The Concept of Law*.[2] Of course those who are
internal to the system as well as those who are external to it
can make 'external' or sociological statements about its rules.
If it is insisted that the rule of recognition is 'political', or
'non-legal', and that alteration of the rule of recognition in
accordance with the conditions laid down in it is a 'non-legal',
'political', or 'revolutionary' phenomenon, then a rather special
sense must be given to these words. There is, at least, a characteristically different political phenomenon that occurs when a
change is carried out in open violation of the procedure mentioned in the constitution.

Is there perhaps an argument in favour of 'continuing
sovereignty', and against 'self-embracing sovereignty', in the
fact that the authority of Parliament to legislate about law-
making and the general obedience of the courts to Parliament
has not been established by statute? As Salmond and others
have said, no statute could establish obedience to statute, for
that 'would be to assume and act on the very power to be conferred'.[3] But does it follow that all aspects of this rule cannot

---

[1] Though non-legal codes and rule books often do not include such a provision
as one of the rules. The Highway Code, for example, has no amendment clause,
thus leaving it inexplicit that the powers of the Minister of Transport constitute the
'highest ideological presupposition' of the motorist, rather than one of the rules
governing motoring.

[2] pp. 107–14.   [3] Salmond, *Jurisprudence*, 3rd edn., p. 125.

be altered by statute? On either theory Parliament in some shape will be obeyed. Is it beyond possibility that the interpretive difficulty about the form which judicial obedience should take, might be affected by legislation? Such a possibility once occurred to Lord Morton of Henryton after listening to an address by Sir Owen Dixon (then Chief Justice of the High Court of Australia) on 'The Common Law as an Ultimate Constitutional Foundation'.[1] After all, the judges know nothing (so it is said) of abstract theories of sovereignty. Still less do they reflect about presupposed ideology or the relationships between norms. To them the matter appears as an undisputed doctrine of common law and as a rule about implicit repeal of statutes. What, Lord Morton wondered, would be the effect of a statute in some such form as the following: 'Whereas it is desirable that the legal doctrine X (implicit repeal) should no longer form part of the law of England, the legal doctrine X shall no longer be part of the law and in substitution there shall be instituted in the law of England the following doctrine'? Was that, Lord Morton asked, a statute to which effect should not be given?

There is another matter on which legislation might have significant impact. At the present time considerable uncertainty exists as to the availability and propriety of remedies to restrain the presentation to Parliament, or for the royal assent, of disputed or purported legislative measures. But presumably there could be legislation to resolve the uncertainty. Suppose that Parliament had provided that (say) ratification of the Treaty of Rome should take place only after having received the assent of a two-thirds majority in the House of Commons and of the electorate voting at a referendum. Suppose it also to be provided that any repeal of this provision should equally require approval by the same procedure to have the force of law. If a subsequent attempt were made to ignore these provisions, or to repeal them by simple majority, the two theories of sovereignty would stand clearly opposed. According to the traditional theory the courts would be faced simply with the question which of two statutes takes priority, and with a clear intention of a later sovereign Parliament to repeal earlier provisions. According to the new theory the appropriate questions would be whether the second measure was in law a 'statute'

---

[1] See 31 *Australian Law Journal* 240. Lord Morton's remarks are at p. 250.

and whether 'Parliament' had succeeded in expressing any intention to do anything. There would be also the question of the appropriate remedy, and at what stage the courts might apply it, if at all.

Suppose further, therefore, that in passing the original protective or 'entrenching' legislation Parliament had explicitly provided, in addition to the special majority and referendum procedure, that a court should on application grant an injunction to restrain the further progress of any measure not passed through the Commons with the requisite majority and which purported to be a ratifying or a repealing bill. Alternatively the same method might be adopted to prevent presentation of the measure for the royal assent. Provisions of this kind might be politically denounced as an unprecedented interference with the legislative process[1] and possibly with the privileges of both Houses and the prerogatives of the Crown. But is there any reason to suppose that an Act of Parliament could not authorize such interference? If it could, it would dispose of one present uncertainty about remedies[2] and at the same time prevent the issue from being raised in the shape of a conflict between two purportedly authoritative statutes. For at the time when adjudication was required on a bill introduced into the legislature there would not on any hypothesis be a later Act of Parliament or any question of implicit or explicit repeal by it. The earlier entrenching statute would have no rival. Could it be disregarded?

If the implications of the revised theory of sovereignty are accepted, its precise application and consequences remain unclear. The general argument, briefly put, is that the doctrine

[1] But to call it an interference with the actions of *Parliament* would beg the question in issue. It could be argued that the courts were assisting rather than hindering the proper working of the legislative process by intervention to prevent the submission of invalid material.

[2] The propriety of early intervention by the courts has been debated in Australia in relation to state legislatures. *Hughes and Vale Pty. Ltd.* v. *Gair* (1954), 90 C.L.R. 203: *Clayton* v. *Heffron* (1960), 105 C.L.R. 214 express doubts about the use of injunctions. However, in jurisdictions where there are constitutional requirements affecting the legislative process it is clear that judicial enforcement cannot be ruled out by arguments resting on Parliamentary privilege in its English setting. Cf. *Bribery Commissioner* v. *Ranasinghe*, [1965] A.C. 172 *Harris* v. *Minister of the Interior* (1952), (2) S.A. 429 (n. 5), *Rediffusion (Hong Kong) Ltd.* v. *Attorney-General for Hong Kong*, [1970] A.C. 1136; and Enid Campbell, *Parliamentary Privilege in Australia* (1960), pp. 85-9.

of Parliamentary sovereignty implies merely that no object of
policy is outside the reach of Parliament, but that to achieve
its purposes Parliament must be properly constituted, and the
constitution and procedure of Parliament may be altered in
such a way as to prevent certain objects from being attained
by any except a specified procedure. This view could be stated
in a number of ways. It could be said: 'Parliament cannot
place any blanket *prohibition* on its future action but can place
procedural restrictions[1] on such action.' Alternatively: 'Parliament may do anything, but the rules which define it may be
altered.'

To all this a number of interpretations could be given. Some
possibilities are:

1. That any reformulation or redefinition of the procedure for
   legislating may be regarded as redefining the legislative organs,
   whether its intention is to incorporate special majority provisions
   or to add extra conditions such as referenda or the assent of
   specified bodies external to the legislative chambers.

2. That whilst a general redefinition is possible, special legislative
   requirements for *ad hoc* purposes will not be regarded as a redefinition of the legislative organs competent to legislate for those
   purposes.

3. That whether for general purposes or for single *ad hoc* purposes
   special procedures that relate to the internal working of, or majorities in, the legislative chamber will be regarded as an amended
   definition of the legislative organs, but not if they take the form
   of additional requirements or assents of external parties, whether
   of the electorate as a whole or specifically named bodies.

4. That in any of the above cases the reformulated legislative procedure will be repealable by the original legislative procedure
   unless the revised or 'entrenched' procedure is also specifically
   made applicable to any repeal of the 'entrenching' Act itself.[2]

The difference between these propositions can be illustrated
by a provision in the 1961 Constitution Act of the South African
Republic. Section 114 of the Act provided that Parliament

[1] The distinction is clear in principle but certain procedures (e.g. a 99 per cent
majority requirement) could in substance amount to a prohibition.
[2] The New South Wales entrenchment upheld in *A.G. for New South Wales* v.
Trethowan, [1932] A.C. 526 was of this 'double' variety. New Zealand's 1956 special
majority requirements were not themselves entrenched by any similar procedure.

should not abolish any provincial council, or abridge the powers conferred on provincial councils under section 84 of the Act, except as the result of a petition from the provincial authority. If proposition (3) is acceptable, the Constitution Act could not be regarded as making Provincial Councils a part of 'Parliament' for the purpose of dealing with their powers, or as constituting a redefinition of the meaning of 'Parliament' for the purpose of legislating on that particular subject. Moreover, if proposition (4) is acceptable, the provision could be repealed, either implicitly or explicitly, by the ordinary legislative process, since no attempt was made to protect the guaranteeing provision itself by making provincial council assent necessary for its repeal.[1]

Which propositions, if any, the British courts would accept remains a matter for the future. It has, in fact, never been necessary for a court in this country to decide the points in issue between the older and newer doctrines of Parliamentary supremacy, since Parliament has never attempted to use its authority to regulate the future by an explicit reformulation of legislative procedure accompanied by entrenchment. But the balance of argument seems to favour one form or another of the newer theory. If valid distinctions can be made between substantive limitations on policy on the one hand and reconstitution of structure, and reformulation of procedure on the other, the traditional theses about Parliament's sovereign inability to bind successor Parliaments and about the enforcement of later statutes, at the expense of earlier ones, simply evade the fundamental issues as to the way in which rules defining 'successors', 'Parliament', and 'statute' may be made and altered.

3. THE PRIVY COUNCIL DECISION IN *RANASINGHE*'S CASE

Some fundamental questions about restraints on the manner and form of legislation were faced by the Privy Council in 1964 in *Bribery Commissioner* v. *Ranasinghe*,[2] an appeal from Ceylon.

---

[1] A similar argument might be applied to Section 1 (2) of the Ireland Act, 1949, which provides that 'in no event will Northern Ireland or any part thereof cease to be part of His Majesty's dominions and of the United Kingdom without the consent of the Parliament of Northern Ireland.' Cf. R. F. V. Heuston, *Essays in Constitutional Law*, p. 27.　　　　　[2] [1965] A.C. 172.

Ranasinghe was prosecuted for a bribery offence before a tribunal set up under the Bribery Amendment Act, 1958. The Ceylon Supreme Court quashed the conviction on the ground that the 1958 Act provided for a method of appointing members to the tribunal which was inconsistent with the constitutional provision regulating the appointment of judicial officers laid down in the Constitution Order in Council of 1946.[1] For the Bribery Commissioner it was argued that, if such inconsistency existed, the sovereign Parliament of Ceylon must be held to have amended the constitution by passing the 1958 Act. It was conceded that the Constitution order provided that any such constitutional amendment should require a two-thirds majority of the total membership of the House of Representatives certified by the Speaker. The 1958 Act had not been passed by a two-thirds majority and did not have a Speaker's certificate. It was contended, nevertheless, that the official copy of the Act must be regarded by the courts as conclusive of its validity.

This argument was rejected both by the Supreme Court of Ceylon and by the Privy Council. The latter's judgment was delivered by Lord Pearce. It was true, he suggested, that the English authorities had taken a narrow view of the courts' powers to look behind an authoritative copy of the Act ('All that a court of justice can do is to look to the Parliamentary roll').[2] But that dictum was laid down in a situation where no governing instrument prescribed the law-making powers and the forms essential to them. Where such forms are laid down 'a legislature has no power to ignore the conditions of law-making that are imposed by the instrument which itself regulates its power to make law'.[3] The conclusion was that 'the Speaker's certificate is a necessary part of the legislative process and any bill which does not comply with the condition precedent of the proviso, is and remains, even though it receives the Royal Assent, invalid and ultra vires'.[4]

Lord Pearce cited *Trethowan*'s case as supporting the Board's conclusion that 'where a legislative power is given subject to certain manner and form that power does not exist unless and

---

[1] S. 55 of the Constitutional Order in Council vested the appointment of judicial officers in the Judicial Service Commission.

[2] *Edinburgh Railway Co.* v. *Wauchope* (1842), 8 Cl. & F. 710, 725.

[3] *Bribery Commissioner* v. *Ranasinghe*, [1965] A.C. 172, at p. 197.

[4] Ibid., at p. 200.

until the manner and form is complied with'.[1] A difficulty often expressed about the *Trethowan* decision is that it was not clear how far the propositions laid down were conditioned by the fact that the legislature in question was a subordinate legislature subject to the provisions of the Colonial Laws Validity Acts. In the High Court of Australia it had been suggested by Dixon J. that the conclusion was a more general one, which might conceivably apply to the sovereign Imperial legislature. A manner and form provision enacted in a United Kingdom statute might, he thought, in certain circumstances compel the courts to consider whether the supreme legislative power had been exercised in the manner required for its authentic expression.[2] Lord Pearce in *Ranasinghe* seemed to imply equally that both non-sovereign and sovereign legislatures may be made subject to procedural rules entrenching parts of the law from simple majority repeal. 'The proposition which is not acceptable', he said, 'is that a legislature once established has some inherent power, derived from the mere fact of its establishment, to make a valid law by the resolution of a bare majority which its own constituent instrument has said shall not be a valid law unless made by a different type of majority or by a different legislative process.'[3] 'This restriction exists independently of the question whether the legislature is sovereign as is the legislature of Ceylon or whether the constitution is "uncontrolled" as the Board held the Constitution of Queensland to be' (in *McCawley*'s case).

This and a further passage, of some interest, suggest that the Privy Council decision may be seen as giving support to a general proposition that a legislature is not fettered in its sovereignty when a simple majority is restrained from enacting its will into law:

A Parliament does not cease to be sovereign whenever its component members fail to produce among themselves a requisite majority, e.g. when in the case of ordinary legislation the voting is evenly divided or when in the case of legislation to amend the Constitution there is only a bare majority if the Constitution requires something more. The minority are entitled under the Constitution of Ceylon to have no amendment of it which is not passed by a two-thirds majority. The limitation thus imposed on some lesser majority

[1] Ibid., at p. 199.   [2] (1931), C.L.R. 394, 426.
[3] [1965] A.C. 172 at 198.

of members does not limit the sovereign powers of Parliament itself, which can always, whenever it chooses, pass the amendment with the requisite majority.[1]

It would seem to follow from this that a Parliament which has by its own act imposed procedural conditions upon the legislative process is no more limited, bound, fettered, or non-sovereign than a legislature which has such conditions bequeathed to it in a constitutional instrument. Those who argue that Parliament cannot lay such conditions upon itself, on the ground that Parliament cannot limit or bind itself, are thereby deprived of an argument. If such conditions are not limitations on sovereignty, it cannot be the impossibility of limiting sovereignty which in itself makes entrenchment legally impossible to a sovereign legislator.

What can be certainly inferred from *Ranasinghe* is that a legislature whose constitutional instrument places *procedural* restraints upon the forms of law-making may not ignore them simply because it is sovereign in the sense of having plenary power to make laws for the peace, order, and good government of the territory. If its constitutional instrument contains no such procedural provisions as to the form of law-making, it, or a simple majority of its members, may legislate so as to repeal by implication limitations on substantive matters laid down in its constitution (according to the doctrine laid down in *McCawley*'s case). This is, in truth, a reinterpretation and a narrowing of the *McCawley* decision. On that occasion in 1920 Lord Birkenhead thought it an 'elementary commonplace' that a colonial legislature with plenary powers could treat the constitutional document which defined its powers as if it were 'A Dog Act or any other Act whatever its subject matter'.[2] This proposition must now be restricted to *substantive* matters in constitutional instruments. Where definitions of procedure or special majority provisions are laid down, they cannot be treated as provisions in a Dog Act might be.

Since *Ranasinghe*'s case did not involve a legislature whose original constituent instrument contained no provisions about the mode of law-making (or which, like the Queen-in-Parliament

---

[1] [1964] 2 W.L.R. 1301, 1313; [1965] A.C. 172 at 198.
[2] [1920] A.C. 691, 703, 704.

in the United Kingdom, has no constituent instrument) it does not directly demonstrate that such a legislature may impose conditions on itself. Nevertheless, it does suggest that some reasons hitherto given for supposing that this is not possible are without force. The decision gives judicial backing to the distinction between procedural and substantive limitations on the legislative process which has been at the centre of all recent discussion of the doctrine of legislative sovereignty. It helps to confirm that existing English authority does not rule out the possibility that the Queen-in-Parliament might legislate so as to provide a special manner and form for specified types of legislation. Though the British 'grundnorm' that the courts must give effect to Acts of Parliament is at present indeterminate as between the rule that the meaning of 'Act of Parliament' can be altered by legislation and the rule that it cannot, the Privy Council at least seems to be edging a little in the direction of 'self-embracing sovereignty'.

4. SOVEREIGNTY, AUTOCHTHONY, AND INDEPENDENCE

The doctrine of sovereignty in its traditional guise has complicated the relations of the Queen-in-Parliament both with Europe and the Commonwealth. If what one Parliament can do, another can undo, a statute which provides for permanent adhesion to or membership in an economic or political union of states may at any future time be repealed, notwithstanding any statutory provision to the contrary. Besides this problem of legal union there arises also a problem about legal separation. In the Commonwealth this has given rise to the discussion of what has been dubbed 'autochthony'. When, as in the Statute of Westminster of 1931, and in the Independence Acts of the post-war years, sovereign independent status has been accorded by Britain to former legally dependent territories, questions have been raised about the mechanism by which new constitutions may best be established, and the independent future irrevocably sealed off from the dependent past.

'Autochthony' has been aptly explained in the following way.[1] Some member nations of the Commonwealth, and some

[1] By Sir Kenneth Wheare, in *The Constitutional Structure of the Commonwealth* (1960), chap. 4.

who have reached independence and left the Commonwealth, may wish to be able to free their constitutions not only from any trace of subordination to, but also from any link with, the original authority of the British Parliament. They demand that their constitutional instrument should have the force of law through its own native authority. 'They assert not the principle of autonomy only; they assert also a principle of something stronger, of self-sufficiency, of constitutional autarky . . . of being constitutionally rooted in their own soil.'[1]

Though this ambition can be graphically and simply described, it envisages a notion which is far from simple. It is not easy to say which constitutions are beyond peradventure autochthonous and rooted in their own soil. This is partly because judicial decisions are lacking on certain points,[2] but also because the notion of an 'independent root' is not itself a clear one. On one possible criterion of separateness, Canada, New Zealand, and Australia are not in a state of autochthony; whilst the Republic of Ireland and India are; and Pakistan, South Africa, and Ghana possibly are. In all except the first three a new constitution has been promulgated and claims made that the People (or God), rather than the British Parliament, in some sense stand behind it. Usually a constituent assembly has been convened to authorize or ratify the process of constitution making. Nevertheless, according to another conception of separateness all, with the possible exception of Canada, are autochthonous and no longer regard the British Parliament as standing behind their institutions. To complicate—or perhaps simplify—the picture: on the traditional Dicey view it is disputable whether any of these constitutions is autochthonous, or indeed whether, in a British legal frame of reference, there can be any such thing as autochthony (since although autonomy can be conferred by a permanently sovereign Parliament, perhaps irreversible autonomy cannot). If we ask what it means to say that a constitution has a native 'root', at least three possible criteria for its existence can be seen. One is whether all processes for operating constitutional change are locally operated. This would only eliminate Canada, whose constitution has still

---

[1] Wheare, op. cit., p. 89.
[2] See especially Sir Kenneth Wheare's discussion of India's constitution, op. cit., pp. 95–100.

not been formally made amendable in Canada, though the British North America Acts are automatically amended at Westminster on Canadian request. Various suggestions have, in fact, been made in Canada for 'repatriation' of the constitution. One such suggestion was a British enactment of a Canada Independence Act to come into effect on a national holiday (though it is difficult to see how national holidays can give the force of law to anything).

A different criterion of autochthony is whether in the setting up of independent institutions the processes necessary for constitutional legislation under existing legislation have throughout been complied with, or whether, in the enactment of constitutional provisions or the setting up of constituent assemblies, legal continuity has been broken, or claims made that it has been broken. Whether it has been broken or not may well be the subject of differences of opinion. The Irish in 1922 did not regard their constitution as having been made under the authority of the Irish Free State Constitution Act passed at Westminster, though it was that Act, on the British view, that gave it legal authority. The independent constitution of Ghana, on the other hand, resulted from a series of legal steps each carried out in terms of the previous law and traceable directly back to the British Independence Act and Constitution Order in Council of 1957.[1] If the criterion is legal continuity, Ghana's autochthony is in question. The same is true of the republican constitution of South Africa. In India the issue would turn upon whether the acts of the constituent assembly which were not assented to by the Governor-General ought to have received his assent according to the intention of the British independence legislation—a matter which neither the British nor the Indian courts have been called on to decide (though the courts in Pakistan held in comparable circumstances that assent was necessary).

A third and completely different criterion for the existence of autochthony[2] is whether, for whatever reason, and with or without a locally operating amendment process, or an intervening

---

[1] See Kenneth Robinson, 'Constitutional Autochthony in Ghana', *Journal of Commonwealth Political Studies* (1961), p. 41, and 'Autochthony and the Transfer of Power', *Essays in Imperial Government*, ed. K. E. Robinson and A. F. Madden (1963).

[2] See Wheare, op. cit., p. 108.

constituent assembly, or a break in legal continuity, the people, or possibly the bench, in the country in question regard the constitution as authoritative because of their own acceptance of it. 'Acceptance' here, however, is ambiguous. People obey, and in that sense accept, laws for a number of reasons and are not normally asked to distinguish between their motives for obeying the law and their reasons for believing it to be valid. But it would not be a contradiction for an Australian to say that he believed the reason for the Australian constitution's validity to be its embodiment in a British Act of Parliament which at the time of its passing extended to Australia, at the same time as he insisted that he 'accepted' it because the rules it contained were enforced by Australians and approved of by his parliamentary representatives, who could alter them if they ceased to approve of them. The difficulty is that words like 'root', 'base', and 'foundation' of a constitution, together with most of their synonyms, and verbs such as 'stem from', can be used in legal, or historical, or sociological senses. It is a historical fact that the South African constitution, for example, had its origin in a British statute and its 'root' in this sense cannot be abolished or cease to exist. If the historical fact is undisputed, is it yet possible to ask whether the legal root is the same as the historical root? Courts in fact are rarely asked any such question as 'what is the legal root of the constitution?' Their answer could only be revealed implicitly in certain circumstances. If, for example, the provisions of existing enactments which at moment A provide the historical and legal roots of the law are ignored by legislators or a constituent assembly, the bench either has to acquiesce or to decide that the transactions in question have no authority.[1] Acquiescence and the upholding at moments B, C, D, etc., of provisions enacted without regard to the original legal requirements could sooner or later be described as judicial acceptance of a new legal root. If there is no such break in legal continuity the question whether the legal and historical roots are the same is academic and is not likely to be put to the test. The courts would only have to answer it if the British Parliament

---

[1] Uncertainty about the attitude of the judiciary may have influenced the decision of the government of the Union of South Africa not to attempt to establish an independent root in the Irish sense. Cf. Ellison Kahn, 'The New Constitution', 78 *South African Law Journal* 244 at p. 257.

were to purport to exercise its authority by extending legislation to a Commonwealth territory despite the declarations made in the Statute of Westminster and subsequent
Independence Acts, or to repeal those Acts themselves. In
that unlikely event, Commonwealth courts would then have to
decide whether such repealing provisions had the force of law,
and whether their own ultimate standard of legality was to be
found in local or United Kingdom legislation. Even then the
question might not be clearly decided, since either of two reasons
might be allotted for denying the force of law to British statutes. It
might be said that there was now a native root or local 'grundnorm', beyond which judicial scrutiny would not go. But, on the
other hand, judges in the common law tradition, especially in
Canada, New Zealand, or Australia, might be more inclined to
say that the United Kingdom Parliament had been finally dis-
abled, by its own provisions conferring independence, from re-
asserting Imperial authority. This, in effect, would be to locate
the logical and legal root of the Commonwealth constitution in the
relevant British Independence Act, or in the Statute of Westminster, which had conferred the charter of independence.

The fundamental question raised by an assertion of 'autochthony' is whether a legally effective abdication of British legislative authority has been made by the sovereign Parliament
of the United Kingdom. If it has, further local operations,
proclamations, and breaches of continuity are superfluous. If
it has not, they are ineffective. For anyone who maintains the
latter, a breach of legal continuity cannot imply legal independence, or legal anything; and the only answer to the question
about an alleged 'new' system's legal root would be that it had
no legal root.

This question suggests that more than theoretical importance
attaches to the issue whether, as was said in *British Coal Corporation* v. *The King*,[1] Parliament 'could as a matter of abstract
law, repeal or disregard Section 4 of the Statute' (of Westminster). In 1931 it was possible to view the declaration in that
section (that legislation should not extend to Commonwealth
countries without a declaration of their request and consent)
as a recognition rather than a denial of the potency of Acts of
Parliament still to extend to the Commonwealth, though one

[1] [1935] A.C. at 520.

tempered by a statement of Parliamentary intention to under-
take such legislation only under certain conditions. It was,
said Professor Berriedale Keith, 'a singular assertion of the
sovereign authority which still adheres to the Imperial Parliament'.[1] Since 1931, however, a number of similar declarations
have been made and they cannot all be plausibly viewed in
this light. The Nigeria Independence Act of 1960, for example,
certainly did not imply by its terms any recognition of a continued ability to legislate for Nigeria under any conditions.
The equivalent enabling section to section 4 of the Statute of
Westminster made no provision for legislation by Nigerian
request and consent but said plainly that from the first day of
October 1960 no Act of the Parliament of the United Kingdom
thereafter passed should extend or be deemed to extend to
Nigeria as part of the law of Nigeria.[2] Its intention was clearly
to impose a binding restraint upon future legislative power in
a particular sphere—an operation that, according to both Dicey
and Professor Berriedale Keith, must have been nugatory or
ineffective.

Anyone who accepts the traditional notion of sovereignty is,
it should be noticed, also, committed to saying that section 2 of
the Statute of Westminster and similar clauses in the later acts
do not mean what they say when they provide that Commonwealth Parliaments shall have power to repeal any British Act
of Parliament in its application to them, including any future
act or the empowering statute itself. This provision seems to
suggest that any British repeal of the Statute of Westminster or
independence legislation could thus itself be repealed in its
application to the Commonwealth country. 'In this way a
Member by the use of powers given to it under one section of
the Statute of Westminster or of an Independence Act might
protect itself from losing the freedom which it had gained under
other sections of the Statute or of the Independence Acts from
being legislated for by the United Kingdom Parliament.'[3] On
the traditional view of continuing Westminster sovereignty,

---

[1] 13 *Journal of Comparative Legislation* (1931), p. 28.
[2] Though the independence legislation for Ghana and Ceylon in 1957 and 1947
both contained the 1931 provision for extension with an express declaration of
request and consent, no equivalent provision was enacted in later independence
legislation such, for example, as that relating to Tanganyika and Sierra Leone.
[3] Wheare, *The Constitutional Structure of the Commonwealth*, p. 34.

however, it is hard to see how any such Commonwealth repeal could succeed in its purpose.[1] In fact s. 2 which, on the face of it, confers repealing powers, is, along with s. 4 which regulates future British action, fundamentally inconsistent with the view that Parliament cannot be bound. It could only be consistent with that view if it were to except the Statute itself from the conferred power of repeal instead of, as in the Nigerian legislation, specifically including it.

It is clear what view the courts in member countries of the Commonwealth would take of the irreversibility of independence legislation.[2] But given that Commonwealth legislation is no longer repealable by the United Kingdom, there is little point and uncertain meaning in the assertion of 'autochthony', or in the denial that a new constitutional settlement derives its legal validity from the old one. If 'autochthony' is proclaimed, to the accompaniment of such exercises as plebiscites and constitutional conventions, awkward logical questions arise. It may be that the people are said to give their authority to the constitution at a referendum, but a referendum itself must be authorized and is only distinguishable from an unofficial poll or a private solicitation of popular opinion by the fact that it is held under lawful authority. If it is so held then the arrangements which are authorized by it are legally derivable from, and have their legal root in, previously existing authority. But it is surely a confusion to identify *continuity* between an old and a new system with *subordination* of the new institutions to the old. What matters, whether in Cape Town or Karachi, is that the new constitutional situation should be *irreversible* and alterable only by the modes of formal amendment embodied in the new constitutional instrument. Given these distinctions, 'autochthony' can be seen to be a vivid but ambiguous metaphor, itself best explained metaphorically. One might perhaps describe an 'autochthonous' desire as a wish on the part of the offspring

---

[1] An approximate analogy would be the following: A is B's slave. B says to A, 'Go free, you may disregard anything I say from this time on.' B then says, 'I take back what I just said. You must come with me.' A says, 'Not so. I now have permission to disregard what you say.' B says, 'But your permission to do so flows from my authority and since I have revoked it your permission no longer exists.'

But here, of course, we know nothing in general about B's rights to make rules.

[2] 'Freedom, once conferred, cannot be revoked', *Ndlwana* v. *Hofmeyr* (1937), A.D. 229, 237.

of the Mother of Parliaments simultaneously to cut the umbilical cord and to deny that it has ever existed.

5. DISPUTED SOVEREIGNTY: THE RHODESIAN CASE

Proclamations of autochthony amount to a rejection of the standards of legality of a previously accepted constitutional system. When this happens and when, with or without violence, a revolution occurs, it is sometimes said that a new regime or system becomes legal or is accepted as valid. But this is a confusing way of speaking. Revolutions do not acquire validity or legality. What happens is that administrators and citizens who transfer their allegiance to a new constitutional system accept different criteria of validity or legality.

During the course of a revolution there may be differences of view amongst those who administer the system as to the proper criteria of validity and as to whom those criteria designate as the source of sovereign legislative authority. The unilateral assertion of independence by Rhodesia in 1965 produced exactly such a difference of view between the judges of the Rhodesian High Court and the judges of the Privy Council. Whilst the former held that lawful authority in Rhodesia could be exercised by the Rhodesian legislature,[1] the latter held that no validity could be accorded to any of the acts of the Rhodesian government or legislature after the declaration of independence and that the provisions of legislation passed by the United Kingdom Parliament still had full legal effect in Rhodesia.[2]

The difficulties of courts in a revolutionary situation were, however, perhaps best displayed by the earlier attempts of the Rhodesian judges to grapple with a situation in which competing claimants to sovereign authority existed.

Under its 1961 Constitution, Rhodesia enjoyed, in practice, internal self-government. In many respects its status was similar to that of a fully independent Commonwealth country. The Prime Minister attended Commonwealth Conferences and Rhodesia exchanged High Commissioners with other Commonwealth countries. By an express convention agreed in 1957, the British Parliament did not exercise sovereignty over the

---

[1] *Madzimbamuto* v. *Lardner-Burke*, [1968] (2) S.A. 284.
[2] Ibid., [1969] A.C. 645.

internal affairs of Rhodesia by legislating on matters within the competence of the Federal Parliament. So Rhodesia was in a similar position to the self-governing Dominions—Australia, New Zealand, Canada, and South Africa—before the Statute of Westminster in 1931 gave those Dominions their formal legal independence and the right to amend their own constitutions. In Rhodesia, despite internal independence existing in practice, the power to amend the constitution was not solely within the legal powers of the Rhodesian Federal Parliament. Hence the unilateral declaration of independence in 1965 amounted to an attempt to seize the amendment power and exercise it illegally.

In 1966 an action was brought to test the validity of detention orders made under the government's emergency regulations—which directly challenged the legality of the revolutionary regime. The High Court's decision in September 1966[1] was that the detention orders must be upheld 'on the basis of necessity and in order to avoid chaos'.

First and quite clearly the Court held that the Government was an illegal organization, acting without authority. Secondly, however, it declared that since *de jure* government was suspended, regulations made by those in *de facto* control of Rhodesia should be upheld to the extent that they were necessary to maintain peace and order and not designed to further the purposes of the revolution. Thus, it was argued, the authority of the 1961 constitution might be upheld, and an attempt made to protect the machinery of justice and to secure the necessary minimum of order even in a territory in which the authority of the law-maker had been usurped.

No attempt was made by the Government to argue that the declaration of independence of 11 November 1965 was a legal act. Instead, it was suggested that the Government and its actions had since become legal because it had conducted a successful revolution and that in successful revolutions those who win are recognized as legitimate rulers. Such successful revolutions, it was said, had taken place in Zanzibar, Nigeria, and Ghana, not to mention the United States.

The High Court in 1966 refused to accept this argument as being applicable to Rhodesia. The fundamental difference, they said, was that states such as Nigeria, Zanzibar, or Pakistan

[1] Judgment GD/CIV/23/66. See also (4) S.A. 462 (1966).

were already sovereign states when their internal changes of regime took place. Where a sovereign independent state changed its form of government by a successful internal revolution, the new state and government might be given *de jure* recognition by other states. But Rhodesia was not in law a sovereign independent state in November 1965 and no change of regime or political declaration or subsequent attempts at ratification could legally make it one.

Since the government, though dismissed by the Queen from their offices, were for the time being in effective control of the country, such of their measures as could properly have been taken under the 1961 constitution would be upheld in the interests of peace and order. But the constitution proclaimed in 1965 was not the lawful constitution and the government set up under it was not the lawful government. It would not become the lawful government until the ties of sovereignty were severed either by consent or by the acquiescence of Her Majesty's Government in the United Kingdom.

The Court went on to say that there was no obligation on Britain to reassert its sovereignty by armed force. Sanctions and other measures had been taken in order to put an end to the revolution. Conflicting evidence was given about the effect the sanctions were likely to have. The Head of the Department of Economics in the University College gave it as his opinion that sanctions might be effective. On the other hand, Government witnesses thought that they would not. The High Court concluded therefore, on the basis of this and other evidence, that it was impossible to say that the revolution had succeeded. Even if the sanctions were to fail, they held, it could not be inferred that Britain would abandon the struggle. The ties of sovereignty could not be said therefore to be 'finally and successfully severed'.

In the United Kingdom steps were taken to reinforce this conclusion. The Southern Rhodesia Act, 1965, and the Southern Rhodesia Constitution Order, 1965, asserted that the colony was still a part of Her Majesty's Dominions. Executive power was conferred on the Governor or on a United Kingdom Secretary of State, and the Rhodesian legislature under United Kingdom legislation ceased to have any power to make law.

In applying what in 1966 they took to be a principle of

necessity, the Rhodesian judges found a principle to guide them
in some of the decisions taken by courts in the United States
after the American Civil War. There the claim to sovereign
legal authority of the rebellious states had been forcibly defeated and rejected. On the face of it, logic might have seemed
to suggest that all measures enacted under the pretended authority of the formerly rebellious legislatures should be deemed to
have no force and effect. But to avoid potential chaos the
Federal courts adopted the principle of distinguishing between
those laws of the rebellious states which were directed
towards the ordinary affairs of life and those which had been
passed with the object of furthering secession and rebellion.
Some sorts of regulatory measures are to be found in any system
of law and order. Rules regulating marriage, property transactions, and the collection of taxes, are examples. Thus, after
the Civil War, American courts were able to give effect to
legislative and administrative measures enacted under illegal
authority, provided they were not hostile in their objects or
enforcement to the purposes of the National government, and
did not infringe the rights of citizens under the Constitution.[1]

A somewhat similar principle was seen by the High Court to
have been implicit in the views of legal and moral philosophers
who had discussed the dilemma of those subject to the laws of
a usurper or tyrant. Here again it was possible to draw some
sort of line between laws imposing no obligation because connected with the usurper's imposition of his illegal authority or
tyranny, and laws whose obligation might be accepted because
they were of the kind which any ruler would have been entitled
to impose, to provide for the ordinary governing of society.

This analogy, though it is hardly one that flattered the government, was applied to the laws and regulations promulgated in
Rhodesia. Given that the *de jure* legislature and executive were
for the time being ineffective, it was argued that effect should
be given to such measures as could lawfully have been taken by
the legitimate authorities under the 1961 constitution. By this
test the detention orders were upheld, since they were made
under the Emergency Powers (Maintenance of Law and Order)
Regulations of 1966, which though illegal were such as could
have been made by the *de jure* government. They did not

[1] *Texas* v. *White* (1868), 7 Wall. 700.

infringe the rights of the citizen as laid down and regulated by the 1961 constitution and prima facie at least they were not in themselves part of the activities associated with U.D.I. or measures hostile to the authority of the sovereign power.

In reaching this decision the High Court was careful to assert that it would not in all cases accept the *de facto* government's assertion that laws or regulations were made in the public interest and for the ordinary purposes of maintaining law and order. It might be, the Court said, that a Minister issuing regulations was considering the public interest solely from the point of view of aiding the revolution.

This decision undoubtedly created considerable difficulties both for the government and for the courts. The regime's law and regulations had to be notionally classified into three groups. First, those predominantly for the ordinary purposes of government and innocent of any connection with the rebellion. Secondly, those whose purpose was ambiguous. Thirdly, those whose purpose was to further rebellion and establish the government in unlawful possession—for example by stifling public criticism of its actions. The extension of the state of emergency was held to be prima facie for the purpose of maintaining order and not for the purpose of sustaining the revolution.

The tests laid down by the court were obviously difficult ones to apply. The regulation, for example, of the armed forces was, in a sense, something which was within the powers of previous legitimate governments. But the maintenance of discipline in the armed forces and the orders issued to them were equally clearly connected with the purpose of maintaining the government in possession. What, after all, was the order preserved by the government for? Any stability or order preserved by a rebellious government is preserved in some measure against those who might otherwise bring about its fall or the restoration of lawful authority. Obviously some things, such as quarantine regulations or punishments for drunkenness preserve order in an ordinary sense, but a large number of other orderings and regulations are essentially ambiguous. Measures to counter economic sanctions are an obvious example. Clearly, economic regulations of a roughly similar kind could, in a sense, have been made under legitimate authority. But not economic regulations with the same purpose. If purpose was to be looked at, there could logically be no analogous measures which a legitimate government could take.

Detention orders were subject to similar ambiguity, as were the censorship regulations put into force by the regime. The latter were clearly a defensive measure against the possible undermining of the government's authority by news and opinions transmitted from outside. If criticism and lawful opposition, which the court declared itself ready to preserve, were to be understood in anything like the sense which the tradition of the common law and constitutional government had given them, the measures taken by the Rhodesian Cabinet in relation to the freedom of speech and publication overstepped the mark by a considerable distance. Governmental analogies with wartime Defence Regulations in the United Kingdom were remote. Even in the worst days of the German *blitzkrieg*, Englishmen were not restricted in the way in which Rhodesian newspaper readers or radio listeners were. Moreover, the American Supreme Court, whose precedents were prayed in aid, could hardly be imagined upholding a censored press as compatible with the rights of citizens in a free country.

The Rhodesian ministers, it may be noted, accepted the jurisdiction of the High Court in 1966 on its own terms. An attempt was made by counsel for the Government to argue that the judges had implicitly taken office and were serving under the terms of the 1965 constitutional document, but the argument was not at that stage tenable. The 1965 document purported to make the validity of the constitution non-justiciable; so if it had been in operation the Government would have had to maintain that the court was incompetent to consider the case which its own counsel was arguing.

Though an attempt was made to validate the 1965 constitution by the Constitution Ratification Bill of 1966, the attempt plainly could not succeed. It was alleged that this Bill became law when signed by the Officer Administering the Government. But it could not become law until that officer had signed it on behalf of the Crown and he could not legally sign it on behalf of the Crown until it became law. As to the office which the Officer Administering the Government purported to hold, it had in any event been repudiated by the Queen as one which could not properly represent her.

The position of the judges in Rhodesia was thus a unique one. They were not in the position of judges in some states where a revolution has taken place which is universally regarded as complete by the governments and peoples of other countries. In such a situation, those whose job it is to apply the law may be willing or may be compelled to take an oath of allegiance to the new Sovereign and apply the law of the new regime. When the American Revolution was complete and England and the European nations acknowledged the American colonies to have severed the ties binding them to the mother country, those appointed to serve as judges in America could regard themselves as servants of a new sovereign state whose *de jure* status was recognized by the world. In England also after the peaceful revolution of 1688 a new allegiance was possible and inevitable. The King to whom allegiance was formerly owed had fled—dropping the Great Seal in the River Thames—and James's judges became the servants of William and Mary.

No one can deny that revolutions have occurred in the course of history. But it is not the job of judges either to act as if historic events had already occurred or to urge them on. The only way in which they can take part in a revolution is to resign their offices or be dismissed.

In 1966 the Rhodesian bench did its best to construct on extra-legal principles a set of guide lines for judges caught up in a revolutionary situation. It is not perhaps logically impossible for a constitution itself to specify rules for such a situation which would authorize obedience to the edicts of a successful group of revolutionaries; but not surprisingly existing constitutions do not do so. If they did the rules would, in their application, run into all the difficulties encountered by the Rhodesian High Court.

In the end the Rhodesian court, like other courts in the Commonwealth[1] and perhaps by implication the Privy Council, accepted a principle modelled on the doctrine of Hans Kelsen,[2] and by analogy on the doctrine of recognition of effectively operating governments by foreign states. The argument,

---

[1] e.g. in Pakistan and Uganda. See *The State* v. *Dosso* (1958), 2 Pakistan S.C.R. 180, and *Uganda* v. *Commissioner of Prisons ex parte Matovu*, [1966] East Africa L.R. 514, and cf. *R. v. Ndhlovu* 1968 (4) S.A. 515.

[2] e.g. in his *General Theory of Law and State* (1945), pp. 117–18, 368–9.

roughly speaking, is that a new, though revolutionary, legal order acquires validity when it becomes, by and large, effective and that all the rules of an existing legal order lose their validity when they cease to be effective. But this treatment of 'efficacy' as a necessary prior condition of validity need not be accepted. Kelsen stipulates for a legal system that its individual rules can only be spoken of as valid if the system is in general efficacious and operative. From this it may be inferred that individual rules can no longer retain their validity when the system ceases to be one that is being effectively used or operated. This may, in fact, accord with many people's instincts about the notion of validity, which connect it with the idea of a rule or practice being in force, or being effective, or deserving to be followed. But Kelsen's is not the only conceivable way of thinking about 'validity'. The term might be used to mark off a purely formal characteristic of a rule that is properly formulated in terms of some criterion that identifies it as one of a particular set of (let us say) 'rule-like statements'. Whether any such set of rules or laws is at any particular moment being operated by anybody, or whether it serves any purpose, or whether its prescriptions deserve to be obeyed, may be treated as quite separate issues. There may be 'valid' rules in an obsolete, or historical, or rejected system, or one postulated in imagination, or on paper. The rules of each system will be valid in relation to their own criteria and it is only in relation to a particular system that questions of validity can be raised. Validity is not a characteristic like 'efficacy' or 'usefulness' that applies to systems themselves or can be lost by one and gained by another. The laws of colonial America and Czarist Russia do not now enjoy or deserve obedience. But these sociological and moral facts may be distinguished from the requirements made—in a timeless sense—in those systems. Thus when Kelsen suggests that it 'cannot' be maintained that men ought to behave in accordance with the norms of an ineffective system, it may be said in reply that it *can* be maintained in terms of the norms of that system itself and that it must, in terms of these norms, be maintained by persons designated as judges in that system. They are not compelled in that capacity to accept the rules of recognition adopted towards usurping regimes by other states. Indeed, they are compelled by their oaths of office not to do so if such rules conflict with the domestic criteria of legality that they were appointed to apply.

Of course judges, like citizens, can in a revolution decide by an exercise of moral and political judgment that it is no longer appropriate or desirable to continue to act in their former capacities and tranfer allegiance to a new sovereign authority on the ground that the upholding of the rules of the pre-existing constitutional system has become pointless or impossible.[1] But they cannot make that decision in their original capacity as judges. Whilst they claim to retain that role they cannot lend their support to the propagation as lawful acts of revolutionary or 'autochthonous' measures.

---

[1] Judicial behaviour is of course one of the major elements on which judgments about the efficacy of governmental systems rest. Professor A. M. Honoré in proposing a possible body of principles for revolutionary situations thus suggests that one rule might be 'When a revolutionary régime is established, so that there is very little possibility of a restoration of the old régime, judges are authorised to diminish the chances still further' ('Reflections on Revolutions', 1967 *Irish Jurist* 268 at p. 273). But since such principles would be rules of morality or prudence it is difficult to see how they could be formulated in any general way and without reference to the moral justification of particular revolutions.

The Rhodesian secession and litigation has produced a wide range of comment. See, for example, R. S. Welsh, 'The Constitutional Case in Southern Rhodesia', 83 *L.Q.R.* 64 (1967); Claire Polley, 'The Judicial Process and the Southern Rhodesian Judiciary', 30 *M.L.R.* 263 (1967); R. W. M. Dias, 'Legal Politics: "Norms behind the Grundnorm" ', 26 *C.L.J.* 233 (1968); S. A. de Smith, 'Constitutional Lawyers in Revolutionary Situations', 7 *University of Ontario Law Rev.* 93 (1968). F. M. Brookfield, 'Kelsen and the Rhodesian Revolution', 19 *Univ. of Toronto L.J.* 326; H. R. Hahlo, 'The Privy Council and the Gentle Revolution', 19 *South African L.J.* 419; R. S. Welsh, 'The Function of Lawyers in a Coup d'État', 1970 *South African L.J.* 168.

IV

JUDGES AND LEGISLATORS

In both Britain and America (as elsewhere) there is an important cluster of questions about the role of the judiciary in the application of law. In each country there have been traditional arguments about, for example, the extent to which adjudication embodies policy or discretion; about the extent to which judges ought to promote certainty or further the ends of justice, and about permissible techniques to be used in the interpretation of statutes and the development of the common law. In the United States, as well as in some Commonwealth countries, there has been in addition a further range of questions about the duties of the judges in applying the provisions of constitutional instruments. Though all these questions raise difficult considerations, some of them are linked and may connect with general differences of opinion about the nature of the constitutional structure, or the relationship between the different elements in it. In England, Bentham's general views about the sovereign role of the legislature were certainly connected with his criticisms of judicial technique, and, more recently, differences between British legislative supremacy and the separation of powers have been explicitly connected by some writers with different approaches to statutory interpretation in the United States and Britain. Differences of opinion about the judicial role may thus be due in part to objective differences in constitutional situations. They may be complicated by incoherences or ambiguities in the way in which judicial behaviour is described; and they may be affected by different assumptions about the relation of the judicial process to social justice and about the general objects to be promoted by judicial action. Each of these possibilities deserves some examination.

I. THE INFLUENCE OF CONSTITUTIONAL AND STRUCTURAL DIFFERENCES

Two constitutional factors may have influenced arguments about the judicial role and judicial interpretation. In the first place the formal relationship between legislature and judiciary may be significantly different in different political systems. Secondly, there may be structural differences in the modes of operation of legislatures.

It has sometimes been suggested that factors of the first kind lie behind differences of approach in Britain and the United States—the one favouring a conservative, restrictive, literal, or even 'wooden'[1] approach to the interpretation of statutes, the other inclining towards more liberal, flexible attitudes. Under the separation of powers, it has been said, Congress issues legislative instructions and the courts obey. But they do it not because they are the servants of Congress but because the constitution places a duty equally on each—on Congress of formulating legislative instructions and on the courts of interpreting them. Parliament, in the United Kingdom, on the other hand, is the sovereign master. Its instructions are subject to no constitutional reservations and this, perhaps, gives rise to a belief in the sanctity of the exact words of the statute.[2] If the theory of legislative sovereignty is taken to be one about the authority or 'will' of a sovereign person or body of legislators, it is not clear that this conclusion necessarily suggests itself. Indeed, the opposite assumption might seem equally plausible, namely that the primary object of those who serve the Sovereign is to find out what the sovereign commanders intended to bring about, and then to put it into effect, even at the expense of doing some violence to the words which they may happen to have used. That conclusion could indeed be drawn from remarks such as Hobbes's: 'It is not the letter but the intendment or meaning, that is to say the authentique interpretation of the law (which is the sense of the legislator) in which the nature of the law consisteth.'[3] In practice the traditional English principles and maxims of interpretation have wavered between two positions—one being that the words in which legislators have couched their instructions merely provide evidence (possibly the best) of their actual aims or intentions; the other being that the actual aims or intentions of legislative persons merely provide evidence of the meaning of the legislators' words (and

[1] Mr. Justice Frankfurter in *U.S.* v. *Monia*, 317 U.S. 424 at 431.
[2] Max Radin, 'A Short Way with Statutes', 56 *Harvard Law Rev.* 406–7.
[3] *Leviathan*, Everyman edn., p. 146.

thereby) of the instruments which emerge from their deliberations. The attitude reflected by the second of these propositions may be strengthened if the Sovereign is considered not as simply a set of natural persons, but an artificial entity whose final command takes the form of an instrument or statute which does not necessarily represent the actual historical intentions of any particular person or persons. That a statute is the joint handiwork of three legislative elements and that the Crown, in assenting to it, cannot be deemed to know or approve what has transpired in either Chamber, is certainly an argument which has been used in England to devalue the suggested usefulness of parliamentary materials as aids to statutory interpretation. Elsewhere, where legislative authority is not merely shared between a number of elements, but parcelled out amongst elements or Chambers acting in different ways or with different majorities for different purposes, the importance or conclusiveness of evidence about the intentions of persons taking part in the process may be seen to be still further diminished. A dictum of the South African High Court clearly reflects this attitude: 'Evidence that every member who voted for a measure put a certain construction on it, cannot', it was said, 'affect the meaning which the courts must place upon the statute, for it is the product not of a number of individuals but of an impersonal Parliament. . . . Its sovereign powers are exercised by human beings but . . . legislative powers were conferred on Parliament, not on them.'[1] In the United States Mr. Justice Holmes once expressed a similar view. 'We ask', he said, 'not what this man meant, but what those words would mean in the mouth of a normal speaker of English using them in the circumstances in which they were used. . . . We do not inquire what the legislature meant; we ask only what the statute means.'[2]

The impact of sentiments of this kind, if taken seriously, is at least to cast doubt upon the conclusiveness (if not necessarily the relevance) of parliamentary materials tending to reveal the views of those who assisted in the passage of legislation. A number of practical considerations also might be used to discredit the view that there is any such object as legislative intention. The form in which statutes pass into law does not in practice

[1] *Swart and Nicol* v. *De Koch and Garner*, (1951) (3) S.A. 589 (A.D.) at 621.
[2] 'The Theory of Legal Interpretation', 12 *Harvard Law Rev.* 417(1899).

derive from plenary gatherings of parliamentarians, all of whom
have considered what they wish to bring about and what
means have been used to bring such an intention into effect. For
the most part in Britain statutes are drafted by civil servants
and approved by a party majority most of whom have not read
the legislation or been present when it was debated. Some important legislation indeed has never been debated at all, if the
guillotine is applied at the committee stage.[1] Statements about
the effect of a Bill's provisions, even when made by Ministers
who have promoted the legislation, are not made in an atmo-
sphere free of bias or conducive to a judicious weighing of the
considerations which may then or in the future be advanced for
or against particular interpretations. Many Bills, even if not
amended at a later stage, are a compromise between different
points of view, and it is not always certain from the ultimate
form of enactment, which viewpoint or policy has prevailed.
Neither is it uncommon to get from a perusal of a debate on
controversial points a number of opposed expressions of opinion
or of misgivings as to the possible ambit and effect of the statute.
This is particularly likely where statutes deal with very general
or controversial subject-matter. Statutes such as the Race
Relations Act or the Obscene Publications Act, or taxation
provisions provide many examples. Legislation on constitutional
matters is equally productive of internal legislative disagreement. In the debate on the Statute of Westminster in 1931, for
example, the powers conferred on the Irish Free State were the
subject of keen controversy. Mr. Winston Churchill thought that
the statute was not obscure on the point. It was, he said, the
plainest Act of Parliament he had ever read.[2] The Solicitor
General agreed with this view, but his opinion of what the Bill
had done was the exact opposite of Mr. Churchill's. Scrutiny
of *Hansard* on such occasions may well induce in a judge some
sympathy with Lord Halsbury's dictum that a legislator is the
very worst person to consult about the meaning of a statute

[1] As happened to the Transport Bill, the Town and Country Planning Bill, and
the Iron and Steel Bill between 1945 and 1950; and to the Housing Repairs and
Rents Bill in 1953–4. Thirty-seven clauses and 7 schedules of the Transport Bill were
not discussed. For the other three Bills the figures of provisions not discussed were
respectively 50 clauses and 6 schedules, 23 clauses and 6 schedules, and 38 clauses
and 5 schedules. The 1971 Industrial Relations Bill had 26 undebated clauses.
[2] 259 H.C. Deb. col. 1194 (1931).

since 'he is very much disposed to confuse what he intended to do with the effect of the language which in fact has been employed'.[1]

Despite, therefore, the numerous dicta about the duty to find the intention of Parliament and despite the respectability of the 'mischief' rule derived from *Heydon*'s case, as to 'extrinsic circumstances'[2] which may throw light on the situation or mischief which an Act is intended to remedy, there has been an undoubted tendency on the part of English judges, most particularly in a class of cases where they were faced with what they took to be plain words in a statute, to shy away from what might seem to be speculation about possible legislative motives and to refrain from using Parliamentary or other historical materials. Originally Parliamentary proceedings were confidential matters, which it was a breach of privilege to reveal and which were not therefore available for consultation in any place outside. In fact the evolution of judicial attitudes seems to be closely connected with the view that the judicial role is to find the law and apply it whatever consequences might follow, and that journeying 'outside' the statute for guidance might lead to essays in legislation or variations in the plain words of statutes. Much discussion in the nineteenth century took place in this context and often within the bounds of a particular argument about the extent to which courts should construe statutes 'equitably' (or 'liberally') so as to avoid absurdities which could not be presumed to have been intended. 'It is infinitely better', Lord Bramwell said, 'to adhere to the words of an Act of Parliament and leave the legislature to set it right than to alter those words according to one's notion of an absurdity.'[3] And: 'If the language of a statute be plain, admitting of only one meaning the Legislature must be taken to have meant and intended what it has plainly expressed.'[4]

---

[1] *Hilder* v. *Dexter*, [1902] A.C. 474, 477.

[2] 'In construing Acts of Parliament, the words which are used are not alone to be regarded. Regard must also be had to the intent and meaning of the legislature [which is to be] 'collected from the cause and necessity of the Act being made, from a consideration of several parts, and from foreign (meaning extrinsic) circumstances, so far as they can justly be considered to throw light on the subject' (*Hawkins* v. *Gathercole* (1955), 6 D.M. & G. 1 at p. 21.

[3] *Hill* v. *East and West India Dock Co.* (1884), 9 App. Cas. 448.

[4] Lord Atkinson in *Vacher and Sons Ltd.* v. *London Society of Compositors*, [1913] A.C. 107 at 121–2.

The strength of the emphasis on the words of the statute in
this 'plain words' situation (enforcement of assertedly 'clear'
meaning versus correction of absurdity or consequential injustice) may well have infected judicial attitudes in situations
which are different—where there is, for example, an admitted
ambiguity of meaning, or where the expressions used are general
and have to be applied to a specific factual situation. The interpretation of constitutional documents obviously gives rise to
such situations and it is clear that in some cases the approach
of English and Commonwealth judges has been affected by the
'literal' or 'plain' words, or 'staying within the statute' approach
which could only have relevance in the context of a different
problem of interpretation. Thus in *Amalgamated Society of
Engineers* v. *Adelaide Steamship Co.* in 1920 Isaacs J. in the High
Court of Australia cited with approval Lord Haldane[1] in
Vacher's case to the effect that speculation on legislative motives
was not a topic for judges to enter on. 'Their province is the
very different one of construing the language in which the
Legislature has finally expressed its conclusions.'[2] In *James* v.
Commonwealth of Australia it was said that 'the true test must as
always be the actual language used'. And in *The Commonwealth*
v. *The Bank of New South Wales* approval was given to statements
that 'the object, the purpose, and the intention of the enactment
is the same', and that 'what the Legislature intended to be
done or not to be done, can only be legitimately ascertained
from that which it has chosen to enact either in express words
or by reasonable and necessary implication'.[3]

A coalition of factors therefore—constitutional arguments
locating Parliamentary authority in an artificial tripartite body;
the original unavailability of Parliamentary proceedings; force-
ful emphasis on the necessity to give literal effect to plain words
in a special class of cases; and possibly some reluctance to
countenance legislative or speculative activity as an acknowledged element in the declaration of law—together combined

---

[1] Haldane said that in arguing an appeal on the construction of a statute he had
once mentioned the necessity to ascertain what the 'mind' of the legislature had
been; but the remark was not favourably received by the Court of Appeal. 'Mind
of the legislature', cried out Lord Esher to me from the Bench, 'and you, Mr. Haldane, have been twenty years in the House of Commons and yet speak of it'
(*Richard Burton Haldane: An Autobiography*, p. 70).

[2] (1920), 28 C.L.R. 129.   [3] [1950] A.C. 235 at 307.

to produce what critics have seen as a restrictive, narrow, or literal approach to the interpretation of statutes.

2. CHARACTERIZATION OF JUDICIAL ATTITUDES

The alleged restrictive, narrow, or literal approach has, however, been an amalgam of different suggested defects. In some judicial arguments reference to the 'literal' meaning of a disputed provision or adhering to the 'explicit' words of the statute may appear simply as a form of assertion that the meaning contended for is correct. Thus Mr. Justice Stone in *U.S.* v. *Butler*[1] could urge upon a majority of the Supreme Court the need for a 'frank recognition that language, even of a Constitution, may mean what it says'. Where what is in dispute is what a particular provision, rightly understood, does say, this use of adjectives such as 'literal' or 'explicit' is plainly question-begging. In the language of critics, 'literal', 'logical', or 'strict' approaches are often by implication approaches in which there is *misapplied* or *misplaced* strictness, logic, or reference to particular words or contexts. The criticisms made of some of the Privy Council's constructions of the Canadian and Australian constitutions suggest various forms of such putatively misplaced activity. The Privy Council refused, in the words of one writer, to see in the British North America Act 'anything of a constitutional nature or to be guided by its historical origins. . . . They have applied to it arbitrary rules of construction which have at times robbed it of its historical context and divorced its meaning from the intention of those who in truth framed it.'[2] Another critic has suggested that 'had Lord Haldane known more of the facts of life and the dynamics of development in those distant Canadian provinces and less of the verbalism of German philosophy, he might not have been so proud of his share in rewriting the Canadian constitution'.[3] If Lord Haldane's philosophy had impelled him to *rewrite* the British North America Act, one might suppose that his method of approach, right or wrong, would deserve to be called broad or legislative;

[1] *U.S.* v. *Butler*, 297 U.S. 1 at 88 (1936).
[2] W. P. M. Kennedy, 'Law and Custom of the Canadian Constitution', *Essays in Constitutional Law* (1934), p. 85.
[3] W. A. Mackintosh, *Federalism*, p. 95.

but the criticism in question shows that whether such an approach is treated as praiseworthy may depend upon whether the interpretation placed on the statute is in the critic's view correct. The restrictiveness attributed by some Commonwealth critics to the Privy Council was in a number of cases, at least in form, repudiated when it was conceded by the Privy Council that a 'large and liberal interpretation'[1] was appropriate. 'There are', Lord Sankey said, 'statutes and statutes; and the strict construction deemed proper in the case, for example, of a penal or taxing statute, or one passed to regulate the affairs of an English parish would be often subversive of Parliament's real intent if applied to an Act passed to ensure the peace, order, and good government of a British Colony.'[2]

In interpreting provisions relating to peace, order, and good government, or to the division of functions between state and federal legislatures the implicit distinction between strict and liberal construction may, in practice, lack any possible application. The problem is likely to be one of applying to particular facts a general term such as 'property and civil rights', or of allotting a meaning in the twentieth century to a provision drafted a hundred years earlier. There may be 'the familiar difficulty of determining which of two alternative meanings is to be given to an instrument, the authors of which did not contemplate the possibility of either meaning'.[3] In these situations broad or liberal construction may implicitly mean lending assistance to some interest deemed to deserve promotion, such as the federal government, social welfare, or particular governmental objectives, and it is assumed that such purposes are in fact more likely to be promoted if judges are willing to make use of historical, social, or economic materials.

Advocates of broad or liberal approaches have been of many different kinds and between them have coined a wide variety of laudatory adjectives. 'Liberal', 'equitable', 'purposive', 'progressive', 'functional', 'historical', and 'policy-oriented' are examples. The condemnation of restrictivist views leads to a comparable variety of epithets, such as 'strict', 'literal',

---

[1] *Edwards* v. *Attorney General for Canada*, [1930] A.C. 124 at 136.
[2] Ibid., pp. 136–7.
[3] *Attorney General for Ontario* v. *Attorney General for Canada*, [1947] A.C. 127 at 148–9, *per* Lord Jowett.

'verbal', 'logical', 'pseudo-logical', 'automatic', 'analytic', 'deductivist', 'mechanistic', and (even) 'positivist'.

A number of different sources for such characterization of judicial methods can be distinguished. There is the fairly straightforward criticism by historians, academic lawyers, and judges themselves, based on dissatisfaction with the multiplicity and inconsistency of canons of construction. There is the criticism which stems from the various forms of realist jurisprudence, more particularly in the United States and Scandinavia; and there is the critical tradition of those from Bentham onwards who have expressed dissatisfaction with the judicial process, from motives which were liberal or progressive in a political sense. From this mixture of theories and motives has emerged, not surprisingly, some confusion in the various senses in which a judicial approach may be said to be 'broad', 'liberal', or 'progressive', as against 'narrow', 'literal', and 'restrictive'.

Judicial method has been thought of in the first way:

(1) If it involves evidence about history or social policy instead of, or in addition to, verbal, grammatical, or logical arguments.
(2) If it manifests a desire to rationalize, harmonize, and develop legal principles.
(3) If it accords with a particular political or economic theory, or furthers the ends of social justice.

Though the same individual may hold 'progressive' views in all three senses, and may connect them,[1] they do not entail each other and it need not always be the case that progressive aims in the third sense are promoted by progressive methods in the first or second senses.

3. JUDICIAL ATTITUDES AND SOCIAL JUSTICE

That the relation between social justice or progress and progressive methods in the first of the senses distinguished is not a

---

[1] For example, 'Some famous judges like Sir George Jessel or Lord Wright have tended to interpret the judicial function as one of active assistance in the *progressive* development of the law. They have *therefore* leaned against the prevalence of linguistic over policy arguments' [italics added] (W. Friedmann, *Law and Social Change in Contemporary Britain*, 1951, p. 245).

simple one can be seen on many occasions when the courts are faced with the resolution of competing social interests. *Liversidge* v. *Anderson*[1] provides an example. There the majority of the House of Lords, after considering evidence about the purpose and operation of the Defence Regulations of 1939, gave what might be called a broad construction to the Home Secretary's power to detain persons suspected of hostile sympathies. In fathoming the intentions of the Home Office they were probably right. On the other hand, Lord Atkin's dissenting judgment was undoubtedly based on a restrictive or literal interpretation of the words 'has reasonable cause to believe', which gave detention powers to the Home Secretary, and that judgment has frequently been praised as upholding the rule of law and the rights of the individual. It is not entirely clear who in this situation were the progressives, Lord Atkin or the majority.

Consideration of the relationship between social justice and judicial method suggests two further possibilities. One is that the purposes or policy written into the law itself might conceivably be unjust, so that discovering and giving effect to the true intention of the legislature might restrict or retard progress or social justice. Another conceivable possibility is that the law is laudable in its object and clearly expressed, but conscious or subconscious judicial bias prevents its literal and socially advantageous application.[2] This latter possibility has in fact been conceived, on both sides of the Atlantic. 'No amount of good drafting', Harold Laski wrote to Mr. Justice Holmes, 'can prevent a strong judge like Bramwell from reading a statute in the context of his unconscious presumptions.'[3] A similar view was expressed in Laski's appendix to the Committee on Ministers' Powers Report of 1932, but elsewhere it was combined with a stronger theory about the bias of the law itself. In this account both judges and law were alleged to reflect class values. In *The State in Theory and Practice* of 1934, and in his essay 'The Judicial Function' (first published in *Politica* in 1936) Laski's complaint was precisely that British judges in the twentieth

---

[1] [1942] A.C. 206.
[2] As it has been alleged happened in *Roberts* v. *Hopwood*, [1925] A.C. 578, where the High Court failed to give a literal interpretation to a local authority power to pay such wages as they 'may think fit'.
[3] *Holmes–Laski Letters*, vol. ii, p. 1372.

century could not 'transcend the class structure'[1] and, like their predecessors who presided at the treason trials of the Napoleonic wars, the American judges who tried Sacco and Vanzetti, and the judges of Nazi Germany, were equally 'officials of the State' and 'instruments of the State power'. Between law and the state purpose, Laski wrote, 'the German method achieves by brute force a coincidence of view that in Great Britain and America is accomplished by deep rooted tradition that the judiciary has rarely sought fundamentally to challenge'.[2] But it can hardly be *distorted application* of the law which on this view results from judicial social preconceptions—for *ex hypothesi* these preconceptions and the State purposes which the law reflects are at one (and it is asking something rather odd of judicial officers to demand that they should make 'fundamental challenges' to the purposes embodied in the law). The real complaint here is that both judge *and* law are at fault.

If, however, it is admitted that the law does not reflect a single set of values and if one part of the law can be conceived of as challenging the principles embodied in other parts of the law, then the bench can meaningfully at least be accused of preferring the old to the new. It was on this basis that Mr. W. I. Jennings (as he then was) could write in the thirties that 'the judges in recent years have been unconsciously led by social conditions to exhibit a bias against social reform'.[3] The common law to which the judges were wedded was replete with presumptions and maxims of interpretation favouring property in the Locke-ian sense. The right of a man to his own was protected by the procedural rules of natural justice and, as Byles J. had said in *Cooper* v. *Wandsworth Board of Works*,[4] the justice of the common law might repair the omission of the legislature where statute had not specifically provided for property rights to be protected by allowing the right of hearing sanctified by judicial precedent. 'Omission' was a pregnant word (the history of judicial interpretation could be written around it), which might innocuously signify a legislative failure specifically to mention something clearly implied and intended, or an absence of any

---

[1] Laski, *The State in Theory and Practice* (1934), p. 175.   [2] Ibid., p. 120.
[3] 'Courts and Administrative Law: The Experience of English Housing Legislation', 49 *Harvard Law Review* 426 at p. 452 (1956).
[4] (1863), 143 E.R. 414.

legislative intention in the matter at all. Since it might be suggested that statutory interference with property rights on a large scale was a development at odds with the individualistic values implied by the common law's presumptions about strict construction of statutes, it could be argued that 'the common law itself is biased against administrative law and . . . on occasion judges have *without in any way offending against the law*, used that bias in such a way as to impede the administrative machine'.[1] Even so, there is inconsistency in this form of accusation. 'Impede' is a loaded word. It is scarcely fair to talk of activities which are curtailed by the proper application of the law as being impeded. If, on the other hand, the charge is that on a proper construction of statutory intention the legislature intended that certain common law presumptions and rules of natural justice should give way, then judges who failed to apply that intention must in some sense have 'offended against the law'. Jennings certainly implied that the courts had—if excusably—treated Parliament's intentions with insufficient respect. In an article in 1937 entitled 'Judicial Process at its Worst'[2] he surveyed the record of the courts in interpreting the Public Health Acts Amendment Act of 1890 which had involved, amongst other things, some fluctuation of judicial views on the meaning of 'public sewer'. In the Public Health Act of 1936, he said, 'Parliament quietly tried to express again and in different words the intention that it had forty-six years ago'.[3] Jennings was asserting here that the setback to the legislative purpose was brought about not by social bias but by the deficiencies of *stare decisis* and by conflicts within the fabric of the law. Some critics, however, have used more purposive language. Professor W. Friedmann, for example, has spoken of 'an attitude of jealousy rather than collaboration in the judicial approach to statute'.[4]

It is perhaps in the administrative law field that the possibilities of disagreement about judicial attitudes have been widest since the 1920s, partly because statutory interferences with property rights have been accompanied by *ad hoc* and not

---

[1] 49 *Harvard Law Review* 426 at pp. 434–5 (italics added).

[2] In the same article it is noted that in *Errington* v. *Minister of Health*, [1935] 1 K.B. 249 (which had just been decided), 'the old doctrine of natural justice has raised its head once more'.

[3] 1 *Modern Law Review* 111 at p. 131 (1937).   [4] *Legal Theory*, 2nd edn., p. 311.

always explicit parliamentary attempts to exclude judicial review. The history of judicial 'resistance' to these attempts is a sphere in which there are possibilities for conflicting generalization. In the post-war years, there were generalizations in plenty about 'the attitude' of the courts towards administrative discretion, the *deference* paid to ministerial responsibility, the *extension* of Crown privilege, and so on. The suggestion of purposive deliberation is clear. A conscious or at least semi-conscious use of judicial powers must, it is implied, have occurred in response to feelings about public policy. More recently (and possibly since about 1965), signs of a hardening of judicial attitudes towards administrative discretion have been detected. But such generalizations are complicated by the fact that the discretion exercised by government departments, administrative tribunals, local authorities, and nationalized industries has many different guises. On the face of it the courts in the last twenty-five years can be portrayed as being 'hard' on tribunals, 'soft' on ministerial departments, sometimes 'soft' and sometimes 'hard' on local authorities. How far differences of view about statutory interpretation have seriously affected the outcome is not easy to decide. Certainly it is not obvious that differences of opinion between one judge and another on this subject have by fortunate chance reflected the respective feelings which they would have about the desirability of judicial intervention, apart from the questions of interpretation involved. In *Smith* v. *E. Elloe R.D.C.*,[1] for example, a majority of the House of Lords held that there was no jurisdiction to review the validity of a compulsory purchase order which the relevant act said should 'not be questioned in any legal proceedings whatsoever', on the ground that, literally interpreted, these words protected even orders obtained by fraud or bad faith. On this issue the Lords split three to two, the minority view being that Parliament had not explicitly included orders made in bad faith and did not intend to. No obvious conclusions follow from this about the 'attitude' of either majority or minority towards compulsory purchase orders, government departments, or social policy, if one accepts the possibility of equally fair and objective, but still different, estimates of what is reasonably implied by ambiguous statutory language. It is reasonably clear, however, that in terms of political interests

[1] [1956] A.C. 736.

served, any particular method of statutory construction may sometimes cut one way and sometimes another. There have been suggestions that in recent years the House of Lords has shown 'a particularly strong addiction to the literal rule'. Unfortunately the alternatives in this controversy are somewhat confused, since it is possible to pay tribute to the doctrine that courts must give literal effect to the words used by the legislature whilst expressing views about what Parliament must have 'literally' intended which are based upon arguments other than grammatical and syntactical ones. 'Literal' meaning suffers from its ambiguous status of being associated historically with narrow or grammatical methods of adjudication and being merely an emphatic synonym for 'true intention', which begs all the evidentiary questions as to the methods and limits which are permissible in establishing it. The assumptions behind Laski's complaint about literalism in his addendum to the Donoughmore Report in 1932 were that 'narrow' or 'literal' construction (that is construction looking primarily to the statutory context and not to the mischief or social purpose aimed at) would both distort the true intention of the legislature and favour the social interests which the bench unconsciously wished to protect. Many 'literal' interpretations of administrative powers have, however, worked against private interests in property, so they can no longer be confidently associated with an individualistic bias. Moreover, though both individualism and a desire to maintain the rights of the courts against legislative restriction on review may have been assumed to march together, the latter field at least has not been remarkable for excessive literalism. Some of the interpretations, for example, which the courts in recent times have placed upon words such as 'final' and 'conclusive' as applied to the decisions of administrative tribunals could hardly have been predicted merely from a working knowledge of the English language.

4. LORD DENNING ON THE JUDICIAL ROLE

The ambivalence of the relationship between particular judicial methods and social values such as justice or freedom emerges clearly from some of the extra-judicial views expressed by Lord Denning. In the Romanes lecture in 1959[1] Lord

---

[1] *From Precedent to Precedent* (1959).

Denning has pursued the thesis that judges should serve the 'fundamental principles of truth and justice'. There is, he suggests, a correlation between the narrowing of freedom and the habits of some lawyers in adhering strictly to precedent and the literal meaning of words. Lawyers, he adds, sometimes take pride in Tennyson's words about freedom broadening down from precedent to precedent, but to stand by precedents, 'however wrong they may be and whatever injustice they inflict', does nothing to broaden freedom.[1] If, of course, strict precedent is contrasted with justice, and *stare decisis* is formulated as standing by decisions 'however wrong', the conclusion is plausible. If, on the other hand, *stare decisis* means standing by decisions when in point, irrespective of the consequences, then the doctrine may or may not work in favour of freedom. Liberality of method and a willingness to create new precedents may indeed work against liberty, and an adherence to established principle (for example against an encroaching executive) may work to augment liberty.

In speaking of the lawyer's task as 'serving fundamental principles of justice' Lord Denning makes a comparison between the lawyer and the scientist: 'Just as the scientist seeks for truth so the lawyer should seek for justice.' But it might be questioned whether the lawyer's relation to justice is analogous to the scientist's relation to truth, if 'lawyer' means 'judge' as distinct from 'law-maker' or 'legal adviser'. Equally debatable is the conclusion that the building up and discarding of scientific laws or principles provides a foundation for the view that 'the principles of the lawyer' should be 'modified' or 'discarded' when found to be 'unsuited to the times'. One may remember Bentham's scorn at Blackstone's remark that the 'reason and spirit' of the law as applied by the judges should ensure that 'when the reason of a law ceases the law ought likewise to cease with it'. ('Were I a corrupt dispenser of the law', Bentham said, 'I could wish for no better warrant for my enterprises.' 'Change of circumstances may happen but change of circumstances may be gradual and may have happened in the eyes of some before it has in the eyes of others. . . . It is for them only to alter the course of expectation who first gave it its direction.')[2] Lord

---

[1] Ibid., p. 1.

[2] *Comment on the Commentaries*, ed. C. W. Everett, p. 123.

Denning concedes that many lawyers would dispute the analogy with science and express a concern with 'the law as it is, not with what it ought to be'. But that approach, he suggests, is that of 'the working lawyer', who applies the law as the 'working mason lays bricks without any responsibility for the building which he is making'. It is not good enough, he adds, for the lawyer who is concerned with his responsibility to the community at large. He, it is implied, should approach his job with something of the architect's attitude. Taken literally, such a proposal might seem to amount to a claim to engage in avowed judicial legislation. It may, however, amount to no more than a claim to a creative role where precedents conflict or where clear legislative direction is absent. A similar difficulty occurs in construing the well-known passage on statutory interpretation in *Seaford Court Estates Ltd.* v. *Asher*. On that occasion it was said by Denning L.J. (as he then was) that

the English language is not an instrument of mathematical precision. Our literature would be much the poorer if it were. A judge, believing himself to be fettered by the supposed rule that he must look to the language and nothing else, laments that the draftsmen have not provided for this or that, or have been guilty of some or other ambiguity. It would certainly save the judges trouble if Acts of Parliament were drafted with Divine prescience and perfect clarity. In the absence of it . . . a judge . . . must set to work on the constructive task of finding the intention of Parliament, and he must do this not only from the language of the Statute but also from a consideration of the social conditions which gave rise to it, and of the mischief which it was passed to remedy, and then he must supplement the written word so as to give 'force and life' to the intention of the legislature. . . . A judge should ask himself the question: If the makers of the Act had themselves come across this ruck in the texture of it, how would they have straightened it out? He must then do as they would have done. A judge must not alter the material of which it is woven, but he can and should iron out the creases.[1]

In a later case he added: 'We sit here to find out the intention of Parliament and of Ministers and carry it out and we do this better by filling in the gaps and making sense of the enactment than by opening it up to destructive analysis.'[2] These

[1] (1949), 2 K.B. 481 at 499.
[2] *Magor & St. Mellons R.D.C.* v. *Newport Corporation*, [1952] 2 All E.R. 1226 at 1236.

propositions were criticized in the House of Lords as 'stated rather widely' and as 'a grave misconception'—'a naked usurpation of the legislative function under the thin disguise of interpretation'. 'The duty of the court', said Lord Simonds, 'is to interpret the words that the legislature has used. Those words may be ambiguous, but even if they are, the power and duty of the court to travel outside them on a voyage of discovery are strictly limited.'[1]

Lord Denning's language has been defended on the ground that he was not, in speaking of straightening out the rucks in statutes, thinking of judicial legislation by analogy, in a matter for which the legislature had failed to provide, but merely of filling out the wording or resolving ambiguities of expression.[2] Despite his earlier reference to 'filling in gaps', Lord Denning has, in fact, said that judges ought not to 'fill in gaps' which they may suppose to exist in an Act of Parliament.[3] But, standing on its own, the metaphorical language of 'gaps', 'rucks', 'omissions', and 'hiatuses' is insufficiently precise to distinguish between these two different activities. One man's rightly straightened ruck in the texture of legislation may be another's improperly filled gap.

Similar difficulties arise about the moulding of common law principles to serve the ends of justice. There may be initiative or boldness where precedent is vague or conflicting and—rather differently—boldness which alters settled principles. Throughout his Romanes lecture Lord Denning compares the attitudes of lawyers unfavourably with those of laymen on juries and in the House of Lords who have, it is suggested, shown greater boldness than the judges in broadening freedom. One such case was *Ashby* v. *White*,[4] in which the King's Bench held that Ashby had no cause of action for the refusal of his vote by a returning officer, the matter being, in the view of the majority of the judges, one of Parliamentary privilege and not within their competence to determine. The bolder House of Lords then created a cause of action in effect, by resolution of fifty votes to sixteen. The laymen in the House

[1] Ibid., [1952] A.C. 189 at 191.
[2] See J. L. Montrose, 'The Treatment of Statutes by Lord Denning,' 1 *University of Malaya Law Review* 37 (1959).
[3] *London Transport Executive* v. *Betts*, [1959] A.C. 213 at 247.
[4] (1703), 2 Ld. Raym. 938.

of Commons, unfortunately, were bolder still and imprisoned Ashby's colleagues and arrested their counsel when they applied for Habeas Corpus—a result which did little to add to the broadening down of freedom.

Other illustrations of judicial timidity are suggested. In *Chapman* v. *Chapman*[1] the House of Lords for lack of precedents held that the Court of Chancery had no jurisdiction to vary the terms of a trust in the interests of infant children. In *London Graving Dock Co.* v. *Horton*[2] lawyers worked injustice by relying on the words of Willes J. (in *Indermaur* v. *Dames*[3]) which were 'carefully chosen, often acted upon and form the basis upon which the duty of an invitor is established'. In *Re Herwin* the court had shown itself 'in bondage to words' by following, contrary to its inclination, the well-settled principle that the word 'children' in a will does not extend to illegitimate children.[4]

Throughout the argument there seems a potential running together of two different propositions—one being that lack of precedents, or unclear precedents, ought not to be allowed to work injustice or to narrow freedom—the other being that where they work injustice even clear precedents or established rules ought to yield to bold views based on moral conviction and the furtherance of justice or freedom.

5. REMEDIES FOR 'RESTRICTIVISM'

Where statutes are concerned, a similar distinction might be made between, on the one hand, bold, broad, or policy-orientated construction where there is admitted uncertainty in the terms of what Parliament has enacted, and on the other hand boldness in rejecting an apparently clear provision by consideration of evidence tending to show that some different result had in fact been aimed at by the legislature. A typical example of the first situation is the 'ruck' or imprecision of general language indicated by Lord Denning in the *Seaford* case. An example of the second type of conflict may be seen in *Inland Revenue Commissioners* v. *Hinchy*,[5] where a bold view was not taken. Here the House of Lords followed a 'restrictive' course

---

[1] [1954] A.C. 429.   [2] [1951] A.C. 737.   [3] L.R. 1. C.P. at 288.
[4] 1953 Ch. at 712. A similar construction was given (Lord Denning still dissenting) to the word 'descendant' in *Sydall* v. *Castings Ltd.*, [1967] 1 Q.B 302.
[5] [1960] A.C. 748.

in holding that a tax evasion penalty of 'treble the tax which
the taxpayer ought to be charged under this Act' meant 'three
times the whole tax chargeable for the year' though it was
reasonably clear that the penalty intended had been 'three times
the amount of tax evaded'. It is in this situation, where there is
some probability or even certainty that the draftsmen had in
mind a purpose or meaning which cannot be collected in the
court's view from the language used, that Lord Simonds's
assertion that the courts do not sit to find out the intention of
Parliament has its bite. This problem seems to need separate
consideration from the problem of resolving ambiguities or applying general terms to particular situations, where there is not in
the same sense any intention of Parliament to contrast with the
words used. Where the courts have said (as in *Hinchy*) that the
intention of Parliament can only be taken 'from the words that
they have used in the Act', or that 'what the legislature intended
to be done or not to be done can only be legitimately ascertained
from what it has chosen to enact',[1] it has almost always been
the first type of situation which was in contemplation (conflict
between language and alleged or suspected intention). But these
remarks can easily and inappropriately be cited as apparently
restrictive judicial declarations against all examination of legislative intention, even over the second range of problems relating
to generality, ambiguity, and 'fringe' meanings (which numeric-
ally is probably the larger range). Conversely, advocacy of more
liberal use of Parliamentary evidence of legislative purposes in
this second range may serve to obscure the issue of principle
which arises when legislative intention is reasonably clear or
discernible, but is in conflict with what has been enacted as
collected from the legislative instrument itself.

What is there to be said about this latter issue of principle?
One point worth noting is that giving effect to the language
where it is thought clear, and where it differs from probable
intention, does not consistently promote any particular social
interest. Sometimes it favours the individual, where a broad or
penal provision or administrative power is restricted in its
scope.[2] On other occasions (as in *Hinchy*) it works to the

[1] *Salomon* v. *Salomon*, [1897] A.C. 22 at 38.
[2] As in *Fisher* v. *Bell*, [1961] 1 Q.B. 394, where the display of a 'flick knife' in
a shop window was held not to be an 'offer for sale' under the Offensive Weapons
Act, 1959, but only an invitation to treat.

disadvantage of the individual if general words are implemented despite evidence of a narrower legislative intention. A further example of such a conflict between narrow intention and broad language can be seen in the Cinematograph Act of 1909. In that Act local authorities were given power to regulate cinema premises. It is clear from the title 'An Act to make better provision for securing safety . . .' and from the short second reading debate (covering only one and a half pages of *Hansard*) that fire and safety risks were the only purpose in contemplation. However, the power to license was conferred in general terms and, when used for the purpose of film censorship, was upheld, the courts refusing to give the general words a restricted interpretation.[1]

In principle such differences between intention and performance are possible in all forms of written instrument, whether statutes, statutory instruments, treaties, contracts, or wills. It may be, however, that different considerations of policy are applicable as between them. In the case of wills and contracts the importance of giving effect to the true intentions of the persons involved might be ranked higher than in the case of a statute where the transaction involves an artificial legislative person and the whole community. It is not simply a question of communication of meaning between legislature and judiciary. Certainty, predictability and the rule of law are involved, even possibly at the expense of partial or occasional frustration of legislative or governmental purposes. Unlike a testator, Parliament can always make a fresh statute. There may therefore be some basis for the view that even clear evidence of legislative purpose should not be allowed to displace the usual meaning of words (where there is a usual meaning) unless a clear indication is given that words are being used in a special or technical sense. A thesis of this kind might be thought to have its strongest application in criminal statutes and in the construction of delegated legislation (where the relevant purposes are in practice departmental, where the statutory instruments will probably not have been debated, and where they may be very readily amended).

The accusation that English rules for the interpretation of statutes are too restrictive has possibly two points. First of all,

[1] See, for example, *L.C.C.* v. *Bermondsey Bioscope Ltd.*, [1911] 1 K.B. 44.

it may be the case that inability to cite Parliamentary material has in the past narrowed the scope for arguing that words which at first seem plain are really problematical. A decision that a particular construction cannot fairly be placed on particular words ought only to be taken after all the circumstances in which they were used are known, and ought to be the end point of an investigation, not a reason for rendering part of an investigation unnecessary.[1] Secondly, it will always be relevant to look for evidence of general legislative objectives in that large range of cases which calls for the application of a general category or concept to particular facts. Whether a building is an 'industrial hereditament' or a house 'unfit for habitation' is something which cannot be clearly collected from the words used.

Two reformative proposals frequently made have been that access to Parliamentary materials should be permitted for direct interpretative purposes, and that memoranda explaining the general objects of legislation should be added to statutes. The English and Scottish Law Commissions have supported the second proposal whilst rejecting the first. Each proposal contains difficulties. As to Parliamentary proceedings some have doubted their relevance, citing the remarks of judges who have denied that it is the job of the courts to ascertain the intentions of Parliament. These remarks, it seems clear, were intended for the most part to convey the belief that the intentions of legislators should not displace their plain enactments where these were found to be so. Such remarks were not designed to deny the existence of legislative intentions or their possible relevance where no plain enactment existed.

If, therefore, evidence of legislative intention is, in at least some cases, relevant, may it be regarded in these cases as sufficiently useful or reliable? On this point it is not difficult to see reasons for scepticism. American critics of the abuse of legislative history have spoken of courts 'fumbling about in the ashcans of the legislative process for the shoddiest unenacted expressions of intention' and Mr. Justice Frankfurter in his *Reflections*

---

[1] It now seems agreed that particular words cannot in themselves be characterized as plain or ambiguous except in the context of the whole statute including its preamble (*A.G.* v. *Prince Ernest of Hanover*, [1957] A.C. 436). This argument can be extended to embrace the whole context in which the statutory words were used.

on the Reading of Statutes[1] warned that 'spurious use of legislative history must not swallow the legislation so as to give point to the quip that only when legislative history is doubtful do you go to the statute'.[2] In the same article Frankfurter pointed to the varying weights which must attach to different types of legislative expression. 'A painstaking detailed report by a Senate Committee bearing directly on the immediate question', he said, 'may settle the matter. A loose statement even by a chairman of a committee, made impromptu in the heat of debate . . . will hardly be accorded the weight of an encyclical.'

In a system such as that in the United Kingdom, where legislative committees do not sponsor legislation, there is no exactly comparable source of committee reports. Equally, however, statements about the meaning of legislation will vary in usefulness as between back-benchers (possibly with constituency or pressure-group interests in mind) and ministerial spokesmen. All such statements will obviously need to be weighed in relation to later statements and subsequent amendments in either House, but they might be expected to have several uses. One would be to confirm that some general purpose or mischief had in fact been contemplated when the Act was passed, when the contrary might have been argued by counsel. Another possible function would be to confirm or deny that certain particular situations had been contemplated as falling or not falling under a general provision. The Standing Committee stage of Bills is particularly useful as a source of this kind. If a particular situation or fringe meaning of a statutory term is in question, reference to the Standing Committee proceedings may reveal one of several things. It may be that, in the debate on the clause in which the disputed provision occurs, no reference was made to the point at issue. Alternatively, it may be that the point raised in litigation was discussed and that differing views were expressed, or that the Minister in charge of the Bill was unwilling to speculate about particular marginal situations which might or might not be covered in the Bill. Again, it might be found that the question was raised, that a number of members, including

---

[1] 47 *Columbia Law Rev.* 527.
[2] Both remarks are quoted (the former from Charles P. Curtiss) in the *Law Commission and Scottish Law Commission Report on the Interpretation of Statutes* H.C. 256 (1969) at p. 33.

the ministerial spokesman, expressed a consistent view, and that no one dissented. Examples of the last two situations could be drawn from the Committee stage of the 1965 Race Relations Act, a statute that has raised a number of difficult issues of interpretation. On the major questions of what acts may properly be included under the heading of 'incitement' or constitute 'publishing' the proceedings would yield nothing of value, both because very different views of the nature of the offence were held by different members and because the ministerial attitude —as very often in such penal statutes—was that the courts must be left to work out the application of the general terms. However, on other points the proceedings would be more useful. The meaning, for example, of 'section of the public' in s. 6 of the Race Relations Act has been in dispute. In *R. v. Britton*[1] the Court of Appeal found the term obscure and gave it a restricted meaning. Reference to the Commons Standing Committee debate on the relevant clause shows that the Home Secretary had explained that the phrase had been taken from the Public Order Act of 1936 and that it was introduced simply to counter the possibility that racial propaganda delivered to a particular gathering or restricted number might be held not to have been published or distributed to the public 'at large'. No one disputed this account or suggested any other meaning which the words might have. In this particular situation, therefore, *Hansard* would have provided the court and counsel with a persuasive means of resolving the point at issue.

The Law Commission have suggested as a possible view that the function of legislative material in the interpretative process might be better performed by specially prepared explanatory memoranda attached to a Bill and modified if necessary during its passage through Parliament. These might be modelled on the explanatory memoranda already attached to Bills on first introduction and on the Notes on Clauses prepared by Departments for Ministers, explaining the purpose and effect of each clause and possibly including practical examples of its application.

A similar suggestion was made by Harold Laski in 1929, in a note to the Report of the Committee on Ministers' Powers, that an accompanying memorandum should set out the purposes

[1] [1967] 2 Q.B. 51.

of the Bill. It is not easy to envisage the exact shape and
particularity of such a document. It might indeed be useful both
to the courts and members of Parliament to set out the origins
of the legislation and its relationship to earlier legislation. But
the promulgation of legislative objects or purposes would at
least in some cases raise difficulties. Many such difficulties may
arise in practice because legislation embodies different and
potentially conflicting purposes. Town-planning legislation, for
example, has for its objectives, amongst other things, both
advantage to the community and fairness to individual property
owners who may be disadvantaged. Industrial legislation has to
combine promotion of the interests of employers and employees.
Thus, a statement of purpose, if not tendentious or disputable,
might have to be so general as to be no more revealing than the
title of the Act. If, at the other extreme, particular instances of
situations covered by the Bill were to be included, a curious
form of delegated legislative activity would be created. If these
statements are available to M.P.s they will be raised and very
often disputed at the Committee stage by backbenchers or the
Opposition. If this is to happen, it might seem preferable that
any such particular assertions about the scope of the Bill as are
envisaged and propounded by the Government should be
formally embodied in the legislation.

Explanatory memoranda which were mainly recitals of the
course of earlier legislation and of the historical antecedents of
the Bill in question would seem more defensible. So, on balance,
would a modest Interpretation Act relaxing the rule against
direct citation of Parliamentary materials. (It is sometimes suggested that too great a burden would be placed on the legal
profession, but *Hansard* is fairly accessible in Britain and relevant legislative material is likely to be quickly embodied in
commentaries and textbooks.) In many cases parliamentary
materials will provide no evidence of any weight and in other
cases they may be irrelevant. It would therefore seem a
mistake to expect very much from either of these expedients.

V

THE SEPARATION OF POWERS

THE relationship between legislature and judiciary is perhaps the single most crucial relationship in a constitutional system. In the United Kingdom there is a concentration of formal power in the legislative organ, which in a certain sense, is superior to the executive and judicial branches of government. In other constitutional systems there is what is frequently characterized as a separation rather than a concentration of powers. The phrase 'separation of powers' is, however, one of the most confusing in the vocabulary of political and constitutional thought. It has been used with varying implications by historians and political scientists. It crops up in a number of places in constitutional and administrative law—in discussions, for example, of judicial independence, delegation of legislative powers, executive responsibility to legislatures, judicial review, and constitutionality of arbitral bodies exercising mixed functions. It is possible, indeed commonplace, for commentators to draw different conclusions both as to whether there is or is not a separation of powers in a given constitution and as to what particular conclusions of law or policy follow from the existence of a separation of powers, even where it is admitted to exist.

I. SOME AMBIGUITIES

One example of such uncertainty is the manifest disagreement which exists about the correctness of Montesquieu's description of English institutions. It has often been suggested that Montesquieu's assertions about the separation of powers in England were inappropriate even when he made them, since, in terms of persons, powers, and influence, the functions of government in England were intermixed. On the other hand, it is possible to argue that in certain senses his description was and is appropriate. Professor John Plamenatz, for example, suggests that, despite what was said by later critics, legislative and executive powers 'were separate when Montesquieu wrote De l'Esprit

des Lois and are still separate today'.[1] Montesquieu knew well
enough, he writes, that the King's Ministers were members of
one or other House of Parliament but, contrasting the exercise
of power in England with its exercise in France, he saw that
the Ministers were not the agents of the legislature nor vice
versa. Equally in England at the present time the Cabinet and
Parliament are different organs and their relationships are
different from what they would be in a system such as the
Russian, in which 'the same body exercises in fact (though not
in name) both the executive and the legislative power, the
Supreme Soviet having no other function than to applaud the
decisions taken by the real rulers of the country'.[2] Of course
the extent to which party solidarity unifies the activities of
formally separate organs is only a matter of degree. Clearly the
degree is very great in the U.S.S.R., smaller in the United Kingdom, and smaller still in the United States. Since the American
style of separation had not yet emerged in 1748, Montesquieu
may perhaps be forgiven for applying the phrase 'separation of
powers' to the British constitution, particularly in relation to the
separation or independence of the judicial power, and particularly also as a way of contrasting Britain with some continental
form of monarchical government.

Some disagreements about the legislative–executive separation of powers obviously turn upon ambiguities as between the
physical or legal separation of persons and the separateness or
independence of functions. In discussions of the constitutional
regime of the French Fifth Republic, for example, it is sometimes asserted that a principle of separation of powers has been
introduced. One simple sense in which this is true is that the
constitution makes legislative and executive office-holding
incompatible. Ministers (though they are not, like American
department heads, both constitutionally and physically separated from the legislative chamber) may not sit as members of
the National Assembly. On the other hand, they are not separated from and independent of the legislative body in the sense
of being immune from dismissal by it, since they must resign
their ministerial offices if defeated on a vote of confidence.[3]

---

[1] *Man and Society*, vol. 1, p. 289.   [2] Ibid., p. 290.

[3] The President is separated from the Assembly since he is not accountable to it,
though it is not in a sense separated from him, since he can, unlike the U.S. President, dissolve the legislature.

Though the physical separation of the American President and his Cabinet from Congress is the feature which superficially attracts attention, it is clearly less significant than the fact that the executive branch can neither be removed by, nor dissolve, the legislature. Neither derives its powers from the other but each is co-ordinate in deriving its powers separately from the constitution.

In relation to the separateness of the judicial power from the legislative and executive branches there is a further striking oddity of usage. The separation of powers doctrine has been used inconsistently both to support and to refute the need for judicial invalidation, or quashing, of legislative or executive action. Here two different metaphorical images seem to be at work. In Anglo-American usage there has grown up the idea that the branches of government, when 'separated', may legitimately check or act upon each other and indeed are separated precisely so that they may exercise such mutual checks. Hence (*inter alia*) judicial review of legislation in the characteristic American sense. In France, on the other hand, the view is maintained that powers which are separate may not interfere in each other's function. Hence the review of legislation or administrative action by the judicial branch[1] is thought impermissible. The powers of government are here imagined as separated, in the sense of partitioned off or isolated from each other. A similar view seems to be held by Hans Kelsen in his *General Theory of Law and State*, where it is said that 'the judicial review of legislation is an obvious encroachment upon the principle of separation of powers'.[2]

A further element of confusion enters into arguments about separation of powers, when what is under discussion is not the policy of separating persons or organs but the separability of the *concepts* of 'legislative', 'executive', and 'judicial' as ways of characterizing governmental actions. In this context opposition to the 'separation of powers' or declarations that the doctrine is outdated or discredited usually imply the view that the notions of what are 'legislative', 'executive', or 'judicial' activities cannot be simply or sharply differentiated from each other. It is not immediately obvious what conclusions about policy, if any,

---

[1] The administrative courts are not constitutionally part of the judicial branch.

[2] *General Theory of Law and State*, trans. A. Wedberg (1961), p. 269.

follow from believing this. It has, however, suggested to some that objections to the exercise of 'adjudicatory' or 'legislative' powers by 'executive' officials are unfounded.

2. FORMS OF SEPARATION

There is then in the apparently simple phrase 'separation of powers' a cluster of overlapping ideas (for example, 'distribution', 'differentiation', 'isolation', 'confrontation'). Not all of these are synonymous and the implications of some are mutually inconsistent. At least the following may be distinguished:

1. The *differentiation* of the concepts 'legislative', 'executive', and 'judicial'.
2. The *legal incompatibility* of office-holding as between members of one branch of government and those of another, with or without *physical separation* of persons.
3. The *isolation, immunity,* or *independence* of one branch of government from the actions or interference of another.
4. The *checking or balancing* of one branch of government by the action of another.
5. The *co-ordinate* status and lack of accountability of one branch to another.

References to the separation of powers may be references to any one or to any combination of these ideas. Most of them can be seen in a definition of the phrase which appears in the official Congressional Commentary on the United States Constitution prepared by Professor E. S. Corwin. The doctrine may be summed up, it is said, in the following propositions:

1. There are three intrinsically distinct functions of government; the legislative, the executive, and the judicial:
2. these distinct functions ought to be exercised respectively by three separately manned departments of government; which
3. should be constitutionally equal and mutually independent; and
4. . . . the legislative may not delegate its powers.[1]

---

[1] *Constitution of the United States of America: Analysis and Interpretation*, 1964 edn., pp. 9–10.

Two things may be said about this definition. In the first place, it is not one to be found in its entirety in any of the traditional authorities from whose writings the theory is normally thought to be derived. In the second place, it is doubtful whether it could be said to fit the political arrangements either of the United States or of any other working constitution past or present.

Historically it is not easy to distinguish recognizable assertions of separation of powers doctrine from other theories. The description of distinct functions of government, for example, may be seen in Aristotle's *Politics*. In England there were theories of mixed government, and of checks and balances between the three Estates of the Realm. Here the balance was not so much between specialized governmental functions as between different total constitutional principles (monarchical, oligarchical, democratic) for allocating sovereign authority, and it is argued that these principles are respectively represented by King, Lord, and Commons.[1] The balance is here between different elements or estates sharing legislative power rather than a balance of legislative against other forms of power. Then there were the theories about the different modes in which royal power was exercised, and the common law doctrine of natural justice which frowned upon the notion of any authority executing and judging in its own cause.

Locke's much-quoted remarks about the separation of powers are related to this last doctrine. It may be, he said, 'too great temptation to human frailty, apt to grasp at power, for the same persons who have the power of making laws to have also in their hands the power to execute them, whereby they may exempt themselves from obedience to the laws they make'.[2] Locke's advocacy of separation is thus a mixture of the natural justice argument and a quite different argument about physical separation. Laws, he says, take only a little time to make and there is no reason for the legislature to be continuously in session. But there is need of a constant and lasting force to

---

[1] Blackstone's exposition of this balance is well known. It is the three estates in Parliament also that earlier writers saw as checking and balancing each other. Bolingbroke wrote: 'The proceedings of each part of the government when they come forth into action and affect the whole are both to be examined and controlled by the other parts' (*Remarks on the History of England, Works*, 1809, vol. 2, pp. 413–14).

[2] *Second Treatise of Civil Government*, chap. xii, para. 143.

execute the laws. Thus the legislators, having assembled and made the laws, may *separate* and 'being separated again they are themselves subject to the laws they have made'.[1] This sense of 'separation'—namely 'dispersal' of the legislative body—has nothing to do with the 'separating', 'isolating', or 'balancing' senses of the term. Locke certainly did not believe in the separation of powers in the sense of 'independence and equality' of executive and legislature; for he held: 'There can be but one supreme power, which is the legislative, to which all the rest are and must be subordinate.'[2] Nor did he deal in any separation of judicial power, which was considered by him as a part of the executive.

Montesquieu, on the other hand, certainly emphasized the need to place judicial and executive power in different hands, and also spoke of the mutual balancing and restraining of the legislative and the executive power. But perhaps, through a running together of the checking and balancing theories of mixed government with the separation of persons doctrine, neither he nor many others down to the present day seem clear as to whether 'checking' of one branch by another is a participation in the other's function and a partial violation of the separation of powers doctrine, or whether it is actually an exemplification of the doctrine, which carries out the very purpose of the separating and balancing off against each other of the three branches of government. Thus legislative impeachment of executive officers, or executive veto of legislation, or judicial review of administrative, or legislative action, are sometimes treated in the one way and sometimes in the other—as illustrations of the theory, or as partial exceptions which need explanation or excuse. Something of this can be seen in the *Federalist* papers. James Madison, in No. 47, suggests that Montesquieu's doctrine did not mean that the separate departments of government might have 'no *partial agency* in, or no *control* over the acts of each other'. His meaning, Madison argues, was no more than that one department should not possess the *whole* power of another. It was not possible to avoid all intermixture of functions. Thus, executive vetoes on legislation, or appointment of judicial officials by the executive, were not contrary to Montesquieu's thesis, though they might be cases in which the

---

[1] Loc. cit.   [2] Ibid., para. 149.

departments had not been kept totally separate and distinct. Here 'partial agency' in another function, and control by one department of the function of another, are clearly treated as departures, though justifiable ones, from some pure principle of distinctness or separation. Yet the balancing theory implies that such mutual checking and control is a part of, and not a departure from, separation of powers theory. In fact American separation of powers theory seems a mixture of ideas about isolating, checking, balancing, and interacting. These were sometimes brought into a sort of consistency by the argument that mutual checks and powers of interaction were necessary practical ways of protecting and preserving the original 'paper' separation or isolation.

What Madison called 'partial agency or control' perhaps raises the question whether all the various ways in which checks may be exercised on one department by another can be properly called 'partial agency or participation' in the other's function. Possibly the power of an executive head of government to veto legislative measures might be called the exercise of a legislative power—at least a negative one—and therefore a partial interference by one agency with the function of another. Impeachment by legislative bodies could certainly be called the exercise of a judicial function. On the other hand, the executive's placing of a veto on legislation, especially if subject, as it usually is, to subsequent legislative overriding, need not necessarily be characterized as a legislative function but simply as one legitimate special function of an executive agency.

The question occurs in its most acute form when it is asked whether judicial review of legislative action is itself participation in the legislative function or merely part of the judicial function. The indeterminacy of the answer to this question permitted both the early proponents and the antagonists of judicial review in the United States to support their arguments by reference to the separation of powers doctrine.

3. SEPARATION OF POWERS AND JUDICIAL REVIEW

A separation between the judicial and the legislative and executive branches obviously exists in both Britain and the United States in the sense that in practice the judges are secure in their offices and have an independent status. But whether the separation of powers doctrine implies the existence of that degree of checking or controlling which has come to be known as judicial review in the American sense is not easy to decide. The right to invalidate legislation obviously in one sense invades the principle that each department has an independent sphere of action and a right to take its own view on matters of constitutionality. On the other hand, the controlling or checking functions of the judicial branch can only consist in impartial application of the law, and where constitutional law places restrictions on legislative power, a duty to declare the law seems to imply a duty to declare when such restrictions have been violated, whether by the legislature or by anyone else.

The Founders of the American constitution were notoriously unspecific about judicial review of legislation. The doctrine eventually won the day and reading its history backwards it seems firmly enough entrenched in the tradition of Coke, Locke, and what Professor E. S. Corwin dubbed the 'higher law background'. It was not, perhaps, from Locke's separation of powers arguments that review gained support so much as from his theses about limited legislative power, property, and vested rights. Even so, the victory of judicial review was not a foregone conclusion.[1] There was a newer doctrine than Coke's about legislative power. The 'honied Mansfieldism of Blackstone', Professor Corwin writes, 'was becoming influential in the later days of the pre-Revolutionary controversy'. Despite some confusion, the upshot of Blackstone's doctrine was that sovereignty and legislative power were to be equated, and this view was later to be cited against Marshall's decision in *Marbury* v. *Madison*[2] by American opponents of judicial review.

The enactment of the Federal Constitution, however, gave the advocates of review an argument proof against Blackstonian jurisprudence and at the same time independent of natural law and Lockian political theory. Once the higher law principles had been reduced to written form they acquired an independent positive authority. Blackstone's sovereign legislative power could be attributed to the constituent people and

---

[1] *The Higher Law Background of American Constitutional Law* first published in 42 *Harvard Law Review* 149 and 365.
[2] 1 Cranch 137 (1803).

its edicts enforced by the courts against all delegates and lesser agencies, including state and federal legislators.

It remained true, nevertheless, that this conclusion was not spelled out in so many words—indeed in any words at all—in the Federal constitution. Historians have suggested that twenty or thirty of the forty delegates to the Philadelphia convention favoured the adoption of judicial review; but their views do not clearly appear. Summing up the proceedings relating to the proposed judicial power, Max Farrand wrote: 'Not a word in all this of that great power exercised by the federal courts to declare laws null and void if they are in contravention to the constitution.'[1] So when Chief Justice Marshall came to consider the question in 1803[2] he had to rely in large part on *a priori* reasoning. It was, he said, 'a proposition too plain to be contested that the constitution controls any legislative act repugnant to it'. From this it followed that the judicial department must either enforce the constitution in a particular case or give effect to a law in violation of the constitution. Much of the argument had already been sketched out in Alexander Hamilton's *Federalist* paper, Number 78. The judiciary, Hamilton said, would always be the least dangerous branch of government, having neither force nor will, but merely judgment. In a constitution of limited powers that judgment must be applied to declare all acts contrary to the manifest tenor of the constitution void. No position was clearer than that every act of a delegated authority contrary to the tenor of the commission under which it is exercised is void. No legislative act therefore contrary to the Constitution could be valid. To deny this would be to affirm that the deputy is greater than his principal; that the representatives of the people are superior to the people themselves; that men acting by virtue of powers may do not only what these powers do not authorize but what they forbid.

Hamilton's essay anticipated a number of arguments which could be urged against judicial review. His conclusions might be thought, he said, to suppose a superiority of the judicial to the legislative power. But in reality they only supposed that the power of the people was supreme to both. Nor, he added,

[1] M. Farrand, *The Framing of the Constitution of the United States*, p. 156.
[2] *Marbury* v. *Madison*, 1 Cranch 137 (1803).

could it be of any weight to argue that the courts, on a pretence of repugnancy to the constitution, would substitute their own pleasure for the intention of the legislature. That might as well happen in adjudicating between two statutes or in every adjudication upon any single statute. The courts must declare the law, and if they were disposed to exercise will instead of judgment the consequence would equally in all cases be the substitution of their will for that of the legislative body. If the observation proved anything it would prove that there ought to be no judges at all distinct from the legislative body.

The hypothetical opponent of judicial review might on some points think himself roughly treated by both Hamilton and Marshall. He would not perhaps deny the repeated assertions that limited power is limited power and that the constitution must prevail over legislation repugnant to it. He could even concede that the judges must do their duty and uphold the constitution. He might, nevertheless, still think that these propositions leave room for argument about who is to decide when the admittedly superior constitutional rule has been violated by the legislature. He might also think it uncertain what precise obligation the constitution, rightly interpreted, allots to the judicial branch as its duty in this field. Assertions that judicial duty is to apply the law are not to the point if what is in issue is whether the law of the constitution implicitly allots judgment in particular cases to the legislative body rather than to the judiciary. As to the argument about the substitution of the courts' will for the legislature, might not the objector add that, in many matters of constitutional repugnancy, will and judgment cannot be simply or tidily separated.

Some of these rejoinders were in fact made in a well-known dissenting opinion by Mr. Justice Gibson in the Pennsylvania Supreme Court in 1825 in relation to state constitutions. He conceded that a constitution and the right of the legislature to pass an Act might be in collision but it did not, he thought, follow, where a constitution did not expressly confer a power of review, that it must be the peculiar duty of the judiciary to determine that fact and to revise and correct the proceedings of the legislative power. To affirm that the judiciary had the sole right to judge when such a collision occurred was to take for granted the very thing to be proved. All the organs of government were in theory of equal capacity. They might be considered superior only in those things for which they had a peculiar capacity. That of the judiciary was the construction of laws when made. To assume that judges should be able to scan the authority of the law-giver was to allot them a superior capacity to that of the legislature rather than a co-ordinate role. Repugnancy to the constitution was not always self-evident, and the legislature was entitled to deference in the execution of its role. Since the legislative role peculiarly involved the consideration of the limitations placed upon legislative power, the legislature should be deemed to have a superior capacity to judge matters of constitutionality.[1]

These arguments might conceivably have prevailed. It was not until 1857 that the Supreme Court again asserted its power against an Act of Congress and some have suggested that but for Marshall's stand in 1803, seventy years of judicial acquiescence might have made opposition to Congressional omnipotence futile.[2] If Marshall's argument had not prevailed in America it might well not have prevailed elsewhere, and a good deal of the world's constitutional history might have been different. In Australia in 1951, for example, it was said (in *Australian Communist Party* v. *Commonwealth*): 'If the great case of *Marbury* v. *Madison* . . . had pronounced a different view [judicial review] might perhaps not arise even in the case of the Commonwealth Parliament; and there are those, even today, who disapprove of the doctrine of *Marbury* v. *Madison* and who do not see why the courts rather than the legislature itself should have the function of finally deciding whether an act of a legislature in a Federal system is or is not within power.'[3] Not all federal systems and written constitutions have favoured review of federal legislation. That point, in fact, was made by James Bradley Thayer in 'The Origin and Scope of the American Doctrine of Constitutional Law' in 1893.[4] The division of legislative powers in a federal system has, however, been a powerful factor in augmenting the policing of state legislative powers by judicial bodies. Even Mr. Justice Holmes believed review of this kind essential,

[1] *Eakin* v. *Raub*, 12 Sergeant and Rawle 330.
[2] See, for example, Samuel J. Konefsky, *John Marshall and Alexander Hamilton* (1964), p. 90.
[3] (1951), 83 C.L.R. 1, 262. [4] 7 *Harvard Law Review* 129, 130.

whilst holding that the United States might survive without a Supreme Court power to invalidate Acts of Congress. On the other hand, the functional separation of governmental powers in both federal and unitary systems has been quite frequently used as an argument *against* judicial review.[1] In reality, arguments from the separation of powers, though frequently mentioned, are ultimately of little force on either side of the controversy. As a consideration in favour of review the doctrine is too vague and (since better arguments exist) superfluous. As an argument against review it is in its commonest forms unconvincing. Kelsen[2] makes use of several such separation of powers arguments. Amendment by another organ of a law issued by the legislature is, he has written, a remarkable *restriction* of its powers which creates a *negative legislature* beside a positive one. Such an annulling organ 'forms an authority *above* the legislator'. The right of the law-applying organs to refuse to apply unconstitutional laws (which right Kelsen holds to exist except where explicitly restricted) must indeed have an impact upon the legislators and upon proposed legislation. But in relation to the legislative organ itself, which is a set of procedures and not simply a body of persons, it could be argued that the impact is not from 'above' or from a position of superiority. The legislative organ, with its procedures and powers as defined in the constitution, might be said to be served, enhanced, or protected, rather than restricted, when declarations are made that preserve its legitimate powers from abuse. There may indeed be situations where constitutional adjudication of this kind could be legitimately described as a form of negative legislation if the criteria enforced are of a broad and general sort (such as the American due process or equal protection

[1] e.g. Learned Hand, *The Bill of Rights* (1958), p. 10: 'It was a plausible—indeed to my mind an unanswerable—argument that it [judicial review] invaded that "Separation of Powers" which as many believed was the condition of all free governments.'

[2] *General Theory of Law and State*, pp. 157, 268 (my italics). Kelsen's views are not clear. He implies at one point that the separation or division of powers is a possible and respectable theory, but one opposed to the idea of democracy (which requires that the legislative organ be given control over the administrative and judicial organs). Elsewhere he seems to argue that there can be no such theory since it presupposes that there are three definable and distinct functions of government which, he suggests, is not the case (as there are only two—creation and application of norms).

requirements) but it need not be the case that all such adjudication is in the same sense 'legislative'. Suppose that a legislature were constitutionally forbidden to exercise its powers on Sundays. Could judicial annulment of an unconstitutional legislative act passed on that day fairly be called 'legislative' or 'negative legislation'? Kelsen does not use the argument which some American opponents of judicial review have used, that each co-ordinate branch of government has the right to take its own view of the constitutionality of laws. Historically this argument for legislative immunity from review seems to be less an inference from the separation of powers than from the idiosyncratic English doctrine in which the legislative body inherits some of the formal characteristics of a court. No more than the related power of the High Court of Parliament to punish contempts is it essentially connected with the exercise of legislative functions as such. The co-ordinateness or equality of the legislative and other functions means simply that all are equally allotted their role by the constitution in the American style of separation of powers. None is supreme in allotting powers to the others. But it does not follow from this that they are equally entitled to exercise any particular function. Their functions and capacities are different and their impacts upon each other must be different in consequence. Adjudication must by definition have an impact upon everything in the system. The subjection of legislators, amongst others, to the law does not make the legislature an inferior branch, or detract from its co-ordinate status.

4. SEPARATION OF POWERS AND POLITICAL QUESTIONS

The doctrine of separation of powers has been invoked in an equally equivocal way in argument about the nature of 'political' questions. Both in the United States and elsewhere there has been a set of loosely related views about certain issues which could be roughly indicated by saying that they suggest that some types of dispute are unsuitable for judicial settlement. The nature of this unsuitability has not always been precisely defined. But feelings about it can be seen reflected in doctrines about 'non justiciability', about 'acts of state' or 'actes de gouvernement', and in the insertion in some constitutions of

'Directive Principles of State Policy' alongside judicially enforceable guarantees of citizens' rights. Typical areas in which
such issues have been thought to arise are international relations,
social and economic affairs, and the organization of political
parties and elections. In one sense the resolution of disputed
questions in these areas solely by executive or legislative agencies
might seem to violate the separation of powers. On the other
hand, like opposition to judicial review in general, the exclusion
of the judiciary from 'political questions' has also been defended
on separation of powers grounds.[1]

The American doctrine of political questions evolved by the
Supreme Court has had mixed roots. In foreign affairs, for
example, analogies have been seen with English doctrine about
acts of state. Here the argument against judicial intervention has
been alleged to stem not from separation of powers needs but
from the notion that an act of state is an 'exercise of sovereign
power' which for that reason 'cannot be challenged, controlled
or interfered with by municipal courts'.[2]

Other independent reasons have, however, been advanced,
such as that courts should not meddle in party politics or 'state-
craft'; that determination of certain questions should be left to
the electorate; or that no clear rules or precedents exist; or that
there might be difficulty in enforcing a judgment on a reluctant
executive; or that another branch of government, the executive
or legislature, is charged with making the relevant determination.[3]

Some of these arguments can be seen in the majority opinion
in *Colegrove* v. *Green*[4] decided in 1946. The case began as a suit
against the Governor and State Officials of Illinois, to restrain
them from holding an election on the ground that electoral
districts in the State were malapportioned, in violation, *inter
alia*, of the equality guarantees in the 14th Amendment to the
Constitution. The majority held that a determination of this
issue would bring the courts into 'immediate and active relations with party contests'. It was hostile to a democratic system,
they said, to involve the judiciary in the politics of the people.

[1] 'Perhaps the most usual explanation for the establishment of the category of
political questions is to be found in the doctrine of the separation of powers', C. J.
Post, *The Supreme Court and Political Questions* (1936), p. 12.
[2] *Salaman* v. *Secretary of State for India*, [1906] 1 K.B. 613.
[3] *Luther* v. *Borden*, 7 How 1 (1849).   [4] 328 U.S. 549 (1946).

Courts ought not to enter this 'political thicket'. The constitution had left the performance of many duties to 'depend on the fidelity of the executive and legislative action, and ultimately on the vigilance of the people in exercising their political rights'.[1]

The boundary line between entering the political thicket and dutifully applying constitutional guarantees of citizens' rights to equality and freedom is, however, obviously a misty one. It cannot be that every decision which has to do with the right to vote is fatally tainted with non-justiciability simply on the ground that voting is a political activity. The English judges in *Ashby* v. *White*[2] were prepared to vindicate the right to vote against an illegal refusal by returning officers, in the face of the argument that elections were a political and 'Parliamentary matter'. In the United States the right to vote has been protected against improper dilution by, for example, miscounting or ballot stuffing.[3] But what of dilution by more indirect means? This question was in issue in 1962 when the Supreme Court in *Baker* v. *Carr*[4] held that the inequality of electoral districts in Tennessee might, if not related to a logical and reasonable formula, amount to a denial by the state to voters of the equal protection of the law. Mr. Justice Frankfurter, dissenting, argued that this was a destructively novel exercise of judicial power in the area of an 'essentially political conflict of forces', which would imperil the Court's necessary detachment from political entanglement. The phrase 'political entanglement', standing alone, is of course vague. It suggests an improper or unwise dealing in political matters which are implicitly contrasted with 'judicial' matters or 'the judicial sphere'. But until it is established what political activities are constitutionally subject to judicial review the phrase must be question-begging. As the majority of the Court suggested, 'the mere fact that the suit seeks protection of a political right does not mean that it presents a political question'. Such an objection, they held, 'is little more than a play upon words'.[5] Mr. Justice Frankfurter, in effect, wished to assimilate or equate the issues in question

[1] 328 U.S. 549 at 556 (1945).   [2] (1703), 2 Ld. Raym. 938.
[3] *U.S.* v. *Classic* 313 U.S. 299 (1941); *U.S.* v. *Saylor*, 322 U.S. 385 (1944).
[4] 369 U.S. 186 (1962).
[5] Brennan J., 369 U.S. 186 at 209, quoting *Nixon* v. *Herndon*, 273 U.S. 536, 540.

to decisions about forms of government, or foreign affairs, or
competing theories of political philosophy. The court, he argued,
was being asked to choose between competing bases of representation. One could not speak of dilution or debasement of the
value of a vote without deciding what it should be worth. The
notion that electoral representation proportionate to population was a basic principle demanded by equality and representative government was unsound. 'It was not the English
system, it was not the colonial system, it was not the system
chosen for the national government by the constitution.' At
this point Mr. Justice Frankfurter seemed to be arguing with
some fervour and force from the bench that Tennessee's electoral
arrangements might not be constitutionally unequal as between
voters. But his major theme was that whether voting arrangements of the kind in question were unequal was not a question
which he as a judge was best fitted to decide, or in which
judicial declarations could effectively or beneficially be enforced.

The majority thought otherwise. Every formulation of the
phrase 'political question', they said, 'has one or more elements
which identify it as essentially a function of the separation of
powers'. There must be a textually demonstrable constitutional
commitment of the issue to a co-ordinate political department
of the Federal Government; or a lack of judicially discoverable
and manageable standards; or an impossibility of deciding it
without an initial policy determination of a discretionary and
non-judicial kind. None of these factors, they thought, was
present. Judicial standards under the Equal Protection clause
were well developed and familiar. It had always been open to
courts to determine that a discrimination reflected no policy, but
arbitrary and capricious action.

There were obvious connections here between Mr. Justice
Frankfurter's reasons for not wishing to enter this particular electoral thicket and his frequently expressed general advocacy of
judicial restraint in reviewing legislative policy. Since both advocates and opponents of this policy on the Supreme Court have
accepted the existence of the separation of powers in the United
States constitution it is very plain that the doctrine offers no
clearer guidance here than it did historically in establishing the
propriety or otherwise of judicial review itself. It does not tell us

whether judges ought to review legislative and administrative action or, if they should, how they should do it, or what, if any, exceptions there should be to the ambit of review.

5. SEPARATION, DELEGATION, AND MIXING OF POWERS

Inferences from the separation of powers principle have in various ways complicated the delegation of functions by legislative bodies to other agencies. The principle has been seen as an obstacle both to the exercise of rule-making powers by bodies other than legislatures and to the exercise of adjudicatory powers by bodies other than courts of law.

In the United States the delegation of legislative power was in principle thought to be prohibited by the constitutional allocation of legislative power to the federal and state legislatures in conjunction with the principle *delegatus non potest delegare*. Congress having had legislative power conferred upon it by the constituent People could not be permitted to abdicate it or transfer it into other hands. In the United Kingdom, where Parliament is itself the only formal source of legislative power, no legal difficulty has been thought to stand in the way of unlimited delegations of rule-making power to the executive, and argument has turned upon the political wisdom of such delegation and the means for its control.

A priori, the force of the maxim, *delegatus non potest delegare*, might well be doubted. The mere fact that a power has been given to a person or body might be thought to leave open the question of the manner in which the recipient should deal with his power. A veto upon his abandoning it or transferring it might be drawn from some explicit condition made when the power was conferred, or it might conceivably be drawn from the context and purpose of the powers in question. But it hardly seems to follow from the mere existence of the act of delegation. Similarly, the act of allocating power to separate bodies or persons in the way in which the United States constitution allocates legislative, executive, and judicial functions to Congress, the President, and the courts does not beyond all question imply that the power allocated to particular persons cannot be delegated, or that no other agencies can be created which may also exercise such powers, or that by their mutual concurrence the recipients of power may not interchange their powers in part or agree to the allocation of mixed powers to new governmental agencies. All such implications would, one might think, have to be explicitly spelled out as a premise of a separation of powers doctrine. But the United States constitution (unlike some of the State constitutions) does not even mention in so many words that the powers of government are to be separated. Nor do the Australian or Indian constitutions. Yet in all of these the assumption that they must be so separated has exercised a powerful (possibly regrettable, possibly unnecessary) influence on political and legal development, and has had to be avoided or circumvented by arguments which do not always carry conviction.

6. THE WITHERING OF
LEGISLATIVE–EXECUTIVE SEPARATION

The progressive breakdown or circumvention of the principle of separation of legislative and executive powers has been more obvious than the avoidance or dilution of the principle of judicial separation from the other two functions.

In the United States various arguments have been used to soften the rigours of legislative–executive separation. The possibility of delegation flowing from conditional legislation, for example, has long been recognized. Thomas Cooley, whilst citing Locke in support of the view that the power to legislate must remain where it has been placed by the governing people,[1] conceded that it was not always necessary that a legislative act should be a completed statute in the sense that what it enjoined should take place as law at the time that it left the hands of the legislative department. It could be conditional and its taking effect made to depend upon subsequent events or actions by executive officials.[2]

A second argument is that statutes may delegate to officials the power to 'fill up the details' of legislative provisions.[3]

---

[1] Locke's remark that the legislature 'neither must nor can transfer the power of making laws to anybody else, or place it anywhere but where the people have' (*Second Treatise of Civil Government*, para. 142) may have much to answer for.

[2] *Constitutional Limitations* (4th edn., 1878), pp. 141–2.

[3] *Wayman* v. *Southard*, 10 Wheat 1 (1825).

A third (and overlapping) argument is that delegation of rule-making powers may be upheld if the delegating statute lays down standards or principles 'leaving to selected instrumentalities the making of subordinate rules within prescribed limits'.[1] The increasing liberality of the Supreme Court in defining what is to count as a standard for this purpose is notorious. The power of a Federal regulatory agency to make rules justified by 'public convenience, interest or necessity',[2] for example, might in earlier times have been struck down as an abdication of legislative responsibility, but is no longer so pictured.

In Australia also, the necessities of economic regulation and the exercise of the defence power by the executive in wartime have obviously promoted the legitimizing of executive legislation which juristic analysis might have been expected to outlaw. The Australian High Court seems to have accepted that the apparent inconsistency of executive legislation with the principle of separation or allocation of powers in the Federal constitution can be accounted for in terms of 'the history and usages of British legislation'.[3] At least three juristic arguments have, however, been mustered in support of this pragmatic conclusion. One is that the true distinction in subordinate legislation is between 'delegation of power to make the law . . . and conferring an authority or discretion as to its execution to be exercised under and in pursuance of the law'.[3] This is simply a variant of the American doctrine about the existence of standards and filling in of details, and is equally difficult to apply as an unequivocal test to distinguish illegitimate discretion from legitimate execution. A second set of arguments flows from the fact that legislative powers are set out in Australia, as in the United States under various heads, e.g. 'defence', 'external affairs', or 'trade and commerce'. Distinctions may be found, therefore, in terms of delegating a part of, or the whole of, a power described by these heads or titles. A law abdicating the whole of the legislative power under a particular head could be described as illegitimate because such a law would not itself fall under any specifiable head of power conferred on the Federal Parliament.

[1] *Panama Refining Co.* v. *Ryan* (1934), 293 U.S. 338 at 421.
[2] The duty conferred on the Federal Communications Commission, upheld in *National Broadcasting Co.* v. *U.S.* (1942), 319 U.S. 190.
[3] *Victorian Stevedoring and General Contracting Co. Pty Ltd.* v. *Dignan* (1931), C.L.R. 73 at 102.

A law abdicating the defence power for example would not be a law 'with respect to' defence, but a law with respect to the transfer or surrender of a federal legislative power. As no such head of legislative power exists, the Australian courts can both allow substantial delegations of power to the executive and pay lip service to the formal allocation of powers in the federal constitution without invoking the American separation of powers doctrine at all. A clinching argument superadded for good measure is that the doctrine *delegatus non potest delegare* has no more application in Australia than it has had in British ideas of legislative power. Although it may be applicable to the law of agency in the general and common law, and adaptable to the relationship of Congress to the sovereign people of the United States, its introduction into British constitutional law is, it is said, inappropriate.

The cases supporting this proposition are those in which the Privy Council has held that the *delegatus* maxim did not apply to colonial legislatures.[1] These decisions aptly illustrate the way in which British (as well as American and Australian) courts have often shouldered aside inconvenient conclusions about the delegation of legislative power. They also suggest the conclusion that 'principal' and 'delegate' are somewhat vague terms as applied to legislators acting under higher authority. The inapplicability of the 'agency' doctrine to legislators has sometimes been argued in Commonwealth countries in terms of the members of a legislative body exercising independent authority not subject to orders from constituents or any other source. But this thesis is at least constitutionally valid in relation to the United States Congress, where the *delegatus* maxim is nevertheless accepted. The argument, moreover, confuses 'subordination' in the sense of subjection of legislators to orders (as from constituents) with the constitutional fact of derivation of the powers of the legislative organ from a higher authority. What the Privy Council in cases such as *R.* v. *Burah* did in effect was not so much to reject the relevance of the language of principal and agent to legislative bodies as simply to insist that colonial legislatures, despite appearances, were to be deemed principals. They held that a colonial legislature was to be

[1] e.g. *R.* v. *Burah* (1878), 3 App. Cas. 889; *Hodge* v. *The Queen* (1883), 9 App. Cas. 117; *Powell* v. *Apollo Candle Co.* (1885), 10 App. Cas. 282.

treated as having 'plenary powers as large and of the same nature as those of Parliament itself' and as being 'sovereign within its powers', despite the fact that such legislatures were not, in terms of their origin or their subjection to the Colonial Laws Validity Act, plenary or primary legislative bodies equal in status to the British Parliament, and despite the fact that 'sovereign within its powers' is simply a contradiction in terms. In fact, the delegation of legislative power by the Imperial Crown and Parliament to colonial legislative bodies was as much a delegation of authority as the delegation of legislative power to Congress by the American constituent body. The Privy Council simply chose to ignore it. (It is not clear even in the United States how much weight is placed on the *delegatus* maxim. It does not account, as the Australian courts have pointed out, for the incapacity of Congress to exercise the judicial power or to confer judicial power on bodies outside the judicial system.) At the same time the Privy Council has been prepared to hold that colonial legislatures, their plenary powers notwithstanding, are prohibited from creating and abdicating power to new bodies armed with a general legislative authority.[1]

Two ways of outflanking prohibitions on the delegation of legislative power can then be seen in the context of British and Commonwealth law. One is to deem delegates not to be delegates. Another is (implausibly) to treat delegation of legislative power as if it meant not simply transfer of a wide discretionary rule-making power, but transfer of a rule-making function plus divesting of the delegating authority of its own powers in the field. It is not difficult for a court to hold that delegation or transfer of powers in this sense has not taken place. Both tactics have been of undoubted assistance in freeing Commonwealth countries from unwelcome implications of the American separation of powers doctrine.

7. SEPARATION OF THE JUDICIAL BRANCH

Certain important differences can be seen in the treatment of the separation principle as applied to the judicial branch. One might have expected the necessity of conferring adjudicatory

[1] *In Re Initiative and Referendum Act* (1919), A.C. 935.

powers on administrative agencies to have exerted the same
pressure on the separation of powers doctrine in the twentieth
century as the need to confer rule-making powers on administrative agencies and executive officials. But the process does
not seem to have been an exactly parallel one. It is perhaps
true that American administrative agencies with their mixture
of adjudicatory and rule-making functions are in some sense a
standing violation of the separation of powers principle, and
in both Britain and the United States minor miracles have been
worked with the concept of the 'quasi-judicial' function. Nevertheless, the idea of the separateness and independence of judicial
power seems to have put up more resistance to the demands of
the administrative State. Congress has been prevented from explicitly making judicial determinations (in part by the separate
though over-lapping constitutional veto on Bills of Attainder);[1]
and both the Australian High Court and the Privy Council
have treated the separation of powers principle more respectfully
when considering attempts to give judicial functions to bodies
other than the originally established courts of law. In the
Boilermakers'[2] case, for example, both the High Court and the
Privy Council emphasized that the allocation of the judicial
power of the Commonwealth to Federal courts prevented (in
the light of the separation of powers principle) any conferment
of a judicial power on non-judicial bodies. Thus the Commonwealth Conciliation and Arbitration Acts could not confer judicial functions on an arbitration body, the Commonwealth Court
of Conciliation and Arbitration. In the course of the judgment
on appeal, Lord Simonds drew a clear distinction between the
departure from the separation principle in matters legislative
and executive, and questions relating to the judicial power. 'In
a federal system', he said, 'the absolute independence of the
Judiciary is the bulwark of the constitution against encroachment whether by the legislative or by the executive. To vest in
the same body executive and judicial power is to remove a
vital Constitutional safeguard.'[3]

---

[1] *U.S.* v. *Lovett*, 328 U.S. 303 (1946).

[2] *R.* v. *Kirby ex parte Boilermakers' Society of Australia*, [1957] A.C. 288. For comment and criticism see J. M. Finnis, 'Separation of Powers in the Australian Constitution' (1968), 3 *Adelaide L.R.* 159, and G. Sawer, 'The Separation of Powers in
Australian *Federalism*', 35 *Australian Law Journal* 177 (1961).

[3] [1957] A.C. 288 at 315.

The proposition that separation of judicial power is a vital constitutional safeguard comes down to this—that certain rights of citizens ought not to be finally determined except by judicial processes as carried out in courts of law. If a constitution were clearly to lay down that all determinations affecting individual rights to life, liberty, and property were to be made by a limited and defined set of judicial persons acting in a particular way, and if it were clear what rights these were, then it might well be that all that a constitutional court could say about separation of judicial power was that it was clearly prescribed by the constitution and must be enforced as written, whatever its merits. But since no constitution does say this, applications of the separation principle by judges and its evaluation as an essential constitutional safeguard must necessarily be subjected to some examination. What does this blanket defence assert? Over what range of activities is it an essential protection of liberty to have liabilities finally determined by the traditional methods of common law courts acting judicially? That, of course, is a policy question wrapped up in a very large preliminary question of definition. Where, as in Australia and the United States, important constitutional issues turn upon the meaning of 'judicial' action, much attention has had to be given to the question of definition in order to distinguish judicial power as understood in the constitution from similar forms of determination which may resemble it or have certain elements of it. One well-known dictum is that judicial power means 'the power which every sovereign must of necessity have to decide controversies between its subjects, or between itself and its subjects . . . [involving] some tribunal which has power to give a binding and authoritative decision (whether subject to appeal or not)'.[1] Another dictum is that the holder of judicial power 'investigates, declares and enforces liabilities as they stand on present or past facts and under laws supposed already to exist'.[2] None of these remarks is precise enough to distinguish traditional judicial activities from administrative adjudication in certain forms. Clearly, whatever constitutional problems may result, there is in all modern states a variety of procedures for determining rights and duties. They range from the procedures of traditionally labelled courts

---

[1] *Huddart Parker* v. *Moorehead* (1908), 8 C.L.R. 330 at 357.
[2] *Prentis* v. *Atlantic Coast Line Co.*, 211 U.S. 210 at 226 (1908).

through bodies which, in some sense or other, might be called tribunals, using methods varying in their degree of flexibility, to procedures which are undoubtedly exercises of administrative discretion or policy and not in any sense exercises of judicial power. The characteristics which entitle a procedure to be called 'judicial' are grouped about the notions of independence of deciding officers, finality of their decision, and the respect for procedural principles of natural justice. If we can assume that a line of convenience can be drawn between the settlement of disputes by administrative discretion and their resolution by independent bodies, whatever they are called, provided that they possess these elements of independence, impartiality, and finality of decision, the important policy question remains: What issues or controversies ought to be resolved by such adjudicative methods rather than by legislative determination or executive policy, if constitutional rights are to be maintained?

Belief in the importance of protecting the judicial power from encroachment by the legislature or executive must at least invoke the idea that there is an appropriate area for its operation. But, again, the separation of powers doctrine, as applied to the judicial function, does nothing to help resolve this policy question and may in some Commonwealth constitutions (such as the Australian) have obscured it.

In the field of property rights, encroachment or invasion of a pre-existing judicial sphere by the executive has certainly reduced the rights of individual property owners. In the United Kingdom (though perhaps less so in the United States) this is no longer treated in principle as lowering a constitutional bulwark. Where, on the other hand, issues arise that affect the freedom of the person, sentiments in favour of judicial determination and separation of powers remain strong. Such feelings about the liberty of the subject may in fact help to explain the strong and surprising adoption of the separation of powers doctrine in 1967 by the Privy Council in *Liyanage* v. *R.*[1] In *Liyanage*'s case[2] it was held that a law passed by the Parliament of Ceylon was void, as being a usurpation and infringement by the legis-

[1] [1967] 1 A.C. 259.
[2] 'Possibly the most remarkable exercise in judicial activism ever performed by the Privy Council' (S. A. de Smith, 'The Separation of Powers in New Dress', 12 *McGill Law Journal* 491).

lature of the judicial power. In January 1962 there had been an unsuccessful *coup d'état*, and a number of the participants were convicted of various offences connected with the attempted overthrow of the government, under two statutes specially passed to deal with the offences. The first, the Criminal Law (Special Provisions) Act No. 1 of 1962 purported to legalize, *ex post facto*, certain departures from existing laws of criminal procedure which had occurred when the alleged conspirators were detained. It also widened the scope of the offences of waging war against the Queen and overawing the Government by criminal force, authorized trial without a jury by three judges nominated by the Minister of Justice, and permitted the admission of evidence of confessions which would have been inadmissible under the general law. The provisions of the Act were to cease to be operative after the conclusion of these particular legal proceedings. A second Criminal Law Act later substituted the Chief Justice for the Minister of Justice as the person to nominate the tribunal of three judges. After conviction by this tribunal eleven of the defendants appealed to the Privy Council on the ground, *inter alia*, that it constituted an assumption of judicial power by the legislature inconsistent with the separation of powers contained in the constitution of Ceylon.

Perhaps the most striking feature of the Privy Council's conclusion about the separation of powers is that it can coexist with a sovereign Parliament. In *Bribery Commissioner* v. *Ranasinghe*[1] the Parliament of Ceylon had been held to be subject to certain procedural limitations in the enactment of legislation, but it was considered that the Ceylon Parliament had had, since the British Independence legislation of 1947, 'the full legislative powers of a sovereign independent state'.[2] Nowhere in the constitution was there any express vesting of judicial power in the courts, as in the United States or Australia. Nevertheless, the Privy Council was prepared to find that there was an implicit intention to leave intact the independence of the judiciary which had been expressed as vested exclusively in the courts constituted by Ceylon's Charter of Justice of 1833. The writers of the present constitution, it was said, had therefore recognized 'the importance of securing the independence of the judges and

---

[1] [1965] A.C. 172. (See chap. 3, p. 53, above.)
[2] See also *Ibralebbe* v. *The Queen*, [1964] A.C. 900.

maintaining the dividing line between the judiciary and the executive'. Thus a distinctive type of limitation which is difficult to classify as substantive or procedural is recognized as being constitutionally imposed upon the plenary powers of the Ceylonese legislature. It must not legislate so as to invade the freedom of the judiciary or so as to exercise under the guise of legislation what can be construed as judicial power. The challenged legislation in this instance was held to display both these faults and hence to be beyond the powers of the legislature.

The Privy Council's reasons for allowing the appeal were delivered by Lord Pearce. He distinguished the constitution of Ceylon from the American and Australian constitutions on the ground that in those countries there had been no federal courts before they were created and invested with power. Thus the absence of any express provisions vesting the judicial power in the courts in Ceylon was not decisive. This view suggests that the existence or absence of explicit vesting provisions is less important than might otherwise have been supposed. No doubt the sovereign British Parliament could in the exercise of its plenary powers invade the independence of the judiciary or inflict legislative punishments on named individuals. In *Liyanage*'s case analogies to the British constitution were dismissed by Lord Pearce with the remark that 'the British constitution is unwritten'. But supposing it to be conceded that the separation of powers is capable of surviving the creation of a legislature with plenary powers and that legislation must not in such a case invade the judicial sphere, what constitutes such an invasion? The most extreme example would presumably be an abolition of the judiciary and an absorption of the judicial power. A less extreme example would be a legislative exercise of the power to punish particular defendants and to define their offence *ex post facto*—to pass, in other words, an act of attainder. In the course of argument in *Liyanage*'s case Lord Guest at one point asked counsel: 'Do you say that in a criminal case a law could say to the judges that they will find the accused guilty? Do you say that this could be incorporated in a law?'[1] There is obviously something paradoxical about the argument that such a legislative act is an exercise of *judicial* power. If a judicial act is characteristically the application to particular facts of a pre-existing

[1] [1967] 1 A.C. 259 at 272.

SEPARATION OF THE JUDICIAL BRANCH 123

rule of law, legislative punishments, especially if *ex post facto*, seem at the very opposite pole from judicial activity. Nevertheless, legislative judgments of this type have been equated with improper invasion of the judicial sphere. One such American dictum[1] was quoted with approval by Lord Pearce, who went on to cite Blackstone to the effect that 'a particular act of the legislature to confiscate the goods of Titus or to attaint him of high treason does not enter into the idea of a municipal law'.[2] This defect he saw in the Ceylonese provisions of 1962. Parliament, he said, might legislate for the generality of its subjects by the creation of crimes and penalties. But the Acts of 1962 had no such general intention. They were clearly aimed at particular known individuals. The pith and substance of both Acts was a legislative plan *ex post facto* to secure the conviction and enhance the punishment of these particular individuals. Their Lordships were not prepared, he added, to hold that every lack of generality in criminal legislation or every *ad hominem* or *ex post facto* act were usurpations of judicial power,[3] but this one in their view clearly was.

Two features of *Liyanage*'s case deserve to be underlined. First, it raises and leaves unrepentantly vague the question, When is a legislature exercising judicial power? Secondly, it equates the separation of powers in relation to the judicial function with two policies—namely the securing of judicial independence from external influence and the avoidance of mingling judicial and legislative functions. It is not obvious that these two policies are indistinguishable or that they are equally undesirable. A recognition of the value of judicial security of tenure and the need to immunize judges from improper influence has been almost universally applauded in liberal societies; but there is no similar unanimity on the value of constitutionally prohibiting the combination or mixing of governmental functions. If the separation of judicial power is used indiscriminately to cover and condemn both these notions, policy may well be confused.

[1] From *Calder* v. *Bull* (1799), 3 Dallas 386.
[2] 1 *Commentaries* 44.
[3] In *Kariapper* v. *Wijesinha*, [1968] A.C. 717 both an intention to punish and a declaration of guilt were held necessary to an Act of Attainder. Though, on this view, all Acts of Attainder invade the judicial function, it is not equally clear that all Acts that usurp judicial power and apply to particular individuals are Acts of Attainder. Cf. *U.S.* v. *Lovett*, 382 U.S. 303 (1946), and the Annotation to *Lovett* in 90 *Lawyers' Ed.* S.C. Rep. at pp. 1945 ff.

8. THE DISUTILITY OF THE 'SEPARATION' CONCEPT

To sum up: The notion of the Separation of Powers seems to suffer from the following disabling deficiencies:

First, it is rarely clear whether, and in what sense, there is such a separation. The argument that legislative, executive, and judicial powers are constitutionally declared to be vested in particular persons or bodies is inconclusive.

Secondly, if there is a separation of powers it is unclear what it is that is separated, since the notions of 'legislation', 'adjudication', and 'execution' have not proved capable of precise definition.

Thirdly, the concept of 'separation' itself has been used to cover the ideas of physical separation of persons, legal incompatibilities between rhles or offices, differentiation of functions, isolation or immunity of agencies, and mutual checking, supervision, or policing of one branch by another.

Fourthly, in considering the mixing of governmental functions, different treatment has been given to the division between legislative and executive functions from that accorded to the division between the judicial and the other two functions. The doctrine provides no guidance as to whether this differing treatment is appropriate or necessary or whether voluntary transfers or partial delegations of function between branches of government are legitimate.

In short, the principle is infected with so much imprecision and inconsistency that it may be counted little more than a jumbled portmanteau of arguments for policies which ought to be supported or rejected on other grounds.

VI

CIVIL RIGHTS

In the United Kingdom a number of things have militated against the protection of civil liberties by any formal consolidation or declaration of constitutional rights. The prejudices of common lawyers and the empiricist leanings of political theorists seem to have combined to create a climate of intellectual opinion hostile to the formulation of citizens' rights in 'abstract' terms (though the common law is full of 'abstract' terms).

Of the arguments traditionally advanced, not all are equally weighty and not all consistent. There is the frequent observation that written documents have in the past been disregarded. There is the expressed fondness for institutional remedies rather than rights—though this is a question-begging statement of the alternatives. There is the feeling that both the splendours and miseries of judicial review had better be left to those who enjoy the separation of powers—that litigation of potentially 'political' questions in a system centred around responsible Ministers and a sovereign Parliament is embarrassing if not ungentlemanly.

Objections to formalized statements of constitutional rights have, however, sometimes appeared to waver between condemnation of them for being too general or abstract, and distrust of them for being too detailed or specific. For example, in 1952 Sir Ivor Jennings suggested that a major defect of the Indian Constitution was a reluctance to trust the Legislatures, combined with a reluctance to allow the courts to engage in judicious law-making through the interpretation of broad and general provisions. If nobody except the constituent assembly can be trusted to make laws, he argued, why not make the laws once and for all and enact a one-clause constitution: 'Nobody shall change the laws of India'?[1] Thus, on the one hand some have objected to broad and general declarations, because their meaning and boundaries are unclear; whilst others have criticized

---

[1] *Some Characteristics of the Indian Constitution* (1952), pp. 82–3.

attempts to remove ambiguity by elaboration of detail, on the ground that this leads to undue rigidity.

In the British situation there are obviously two distinct sets of difficulties which proponents of constitutional flexibility may invoke against attempts to declare fundamental rights. These are: (1) the entrenchment difficulty, and (2) the interpretation difficulty. In Britain the first has probably been the more important—so much so that it has prevented any independent consideration of the second. In the Commonwealth, too, the doctrine of Austin and Dicey has been thought to stand in the way of fundamental rights legislation by sovereign Parliaments. It has thrown doubt on the efficacy of New Zealand's attempt to entrench fundamental parts of the constitution against future legislative invasion and it has partly dictated the form of the Canadian Bill of Rights.[1]

None the less, the Canadian and New Zealand examples show that it is a mistake to think of constitutional protections in terms of all or nothing. The choice is not simply between, on the one hand, a legislature subject only to the restraints of public opinion and political opposition and, on the other, a system in which all forms of legislative policy are subject to constitutional prohibitions.

1. PROCEDURAL ENTRENCHMENT

There is, for example, the possibility of producing constitutional protections through procedural entrenchment. If revision of the orthodox sovereignty doctrine were to be accepted it might be possible to guard against the abuse of power without resorting to the device of a Bill of Rights, and without making the resulting justiciable issues turn upon principles of interpretation with which the common lawyer in the English courts is unaccustomed to dealing. Professor R. F. V. Heuston has remarked that 'the common law has found it almost impossible to transmute into satisfactory judicial decisions the important but curiously evasive principles of natural justice. Those who have

---

[1] Any of its provisions may be ousted by later statutes of the Canadian Federal Parliament; but unless expressly declared to operate notwithstanding the Bill of Rights 'Every law of Canada shall . . . be so construed and applied as not to abrogate, abridge or infringe' the rights set out in the Bill. See *R.* v. *Drybones* (1970) 9 D.L.R. (3rd) 473.

written on the topic seem to be mainly speculative jurists trained in Germany or North America; there is something about their writings which is peculiarly irritating to an English lawyer; he cannot explain very clearly why this should be, but so it is.'[1] It may be that members of the English bar will one day have to accomodate themselves to the unwelcome embrace of Continental jurisprudence. But meanwhile it is certainly true that there exists in Britain, in both political and judicial circles, a reluctance to see the judiciary saddled or entrusted with wide issues of policy such as are involved in concepts of 'due process', 'equal treatment', or the abstract freedoms enunciated in the traditional type of Bill of Rights. So there seems, on the face of it, a compromise congenial to the English condition in the hope that we need no longer be faced with a choice between 'the might of Leviathan [and] . . . isolated strongpoints labelled "fundamental rights" '.[2] Selected strongpoints might perhaps be defended by procedural entrenchments or by enhanced majority provisions which would prima facie require the judges who interpret and enforce the law merely to be able to recognize the difference between a half and two-thirds majority rather than apply their minds to such questions as whether the legislature has infringed 'those canons of decency and fairness which express the notions of justice of English-speaking people'.[3]

But a distinction and a caution may be necessary. The distinction is between the concepts of natural justice and fundamental rights in themselves and the enunciation of generalized or 'abstract' provisions or prohibitions. No one is committed to any particular beliefs about justice or morality by wishing to impose even the most 'abstract' limitations on the exercise of legislative power. A constitution may, but need not, reflect or mention such beliefs. It may rather differently, like the Canadian Bill of Rights, declare that there exist and have always existed certain rights and freedoms, but still without attaching itself to any particular moral or philosophical tradition. Canadian citizens may believe that their Bill of Rights speaks truly

[1] Heuston, *Essays in Constitutional Law*, pp. 28–9.
[2] Loc. cit.
[3] A description by Mr. Justice Frankfurter of the requirement of due process and equal protection of the laws placed upon the states by the Fourteenth Amendment to the United States Constitution. *Malinski* v. *New York* (1945), 324 U.S. 401, 416.

whether they happen to be natural lawyers, intuitionists, or utilitarians (unless, like Jeremy Bentham, they object to the language of moral 'rights' as in itself implying natural law beliefs). Alternatively, a constitution may simply place restrictions on legislation or empower judges to enforce specified 'abstract' freedoms—for example, of speech, press, or movement—without giving any indication, in its preamble or otherwise, of the reasons for protecting these particular activities; and a judge who had no personal belief in the 'fundamental' importance of free speech could in principle apply the concept in his decisions as efficiently as a judge who had strong personal convictions in the matter. Although it happens, therefore, to be the case that fundamental moral rights have usually been protected by abstract declarations of a kind which English judges have little experience in, or taste for, applying, abstractness and morality are not the same thing. Blanket prohibitions or abstract generalities may protect interests which are not basic moral interests (for example, the separation of powers or the division of functions in a federal state) and basic moral interests need not be protected by abstract declarations and prohibitions. It is the possibility of using less abstract means, that the new concept of sovereignty in fact suggests.

The necessary warning may be that the judicial role would not in all cases turn out to be as simple as might be at first envisaged, and could embody something of the same kind of uncertainty and policy judgment as the traditional Bill of Rights adjudication. Suppose that entrenchments based upon special majorities were introduced (assuming this to be possible) into a Parliamentary system. On the face of it, it is a simple enough matter for the courts to decide in disputed cases whether or not Parliament has acted by the required majority. No form of metaphysical speculation is required for that. But the question will very often arise whether the object of legislation is of such a kind that the entrenched procedures or special majorities are or are not required by the law. This may be more complex. Difficulty will not arise where the legislative object can be simply and unambiguously described. If an entrenching provision has stipulated that the House of Lords shall not be abolished except by a seventy-five per cent majority in the lower House, it will be fairly clear whether the legislation in dispute is or is not a bill to abolish[1] the House of Lords. But many potential legislative purposes embody an area of vagueness, and the nearer one approaches to interests such as speech, movement, and religion the more noticeable this becomes. Before the court can decide the appropriate procedure it may be necessary to reach a conclusion as to whether the impugned statute can properly be said to impinge upon, for example, religion, speech, or movement, and the un-English imponderables typical of the American First Amendment provisions[2] are reintroduced. Procedural restraint on power will not necessarily, therefore, make possible the protection of civil rights and simultaneously preserve the bench from any need to depart from the customary exercises in statutory interpretation, unless much more detailed entrenching provisions are employed. The problem of legislative evasion also arises. The South African case *Collins* v. *Minister of the Interior*[3] illustrates the judicial uncertainties which occur when a simple majority of legislators use their powers to bring about indirectly in a number of steps a general object which can only be directly achieved by the entrenched special majority procedure.

2. ENFORCEABLE SUBSTANTIVE RIGHTS

Another alternative to the traditional Bill of Rights might be to specify certain principles as entirely subject to judicial policing and others—perhaps in the economic field for example—as completely modifiable by express legislative decision without judicial intervention. The use of non-justiciable principles of state policy approximates to such a formula, but it has not usually been adopted for the more specific[4] contents of Bills of Rights.

[1] Though there might be doubtful cases—e.g. if a proposed bill removed all its powers but did not formally dissolve the institution or put an end to the issuing of writs of summons.

[2] 'Congress shall make no law respecting an establishment of religion or prohibiting the free exercise thereof; or abridging the freedom of speech, or of the press. . . .'

[3] 1957 (1) S.A. 552 (A.D.). Under the South Africa Act, 1909 a Separate Representation of Voters Act could only be passed in a joint legislative session by a two-thirds majority. The Government secured by simple majority an amendment of the electoral system to the Upper House. This produced a two-thirds government majority which was used in turn to pass the voting legislation.

[4] The notion of 'specificity' is not unambiguous. It has been used in the sense of referring to an easily identifiable historical mischief at which the constituent legislators were aiming, and also to imply the use of particular concrete terms which appear to raise no issue of vagueness or interpretation.

To favour the judicial protection of certain rights is not necessarily to undervalue the effect of other preservatives of civil
liberty. In the United States Mr. Justice Frankfurter often emphasized that courts are doing part of a job which depends
equally on 'local functionaries, on the police and prosecutors, on
the skill and the public spirit of the bar'.[1] He also suggested that
the liberties defined in the American Bill of Rights are living
realities in the daily lives of Englishmen without any formal constitution because they are 'in the marrow of the bones of the
people'. This suggests an implausible capacity for virtuous living
which might be qualified in the light of more cynical explanations. Jeremy Bentham's will do. The boasting and toasting of
English liberties, he thought, concealed the fact that they had all
been mere by-products of a struggle between factions whose
needs they happened to serve. Of the freedom of the press he said:

> It is not the Whigs we have to thank for it any more than it is the
> Tories. The Tories . . . would destroy it, once assured of their never
> being in a condition to have need of it. The Whigs would destroy it
> with equal readiness. . . . But this has never been in their power;
> and to that impotence we are indebted for the zeal of both parties in
> behalf of the liberty of the press, and the support they have given
> to the people in the exercise of it. Without this arm they could not
> fight their battles; without this trumpet they could not call the
> people to their aid.[2]

Granted, however, whether by accident or design, the existence of institutions which in part provide a substitute for a Bill
of Rights, there remain the questions, first whether such a condition of life might be improved still more by the addition of a
Bill of Rights, and secondly whether its absence leaves any gaps
in the existing constitutional pattern. In the United Kingdom
there are certainly vague and debatable areas in the civil rights
field. Even without judicial review, much may turn on the attitude of the bench. Judicial glosses on the law of seditious libel,
for example, have modified it so that its uncertain ambit is now
reasonably satisfactory even to philosophical and political radi-
cals. The same is true of the law of blasphemy. At the same time,
in the absence of any positive public commitment to the values
incorporated in the first article of the American Bill of Rights,

---

[1] *Mr. Justice Holmes and the Supreme Court* (2nd ed. 1961), p. 86.
[2] *Bentham's Handbook of Political Fallacies*, ed. H. A. Larrabee (1952), p. 158.

it is possible for judicial discretion in interpreting the common law to work in a direction adverse to freedom of speech or publication. In *Shaw* v. *Director of Public Prosecutions* the claim was made that 'there remains in the courts a residual power to enforce the supreme and fundamental purpose of the law . . . to conserve the moral welfare of the state . . . to guard it from attacks which may be the more insidious because they are the least prepared for'.[1] The proposition is not of course that the judges can control Parliament but that where Parliament is silent and the common law vague, the bench may in effect legislate against forms of immorality not already clearly and specifically illegal. An implicit major premise of this kind is obviously in potential conflict with liberal principles or prejudices about free expression and action. There may also be justification for the complaint that governmental application of the Official Secrets Acts, together with the working of the laws of contempt and libel have gradually become restrictive of a reasonable right of public criticism by individuals and the press.[2] The state of public liberty in this area can only be estimated by working through a number of branches of the law, particularly those relating to police powers, state security, and public meeting. Powers of search and interrogation have never been thought deserving of statutory codification, the one depending upon judicial decisions whose implications are unclear and the other being governed by administrative practice in the Judges rules.

3. JUDICIAL ACTIVISM AND RESTRAINT

If it were decided to enact any general principles covering the rights of citizens in these areas there would, however, remain a major problem about which constitutional instruments are invariably silent. This is the question as to the proper degree of judicial restraint and the attitude to be adopted by those interpreting the Bill of Rights towards the legislative and constitutional judgment of democratically elected parliamentary and

[1] [1961] 2 All E.R. 466 at 452.

[2] The Chairman of Britain's largest newspaper some years ago said: 'If there is a corrupt police force in the provinces, and there is at least one, it is impossible for us to comment, because immediately the chief constable would sue us for libel; so would the Watch Committee; all your witnesses would run away and you would just have to pay up.'

local representative bodies. Great heat has been engendered amongst judges, politicians, and political scientists by this question in the United States and it behoves those who are thinking of trading in fundamental rights to consider what has been said by them.

Commentators have often tagged the opposing philosophies as 'activist' and 'passivist' doctrines. Passivists believe in restraint when reviewing acts of the legislature. Activists believe in something else which it is not easy to describe in a neutral fashion, since their opponents would undoubtedly call it lack of restraint and they themselves might call it 'believing that the constitution means what it says'. The conflict is particularly clear-cut in relation to the guarantee in the First Amendment to the Constitution that Congress shall make no law abridging the freedom of speech. Perhaps the activist view might be put into the form that this places an obligation on the judicial branch of government to make its own direct judgment whether an act of the legislative branch of government does infringe the freedom of speech. Those who oppose this view hold that the primary duty of reconciling social and individual interests lies with Federal and State legislatures, and that it is not a fitting exercise of judicial duty to overturn this considered judgment except in the clearest and most extreme cases (though what constitutes clarity and extremity can perhaps only be exemplified and not defined).

This issue, leaving aside its transatlantic complications, arises wherever constitutional guarantees are made justiciable. It arises in the enforcement of any written instrument, such as the Treaty of Rome or the European Convention of Human Rights (to whose provisions the United Kingdom government and Parliament have, since 1961, made themselves subject).

One of the most generalized of the arguments used by supporters of judicial restraint is that any other approach is incompatible with a faith in democracy. It is, Mr. Justice Frankfurter suggested, a vicious teaching which 'encourages a belief that the judges may be left to correct the result of public indifference to issues of liberty in choosing Presidents, Senators and Representatives'. But constitutionalism entails that this is precisely what judges must at least on some occasions do. A Bill of Rights itself implies that government cannot be left entirely to the instincts of legislators or preserved by a faith in democratic majority judgment. The question is what part such faith should play and in what issues. If judicial reversal is to take place in any case (which is admitted) then its effect and function must in those cases be to correct the effect of what is judged to be public or legislative indifference to the rights of individuals or minorities.

The argument against having an enforceable declaration of rights in a constitution is often presented as leading to a choice between the decisions of democratically elected representatives who will have their way if there is no fundamental rights legislation, and on the other hand non-representative judges who will have their way if there is. This leaves out of the account the fact that on many issues which might be expected to arise the choice, in effect, would not be between parliamentary decisions and judicial decisions, but between executive or departmental decisions and judicial decisions. It is characteristic of civil liberties issues (as a glance at any American textbook reveals) that they concern questions about the application of uncontroversial general principles to situations often unforeseen by the legislature or by anybody. General principles may be widely accepted but particular instances which hinder, embarrass, or complicate policy-making are less easily recognized or admitted. It is administrators who are particularly liable to find themselves in this position. Governmental agencies in any country—and not the least in the United Kingdom—are rarely completely free from the temptation occasionally to refrain from securing the maximum possible degrees of publicity, procedural fairness, and public criticism where their own decision-making processes are concerned.

4. CIVIL AND ECONOMIC RIGHTS

These values of free criticism and natural justice are in fact closely connected with what have sometimes been thought of as the classical civil liberties and the procedural rule of law. Contrasted with them have been 'economic' or 'social' liberties—sometimes because these have been thought more important and sometimes because they have been thought to modify the traditional rights and liberties in various parts of the world and in

various stages of national development. Whether or not either
of these propositions is true, it is clear that even in western European societies less agreement exists about social and economic
rights than about what, in principle at any rate, constitutes
justice in administrative and criminal spheres. One has only to
recall the views expressed by Professor A. V. Dicey in *Law and
Opinion in the Nineteenth Century*, or the differences in the 1930s in
the United States Supreme Court as to the constitutionality of
the New Deal legislation, to see the relativity through time and
place of ideas about economic freedoms. Dicey (in 1914) himself
set out to show the difference half a century might make. He
contrasted the 'universal belief' of 1860 in Mill's 'simple
principle' of individual liberty with the legislative output of the
late nineteenth and early twentieth century—with the statutes
providing for old age pensions, national insurance, school meals,
and the mentally deficient. (He was somewhat shocked that the
recipients of pensions under the Act of 1908 should continue to
be permitted to vote.)

Contrast our feelings about these evaluations with our certainty that outside the sphere of welfare and economics Dicey's
views remain essentially sound. The prescriptions of Dicey's
rule of law in the area of free speech, public meeting, and legal
guarantees against officialdom are widely regarded as applicable
today. Discretion in the hands, say, of the police is not thought
more obviously desirable or necessary than it was in 1900. Most
liberals are prepared to feel that there is nothing mutable or
'culture-relative' about the desirability of being able to criticize
the Government or of being entitled to a freedom from police
behaviour of the kind we should call arbitrary. Nor would they
be easily persuaded to amend this view by being invited to consider the infinitely varied necessities of government in Ghana,
Eastern Germany, Rhodesia, Greece, or South Africa.

This, if it is so, is one argument in favour of a distinction in
any Bill of Rights between civil and economic protections. One
might well wish to include the former whilst excluding or reserv-
ing judgment on the latter. Nobody is very much of an expert
in elaborating and applying the economic rights of man—and
judges less so than many.

Equally difficult issues are raised by the sort of right that is
defined in the American Fourteenth Amendment guarantee of

'equal protection of the laws' and which has been adopted in
many other constitutional documents, as for example those of
India, Germany, and Japan.[1] The declaration of fundamental
rights drawn up by the International Commission of Jurists at
New Delhi in 1959 provides that 'The Legislature must not discriminate in its laws in respect of individuals, classes of persons,
or minority groups on the ground of race, religion, sex, or other
such reasons not affording a *proper basis* for making a distinction
between human beings, classes or minorities'.

It would not be going too far to say that the problems that
most bedevil constitutional adjudication throughout the world
are those set by the need to identify proper bases for distinctions
between citizens and to make precise the permissible liberties
of citizens. Naturally so, since equality and liberty are at once
the most widely shared values in liberal democratic societies and
the most contentious in application.

[1] 'The State shall not deny to any person equality before the law or the equal
protection of the laws within the territory of India . . .' (Indian Constitution, Art.
14). 'All persons shall be equal before the law' (Federal Republic of Germany,
Basic Law, Art. 3). 'All of the people are equal under the law' (Constitution of
Japan, Art. 14). Each document also specifically forbids discrimination on grounds
of sex or religious belief.

The European Human Rights Convention provides (Article 14) that 'The
enjoyment of the rights and freedoms set forth in this Convention shall be secured
without discrimination on any ground such as, sex, race, colour, language, religion,
political or other opinion, national or social origin, association with a national
minority, property, birth or other status.'

VII

EQUALITY UNDER THE LAW

In an obvious, but notoriously diluted sense, a law-maker is concerned *ex officio* with promoting equality of treatment. To deal with men by general rules rather than individualized or unpredictable fiat is to treat them in at least one respect equally. But this is not to say very much, since a rule which applies equally to all may make different provisions for some as against others. This, amongst other things, would make it difficult for a modern legislative sovereign assembly to know whether it had complied with the recipe for legislative action which Rousseau prescribed in the *Contrat Social*. Rousseau there demands that the general will, besides being respectably general in its origins, must in its substance aim at generality and equality. Equality and generality of aim are exemplified in a number of ways. 'Law must be', it is said, 'applicable to all.' It must not seek to achieve 'a merely individual or limited end'. It must not seek to 'judge an individual person or an isolated fact'. It must not purport to determine specific rights arising out of a situation not previously regulated by general agreement. It 'changes its nature when called upon to pronounce upon a particular object'. It must not lay 'a heavier burden on any one subject than on another'. And so on. 'Every authentic act of the general will lays the same obligations and confers the same benefits on all.' The Sovereign 'knows only the nation as a whole and does not distinguish between the individuals who compose it'.[1]

Such a myopic legislator, we may suppose, would make heavy weather in our times. The lieges are not all of a lump. There are producers and consumers, officials and non-officials, farmers and manufacturers, soldiers and civilians, married men and bachelors, adults and minors. What is to be understood by treating them all alike or imposing the same burdens on all, when their situations, capacities, duties, and obligations are different and ought to be so? On the other hand, is not constitutional

---

[1] J.-J. Rousseau, *Social Contract*, book 2, chap. iv.

theory replete with dim and less dim reflections of Rousseau's specifications? No Bills of Attainder. The rule of law, not men. The equal protection of the laws.

Given, in particular cases, acceptable reasons for differences in treatment, the prescription of equality in law, as in morals, seems sometimes to fall away into an empty formality—namely that all deserve equal treatment unless good reasons prescribe otherwise. Of course, at some times and places, tautologies may strike fire. Mr. Gladstone's famous truism of 1864 is an example. 'I venture to say that every man who is not presumably incapacitated by some consideration of personal unfitness or of political danger is morally entitled to come within the pale of the constitution.'[1] Lord Morley tells us that this 'thunderbolt of a sentence' threw the House of Commons into an uproar. Perhaps the House of Commons was not listening very carefully! Clearly the notion of equality, formulated as absence of disqualification, or of irrelevant discrimination, does not advance the argument very far.

I. EQUAL SUBJECTION TO LAW

It cannot be said that there are many startling similarities between the views of Albert Venn Dicey and those of Jean-Jacques Rousseau. But one shared characteristic is an insistence on the equal application of law. By the rule of law Dicey understood, amongst other things, 'the idea of legality or of the universal subjection of all classes to one law administered by the ordinary courts'. Equality before the law, understood as the equal subjection of all classes to a common rule, might at least be contrasted significantly with chaos or lawlessness, but it does not in itself imply any qualitative view about the sort of law to which all are subject. At least three senses might be given to the 'rule of law', of which this first would be the minimal sense. The three senses, or programmes, might be:

1. Everyone (equally) to be covered by, or subject to, general laws, rather than exposed to chaos, individualized commands, or mob rule. Englishmen, as Dicey insisted, are ruled by the law, and by the law alone. 'A man may, with us, be punished

---

[1] John Morley, *Life of Gladstone* (1908), vol. 1, p. 569.

for a breach of law, but he can be punished for a breach of nothing else.'[1] No subject of Queen Victoria in 1885, it must be admitted, would have been much astounded by this proposition.

2. Everyone (equally) to be covered by some body of law which is impartially applied without fear, favour, or anything similar, by an independent judiciary. In this sense South Africa and Rhodesia are at the present time governed by the rule of law, though some of the law in question is in substance abominable.

3. Everyone (equally) to be covered by an impartially administered body of law, which meets certain criteria of precision, equity, and justice. Professor Lon Fuller has called these conditions 'the inner morality of law'.[2] Alternatively, one might perhaps call them the ethics of legislation.

The rule of law in its English context has (like due process of law and natural justice) been mainly expounded in the senses mentioned in 1 and 2—primarily, that is to say, as a procedural concept. The rule of law is not, in Dicey's view, violated when the King's most Excellent Majesty, by and with the advice of the Lords and Commons enacts that the Bishop of Rochester's cook be boiled to death without benefit of clergy,[3] or when the Queen-in-Parliament makes a retrospective legislative adjudication on a claim, so as to nullify, *ex post facto*, a judicial decision inimical to the Crown.[4]

Nevertheless, in two ways Dicey's doctrine was not merely procedural. The equal rule of law, as he expounded it, involves at least one substantive requirement. It must not permit overwide powers of discretionary action to be conferred on officials. It prescribes also a requirement of equal access and subjection of all private and public persons to the same judicial tribunals. It omits, however, to register the truism that the law which all citizens find when they get to the common courts may make unequal provision for some as against others. The same law that bound all could say that the Crown could not be sued, and that

---

[1] *Introduction to the Study of the Law of the Constitution*, 10th edn., p. 202.

[2] *The Morality of Law* (1964), chap. ii.

[3] 22 Henry VIII c. 9: 'It is ordained and enacted by authority of this present Parliament that the said Richard Rose shall be therefore boiled to death. . . .'

[4] War Damage Act, 1965. See *Burmah Oil Co.* v. *Lord Advocate*, [1964] 2 All E.R. 348.

policemen and State officials should have powers, privileges, or legal defences not open to private citizens. At the same time, the prohibition on the creation of wide discretionary powers assumed in its original expression that there could be no valid justification for such powers, based on relevant differences between citizens and officials. Dicey's implied ideal stands rooted in a situation in which the State and its agents confront individuals in a condition of Rousseauite equipollence. A large slice of English controversy about the rule of law has been about the workability of this assumption—in effect, about the equality of public and private persons.

2. EQUALITY OF STATE AND INDIVIDUAL BEFORE THE LAW

It is in one way plain that the State and the individual, or the community and citizen, cannot be equals. One imposes its will upon the other. We can, however, significantly debate which community purposes require the community's agents to be given significant legal privileges not shared by private persons or collectivities. It is especially necessary to put the question in this form in the common law world, where by theory and tradition the law knows only private persons. Secretaries of State, civil servants, and policemen are equally the Queen's subjects. 'With respect to the argument of State necessity, or the distinction that has been aimed at between State offences and others, the common law does not understand that kind of reasoning, nor do our books take notice of any such distinctions.' And 'by the laws of England every invasion of private property, be it ever so minute, is a trespass'.[1] Into this framework of private rights and private law, a statutory body of public powers and public law has had to be fastened. For reasons which do not surprise us, but perhaps ought to, this has not resulted in any great growth of official privilege or discretion in the area of civil liberties. The relations of policemen with citizens are largely conducted as relations between one citizen and another. Law officers make arrests, lay informations, and prosecute offences, protected at vulnerable points by only a minimum of

---

[1] *Entick* v. *Carrington* (1765), 19 State Trials 1030 *per* Lord Camden C.J.

statutory armour. But in the field of economic and administrative relationships a different kind of transaction appears. Where
the use of natural resources (and particularly land) is concerned
the rules have changed. In the nineteenth century English
courts may be said to have acted upon the assumption that their
business was to hold an equal balance between citizens and
officials. An interference with the property rights of Englishmen
often gave rise to disquisitions upon the rules of natural justice
(*audi alteram partem*, and no man to judge his own case). These
two rules rested upon the assumption of a fairly conducted legal
combat between two parties viewed essentially as equals by the
arbitral tribunal. The analogy has become steadily less applicable to twentieth-century contests between the Crown and
individual property-owning litigants. When governmental agencies initiate action they are conceded to be judges of the merits
of their own proposals. At least one of the rules of equal judicial
combat cannot apply. Indeed, its disappearance may even imperil the application of the other (*audi alteram partem*) rule. This
did in fact happen in one sphere of English administrative jurisprudence, and the right to a fair hearing is only now being
established as an independently valid claim of the citizen,[1] even
when no longer conceived as engaged in an equal judicial contest with State officials.

Administrative justice in fact poses a dilemma. It can never
be literally true that for all disputes between official agencies
and individual citizens recourse should exist to an independent
third party. Yet we aim to provide such recourse in a significant, if vaguely delineated, set of cases. What should define such
cases? An answer sometimes suggested is roughly that official
action which affects all equally, for example, raising a tax or
recruiting an army, does not give rise to a dispute or a right of
appeal (as distinct from political or electoral redress) whereas
action affecting citizens in an individual capacity alters the
case. But what is an individual capacity? A change in governmental policy or the cancellation of a defence contract may
affect workers in a particular town or factory in a way not shared
by the general population. But we do not admit these cases as
creating a right of appeal or review. Nor without circularity

[1] See *Ridge* v. *Baldwin*, [1964] A.C. 40. H. W. R. Wade, *Administrative Law*, 2nd
edn., chap. 3, pp. 185–98.

can a criterion be laid down in terms of State action affecting rights rather than privileges, since the classification of a potential claim as a right will in part at least depend upon the remedies available to vindicate it. Historically the question may be put in this form. For which purposes have legislators been willing to subject governmental action to fixed rules, and for which purposes have they been inclined to leave the Government free to formulate and enforce *ad hoc* policies? Typical of the first sphere is criminal, and some social service, legislation; typical of the second, diplomacy and foreign affairs. The latter sphere is necessarily marked by inequality of citizen and State (considered as government agencies). Some advocates of administrative justice argue or imply that the sphere of fixed rules ought to be as wide as possible. But this conclusion is not obvious. The sort of equality which exists between defendants and prosecutors does not fit every possible form of public–private relationship.[1] Perhaps the only generalization which can be made here is that the analogy breaks down wherever government is both party to an issue and a protector of some admitted general or national interest such as scarce natural resources or national security.

3. DENIAL OF EQUALITY

The traditional English rule-of-law man confined his concern for equality and legislative ethics to a veto upon excessive delegation of discretionary power. Predictability of action and the avoidance of procedural privilege were the values he had in mind. As a good Austinian and loyal exponent of the sovereignty of Parliament, he had no truck—at least no professional truck —with the avoidance of substantive privilege in law. Let the Queen-in-Parliament clearly place unequal burdens on one class of subjects compared with another and the subject knows where he stands. If where he stands is uncomforatable or unjust, that is no concern of jurisprudence or judges. It is a part of politics and a task for moral judgment with which legal tribunals should have as little as possible to do. The traditionalist may suspect that the question raised by the rule of equal law in the American (and Indian, German, and Japanese) sense can only be answered

---

[1] A point conceded by Dicey in 'The Development of Administrative Law in England', 31 *Law Quarterly Rev.* 148 (1915).

by a tribunal which is openly legislative. Setting this aside as mere prejudice against judicial review in any form, there remains perhaps a question whether the application of equality guarantees does not involve a creative and legislative burden greater than that which a judicial tribunal can comfortably carry.

In the jurisprudence of equal treatment, as in thinking about equality outside the law, there can be seen a certain indecisiveness about which of two positions to occupy. Argument begins with the acknowledgement that equality before the law does not require every person to be treated in the same way, but only requires similar treatment for those in similar circumstances, or an absence of discriminatory treatment except for those in different circumstances. But sometimes this view is asserted by treating equality as simply having this meaning (i.e. not to be understood as 'treating all alike'), whilst at other times it is asserted that equality cannot be absolute; that it must be balanced against other requirements; that proper classification and discrimination may take place, and that when this happens legislation may justly produce constitutional *inequalities*.

Whether we say that equality may be qualified or modified, or whether we say that acceptable departures from identical treatment do not detract from or qualify the principle of equality, the criteria upon which qualification of, departures from, or applications of, the principle take place, are obviously crucial. The notion of different situation or circumstance carries a certain ambiguity. A recent commentary on the Indian constitution explains that legislative classifications or discriminations for those in different circumstances may relate to geographical differences or differences in time.[1] Bombay may be treated differently from Madras. A reform may be introduced earlier for some than for others. It is clear, however, that the differences in situation do not consist simply in the different geographical or temporal situations themselves, but in the way these situations are evaluated and related to the legislative facts in question. The briefest excursion through equal treatment litigation reveals that this relationship and evaluation has been characterized in a number of ways. It being agreed that legislators may select different persons or groups for different treatment, since 'classi-

---

[1] G. N. Joshi, *Aspects of Indian Constitutional Law* (1965), p. 80.

fication is inherent in legislation',[1] various things may be said about the conditions necessary to reconcile such classification or discrimination with the guarantee of equality. For example:

1. That between classification and legislative objects there must be *some nexus*.
2. That classification must be based on an *intelligible* differentiation.
3. That classification must be based upon some *real and substantial* distinction.
4. That classification must be *relevant* to the object of the legislation.
5. That classification must be *rationally related* to the object.
6. That classification must be *fairly related* to the object.
7. That classification must not be *capricious or invidious*.
8. That classification must not be *arbitrary*.
9. That classification must be *reasonable*.
10. That classification must be *just*.

These formulae are plainly not equivalent. Arranged in this way they might be seen as a series of increasingly high hurdles. Roughly speaking, and in ascending order of severity, three kinds of classification may be separated out, namely that which is intelligible, that which is relevant, and that which is just or reasonable. A distinction between two persons or classes which is intelligible or real may not be for some purposes relevant, and a distinction which is relevant to the purpose in hand may not be sufficiently relevant to be reasonable, fair, or just. The use of the word 'arbitrary' perhaps tends to conceal the difference between the second and third tests (i.e. between relevance and reasonableness) since 'arbitrary' is sometimes used to mean 'irrelevant or capricious' and sometimes to mean 'unjust or unfair'. The distinction between the two tests is important. Compare, for example, a legislative proposal to tax red-haired men, with a proposal to tax the owners of gambling clubs. In both cases the distinction between tax-worthy and un-tax-worthy class is intelligible and existent. In the red-haired case the tax would fail to pass the test of both relevance and reasonableness. In the gambling case the tax would pass the test of relevance but not necessarily that of reasonableness. There might be several

[1] Frankfurter J. in *Morey* v. *Doud*, 354 U.S. 457 at 472 (1957).

reasons for not thinking it reasonable. Though having a high income is a relevant reason for being taxed, one might still think the tax inequitable and unfair because other entertainments, vices, or sporting facilities were not taxed at all, or because the tax was too severe, or because one thought that the owners of gambling premises performed a service to the community.

When courts apply tests to legislative classification, it is not always clear what hurdle, higher or lower, they are requiring the impugned legislation to clear. Sometimes they seem satisfied with mere relevance; at other times more is demanded. Even if it is clear which test is being applied (though especially if it is the second) decisions are often unpredictable because of the different ways in which a large number of possible differences between persons or situations may be weighed.

Many Fourteenth Amendment cases illustrate this point. As Mr. Justice Jackson said (in *Railway Express Agency* v. *New York*) :[1] 'The equal protection clause ceases to assure either equality or protection if it is avoided by any conceivable difference that can be pointed out between those bound and those left free.' Yet in this case, which involved an attack on New York traffic regulations prohibiting advertisements on some vehicles but not others, a number of differences between the two classes of vehicles was pointed out. Some carried paid, others unpaid, advertisements. Some were more of a traffic distraction than others, etc. All these differences were relevant to the purposes of the regulations, but not necessarily thereby reasonable bases for the discrimination. Another feature of the prohibited advertisements mentioned in argument was that they were less of a traffic distraction than displays on Times Square. This feature, however, was finally ignored. (It was no requirement of equal protection that all evils of the same genus be irradicated, or none at all.) Which features of the situation produced by legislative classification will strike a court as relevant and reasonable seems in many cases unpredictable. In *Goesaert* v. *Cleary*[2] Mr. Justice Rutledge, Mr. Justice Douglas, and Mr. Justice Murphy thought that a Michigan law, prohibiting the licensing of female bartenders unless they were the wives or daughters of the male owner of a licensed victualler's establishment, made an invidious distinction between male and female owners of bars. The

[1] 336 U.S. 106 at 115 (1949).   [2] 335 U.S. 464 (1948).

majority of the court, however, whilst conceding that Michigan could not 'play favourites among women without rhyme or reason', or produce 'irrational' discrimination, considered there to be a possible basis in reason (relating to the hazards of unprotected barmaids) for Michigan's action, and therefore upheld the regulation. This, perhaps, fell some distance away from a test of reasonableness. To assess that would have meant considering and weighing the counter-arguments to Michigan's belief, but this the majority were unwilling to do. The constitution did not require legislation, they said, to reflect sociological insight or shifting social standards. So, though the classification might rest, we may infer, on outmoded social standards or lack of legislative insight, Michigan could have had an intelligible and relevant, though possibly insubstantial and unreasonable, basis for its discrimination.

One of the features of the situation which is frequently rejected as decisive in equal treatment arguments is that the legislature has omitted to act in some similar situation alleged to be relevant. In an Indian case a section of the penal code was upheld, though it penalized adultery by men and not by women.[1] In Germany it has been held that the criminal punishment of male homosexuality does not violate equality by reason of not punishing lesbianism.[2] When apparently relevant features of a situation are discarded, it may be said that 'mathematical' or 'abstract' symmetry is not required by equality,[3] or that in determining the reasonableness of a classification attention may be paid to 'the established usages and customs and traditions of the people'[4] (though this consideration has become unfashionable), or that equality does not demand an attack on all evils at once. At other times, however, omission to act in some other case deemed equally evil is stigmatized. 'Sterilisation of those who have thrice committed grand larceny with immunity for those who are embezzlers is a clear, pointed, unmistakable discrimination.'[5]

[1] *Aziz* v. *State of Bombay*, 1954 S.C.R. 930.
[2] 6 B. Verf G.E. 389 (1957). Article 3 of the Basic Law states that '(1) All persons shall be equal before the law; (2) Men and women shall have equal rights; (3) No one may be prejudiced or privileged because of his sex, descent, race, language, faith, homeland, and origin, or because of his religious and political views'.
[3] *Patsone* v. *Pennsylvania*, 232 U.S. 138 at 144 (1914).
[4] *Plessy* v. *Ferguson*, 163 U.S. 537 at 550 (1896).
[5] *Skinner* v. *Oklahoma*, 316 U.S. 535 at 541 (1942).

It has been suggested by Indian commentators that 'frivolous' cases have sometimes been brought forward involving allegations of inequality. A sales tax on hides and skins is attacked because no tax is placed on other articles.[1] But it is not obvious why this contention is any more frivolous than any other disputes about denial of equality. Is it more frivolous than, say, the question whether a legislature would be denying equal protection if it provided for the taking over by the government of a particular firm or industry as compared with any other firm or industry? To nationalize one industry and not another—coal, but not steel—is obviously a form of discrimination. But what sort of test can be applied to the classification problem here? What foot-hold has an interpreter of equality between abstract symmetry and mere political preference? Is a guarantee of equality any different in its application from a guarantee of justice?

4. EQUALITY, PRIVACY, AND LIBERTY

A clash between equality on the one hand and liberty on the other occurs particularly where the equality concerned is that of access to publicly and privately supplied facilities of important kinds. The demands of equality and one sort of liberty (the liberty to supply and associate) reinforce each other. Equal treatment cases involving segregation of races or classes could equally well be argued in terms of a denial of liberty to each class to associate with each other. On the other hand, the demands of equality are potentially at odds with another sort of liberty —the liberty to withold, withdraw, or disassociate. The United Kingdom, stepping cautiously into the field of race relations legislation, is only now encountering the clash of principles long implicit in the Fourteenth Amendment and American State and Federal anti-discrimination measures in employment, pub-lic accomodations, labour organization, and property disposal. The boundary between what is thought just and unjust remains unsettled. There is, it is supposed, a sphere of private relation-ships which ought not to be subject to official enforcement provisions. The phrase 'private relationships' is, nevertheless, likely to beg questions. Here (as in the argument about the

---

[1] *Syed Mohammed* v. *State of Andhra*, 1954 S.C.R. 1117.

enforcement of criminal sanctions in matters of private conduct or morality) 'private' is used ambiguously both to describe a physical context ('in private') and to characterize activity as meriting immunity from public intervention. Though some matters of private morality in the second sense happen usually to take place 'in private' this second proposition is no guarantee of the truth of the first. Wife-beating or homicide within four walls is not immune from social intervention. Similarly, in arguments about discrimination, we may be told that 'it is both possible and desirable for governments to make unfairly discriminatory practices, except in the sphere of primarily private relationships, illegal'.[1] But criteria of privacy are badly needed to rescue this advice from vacuity. The limits or boundaries drawn in anti-discrimination programmes tend to be a cluster of *ad hoc* exceptions. Small businesses or housing projects below a certain size, or domestic employment, may be exempted from enforcement measures, and this is sometimes justified in terms of privacy and the right of free association. But if a right of free association or dissociation is a justifiable principle, why should it be restricted to small groups? Whether a discriminatory practice is classifiable as a private or public discrimination is not always easy to decide; and both inside and outside the law we still need a clear rationale for the extension of anti-discrimination measures from State and public operations and services in the most obvious sense into the field of communal and domestic activity. Proceeding from the certain to the less certain we might, perhaps, set out in descending order of conviction the fields in which we believe prohibition of discriminatory practices, based on race, sex, or religion, to be justified:

1. State and governmental services.
2. Services offered to the public generally.
3. A service financed or subsidized from public funds.
4. Important professions or occupations regulated or licensed by Statute.
5. Services or occupations in which large numbers are employed.
6. Services, provided by individuals, which are economically important or of which the supply is scarce.

[1] *Report on the Constitution of Rhodesia and Nyasaland*, 1960 (Cmnd. 148, p. 78).

What stopping points are there along this line? Obviously a principle of free choice and a policy of protecting it enters at some point. But the right to free disposal of economic resources has already suffered a serious loss of esteem, and further restrictions on it are not inconceivable if the avoidance of inequality and discriminatory practices is generally thought to be sufficiently important.

In the United States the distinction between public or state discrimination, and private or individual discrimination, has been a difficult and disputed one. It has been necessary to pursue it because the Fourteenth Amendment provides the Supreme Court with a double-edged problem. Not only does it require a decision as to whether a difference of treatment amounts to a denial of equality, but it also demands a resolution of the question whether any such denial is, or is not, the result of state action.

One thing that complicates the distinction between private and public (State or governmental) activity is the existence of quasi-governmental institutions. Many kinds of agencies, whether called boards, commissions, corporations, or authorities, as well as local government and educational bodies, are connected with, and are, in some sense or other, part of the governmental or administrative process. There may be many different tests, applicable for different purposes, to the question 'What is a public or a governmental body?' It may, for example, be necessary to delimit the 'province of government' in order to decide the proper boundaries of executive or crown privilege, or for the purpose of adjudicating on alleged libels on public officers. But it is not clear that the same tests are morally or legally appropriate to the task of distinguishing public from private discriminatory action. Many bodies that are not directly agents of government play a part in formulating and administering public policies.[1] Other bodies pursue policies that are directly or indirectly supported, encouraged, or subsidized by the State. But if the idea of State action is spread so thinly that it is held to exist where the State uses its resources to encourage, subsidize, or licence individual activities, it becomes difficult to see where any line can be drawn between the public and private sphere.

[1] Cf. Warren C.J.'s remarks in *Curtis Publishing Co.* v. *Butts* and *Associated Press* v. *Walker*, 388 U.S. 130 at 163 (1967) on the blurring of 'public' and 'private'.

State subsidies and tax exemptions are enjoyed by almost every-
body, and everything that individuals do is done, in a sense,
under the law and subject to its rules.

A number of arguments have been used to extend the American Fourteenth Amendment veto on state discrimination to cover
the acts of private individuals, which prima facie lie outside it.
One such argument is that the states are implicated in individual discriminatory activity if they assist or enforce it through
their laws or legal machinery—for example, by allowing state
courts to enforce a racially restrictive covenant placed on the
use of property by an individual.[1] But the argument that every use
of official machinery to enforce a discriminatory act by an individual involves an endorsement of it seems too general. The
mere use of trespass laws or other remedies, for example, to enforce the exclusion from private property of persons of a particular race, class, or colour, could hardly be said to involve such
an endorsement. Nevertheless, some weight seems to have been
given by the Supreme Court precisely to this argument. In a
number of cases the Court has reviewed convictions obtained
in state courts of trespassers engaged in sit-ins in restaurants,
lunch counters, and department stores. In some cases local laws
positively required segregation.[2] In other cases no positive requirement was made, but state involvement was inferred on the
ground that the state permitted its laws to be used to enforce
discriminatory exclusion. The temptation to use such an argument possibly derives from the fact that other morally relevant
differences are perceived in the exclusion of particular classes
of citizens from such facilities as shops or restaurants as compared
with their exclusion from private homes or individual social or
business arrangements. What is in issue, however, is the force of
this distinction itself. *Bell* v. *Maryland*[3] saw some division of
opinion in the Court on the point. The majority, reversing the
convictions of Negroes who had refused to leave a segregated
restaurant, held that keepers of inns, public conveyances, and
places of public amenity, were in a crucially different position
from private householders. Private property was involved but
it was 'serving the public'. Two points might be made about

[1] *Shelley v. Kraemer*, 334 U.S. 1 (1948).
[2] e.g. *Peterson v. South Carolina*, 373 U.S. 244 (1963).
[3] 378 U.S. 226 (1964).

this use of the word 'public'. In the first place, the contrast with 'private' or 'individual' that is implied when these terms are contrasted with 'public' in the sense of 'people at large' or 'the general public' is not that which is made when 'private' or 'individual' are set off against 'public' in the sense of 'official' or 'governmental'. One cannot therefore infer from the premise that service to the 'public' is involved the conclusion that governmental or 'State' action is involved. In the second place the question to be decided about services offered to, and relationships with, the public in general is precisely what degree of choice or discrimination by individuals they may permissibly embody. Mr. Justice Black, for example, in a dissenting judgment in *Bell* v. *Maryland* saw no obvious difference between the right of a storekeeper or restaurant owner to choose his customers and the right of a householder to choose his guests or a property owner to choose his social or business associates.

Mr. Justice Black's argument in this and similar cases was that nothing in the Fourteenth Amendment prohibited discrimination by private persons who offered goods or services, or compelled them to offer their services to the public at large without exception or restriction. This was not to assert that the constitution positively guaranteed such rights to discriminate or prevented encroachment on them by legislative action. Congress has the right to 'enforce by appropriate legislation' the provisions of the Fourteenth Amendment. Though it might seem that no such legislation could properly extend the provisions of the Amendment to actions which it did not itself embrace, there remains the possibility of legislation against private discrimination under some other head of Congressional power. When the Civil Rights Act of 1964 and its successors did place widespread restrictions on discrimination in the offering of employment and accommodation, one constitutional ground for such Federal action was found in the power to regulate inter-state commerce. In *Heart of Atlanta Motel* v. *U.S.*[1] and *Katzenbach* v. *McClung*[2] Title II of the 1964 Civil Rights Act was sustained in its application to discrimination by a hotel owner in Georgia and a restaurant owner in Alabama. In the first case it was argued that seventy-five per cent of the hotel guests were from outside the state and that, in refusing to rent rooms to Negroes the hotel was creating

[1] 379 U.S. 241 (1964).   [2] 379 U.S. 294 (1964).

an impediment to inter-state travel and commerce which Congress could properly attempt by legislation to remove. In the second case the argument was more recondite. The Government made no claim that the state of Alabama supported the restaurant owner's refusal to serve Negroes in his dining room. But it was asserted that forty-six per cent of the food served consisted of meat bought from a local supplier who had procured it from outside the state, and this was held to be sufficient to place the restaurant owner within the sphere of Federal regulation.

In the matter of property sales, also, the Court has held that a state may involve itself in, and in a sense encourage and promote or endorse private action by repealing laws against discrimination in the housing market.[1] Here the dissenting minority (Harlan, Black, Clark, and Stewart JJ.) criticized the majority's notion that a state could be said to be involved in or to promote discrimination by permitting the discriminatory acts of individuals. Indeed, it would seem that there is no individual act of discrimination that cannot be transmuted into 'official' discrimination if a state denies equality of treatment whenever it fails to enact and retain legislation prohibiting such discrimination.

In Britain, without the complication of states' rights or the Fourteenth Amendment, legislative prohibitions have been unambiguously applied to private discrimination; with, however, some curious inconsistencies. 'Discrimination' is defined simply as 'less favourable treatment based on colour, race, ethnic, or national origin' (with no reference to sexual or religious differences of treatment). To this provision the Race Relations Acts of 1965 and 1968 have added a jumble of exceptions permitting forms of discrimination by private householders, small employers, and firms attempting to secure a racial balance in the employment of labour. Further exception-creating provisions relate to accomodation in ships, benefits arising under charitable instruments, and employments where the attributes of persons of a particular nationality are specially related to the tasks involved. Still further oddity arises from the provisions relating to advertisement, which make it unlawful to advertise an intention to do acts which the legislation itself states to be lawful—for

---

[1] *Reitman* v. *Mulkey*, 387 U.S. 369 (1967), held an amendment to the California state constitution protecting the right to sell, lease, or rent property at the individual's absolute discretion to be in violation of the Fourteenth Amendment.

example an intention to offer employment to a French pastry-cook or a Finnish language instructor.

Some of the discriminatory activities treated as permissible by the legislation rest for their justification upon an implicit rationale of preserving an individual right to discriminate or exercise free choice in 'private' or domestic contexts. Others do not. Here the law reflects the moral perplexities of citizens. Equality is a matter of eliminating differences of treatment between persons, based upon irrelevant distinctions. What is hard to determine is how far majority decisions should be enforced by legal sanctions in the absence of a social consensus and, in any event, which of many individual characteristics are irrelevant for which purposes. Skin colour is the most obvious candidate for consideration as a characteristic that is almost everywhere and for almost all purposes irrelevant to the treatment which one person receives from another person. But to what extent should law and policy attempt to eliminate differences of treatment based on other human characteristics such as wealth, poverty, age, health, intelligence, or sex? An obviously relevant factor is whether a particular characteristic is counted as an endowment outside the individual's control, or an achievement for which he is responsible. Unfortunately we are not entirely certain which are which, or to what extent it is relevant that some original endowments for which individuals are not themselves responsible can be affected by their subsequent efforts. Intellectual capacity and poverty raise difficult questions here. In both Britain and America we think equality to be violated if certain legal or medical services are denied to those unable to pay for them. But we do not yet feel compelled to the same conclusion because there is not equality of access, say, to public transport, without regard to individual ability to pay the fares. Nor should we argue that the State is involved in, and endorsing, discriminatory treatment when it allows its laws to be used by private institutions to exclude those who are unable to afford the price of admission. There are a number of issues here (as equally in the disposal of property after death) on which society has not yet cleared its mind.

The application by courts and legislatures of the principle of equality illustrates, as clearly as anything could, the fact that equality is only one of a number of ends that liberal democratic communities seek to implement. Others are freedom, security, justice, and welfare. When these values clash there may be different ways of describing what is at issue. The jurisprudence of equal treatment shows how those who apply notions of equality to particular cases start out from an assumption that equality is not mere uniformity, sameness, or identity of treatment. Legislatures or societies may classify different persons or groups of persons and treat them differently, if the basis of classification meets certain requirements. Equality, it is argued, will not be violated if young and old, or rich and poor, or tentmakers and musicians, are treated differently if there are relevant differences between them and good or sufficient reasons for the differences of treatment. What the analysis of good reasons in the cases fails to bring out, however, is that if *every* departure from identity of treatment for which there are good reasons is treated as merely filling out the meaning of 'equality' properly understood, then no room is left for any recognition that some departures from identity of treatment might be better described as creating exceptions to the application of the principle of equality. The difficulty is to distinguish between the two situations. In the one a departure from sameness of treatment is undertaken out of a respect for equality, and to restore individuals to some position of comparability with others, which is regarded as having been lost or disturbed. In the other a difference of treatment reflects a deliberate and justifiable rejection of the claims of equality out of respect for the claims of some other value such as liberty or security.

There is, as we shall see, a similar temptation in legal and moral arguments about the application of the concept of liberty to argue that because 'liberty' does not mean 'unfettered licence' and because restraints on action may sometimes be justified in terms of protecting the liberty of others, that all proper restraints on freedom of action may be considered as part of the concept of 'liberty' properly so called. But if all or too many justifiable discriminations and justifiable restraints are fed into the ideas of equality and liberty in this way, the specific roles of equality, liberty, security, and justice as distinct and potentially clashing segments of morality are obscured.

VIII

FREEDOM OF SPEECH AND ASSEMBLY

THE relatively brief history of human thought about freedom of speech is full of high-sounding declarations qualified by necessary reservations. Voltaire, who wrote a treatise on Tolerance in 1763, is credited with the observation that he might disapprove of what his opponent said but would defend to the death his right to say it. Whether Voltaire either said this or believed it may be open to doubt. The French critic Émile Faguet said about him, unkindly, that he was always of three opinions about the liberty to speak and write—first, that it was an excellent thing; secondly, that it should be confined within very narrow limits; and thirdly, that it should be absolutely denied to those who did not think as he did. Whilst conscientious exponents of freedom of expression have always conceded that there are limits to the exercise of the freedom to speak, write, and communicate, they have not made very much progress towards saying exactly what the proper limits should be. In 1789 the Declaration of the Rights of Man maintained that 'No one should be called to account for his opinions so long as their manifestation does not upset public order as established by law'. In the twentieth century many constitutional declarations have either made free speech subject to 'such limitations as are prescribed by law', or allowed it to be limited by laws 'reasonably made in a democratic society'. Some constitutional instruments have gone further. The Constitution of Malta for example provides that no person shall be hindered in the enjoyment of his freedom of expression:

Except to the extent that the law makes provision that is reasonably required in the interests of defence, public safety, public order, public morality or public health, or for the purpose of protecting the reputations, rights and freedoms of other persons or the private lives of persons concerned in legal proceedings, or preventing the disclosure of evidence received in confidence, or maintaining the authority and independence of the courts, or regulating telephony, telegraphy, posts, wireless·broadcasting, television, public exhibitions or public entertainments.[1]

By contrast the United States Bill of Rights provided simply that Congress 'shall make no law . . . abridging the freedom of speech or of the press', and the Supreme Court has had to decide what restrictions and exceptions to create, without any assistance from the Founding Fathers and very little from Anglo-American political philosophy.

It is perhaps a striking fact, considering the importance of the principle in the western world that very few political or legal theorists have given much sustained attention to it.

In England most liberals, when in need of theoretical buttressing for their views, turn to John Stuart Mill's defence of free expression in the essay *On Liberty*.

I. MILL'S DEFENCE OF FREE EXPRESSION

In *On Liberty* Mill defended systematically a version of the view expressed aphoristically in Voltaire's alleged remark. On the face of it one might suppose Voltaire to be saying something contradictory—i.e. that he both disapproves of a doctrine and in some other sense does not disapprove of its expression. It might perhaps be suggested that all that is being approved or defended here is human freedom. One can disapprove of what is said whilst approving the freedom of the agent to say what he sincerely believes. But this in itself seems hardly adequate. No one would say, simply because he approved of human freedom of choice, that he disapproved of someone's *action*—beating his wife, for example—but would defend to the death his right to do it. Our toleration, and in some sense approval, of the actions involved in men speaking their minds whilst we disapprove of the content of what they say, obviously requires some stronger and special justification.

In the light of Mill's general theory that society is not entitled to suppress acts which can be considered self-regarding in that they do no assignable damage to others, it must be supposed that he classes the expression of opinion as a self-regarding action, since he says that no government, however good or representative,

---

[1] Malta Order in Council, 1961.

has the right to suppress it. Those who for any reason believe Mill's general distinction between self-regarding and other-regarding actions to be faulty may for that reason equally have cause to think that his insistence on the absolute immunity of speech is indefensible. They may want to say that the unwisdom of interfering with opinion is merely a matter of expediency and economy[1] rather than general principle and that speech should have no more guaranteed immunity of status than any other action which may in appropriate circumstances be subjected to social or legal penalties.

Mill, however, does not explicitly draw out his free speech doctrine from his general thesis about self- and other-regarding actions. He bases it very largely on an independent argument about what he dubs the 'assumption of infallibility'. All silencing of opinion, Mill tells us, is an assumption of infallibility. This argument of Mill's has been attacked by bad arguments: but can it be defended by good ones?

The word 'discussion' (alternatively 'opinion' or 'doctrine') is important. Mill did not say that all silencing of 'speech' is an assumption of infallibility. Indeed, he conceded that some forms of speech may do definite and assignable damage to other individuals, or to society, or may constitute instigations to criminal action. Thus we are not prevented by his criterion from suppressing libels or the revelation of State secrets or verbal attempts to procure the commission of riots, violence, or crimes. On the other hand, the 'damage' criterion would be empty if it did not place some restriction on the types of activity which can properly be made criminal. The 'liberty of professing and discussing as a matter of ethical conviction any doctrine, however immoral it may be considered', certainly on Mill's view, implies freedom to advocate the desirability of committing acts which society happens to have declared to be crimes. In discussing tyrannicide Mill says not only that the lawfulness of it may properly be discussed but that instigation to it in a particular case may be punished only if an overt act has followed and a probable connection can be established between the act and the instigation.

---

[1] 'There are no doubt a number of reasons which make it more expedient to control men's actions rather than their opinions. . . . Economy is the true utilitarian explanation of why it is better to control men's actions rather than their beliefs' (John Plamenatz, *The English Utilitarians* (1958), p. 128).

This appears to mean some other overt act by someone other than the instigator and other than the act of instigation—which may well be overt enough. Mill seems inconsistent here. What he presumably ought to be saying is that if an act is mischievous or damaging to others or to society, society may properly make it criminal and suppress such speech acts as are so closely connected with the commission of the act as to be part of it or to be counted as attempts to do the act; but that something to be called discussion, advocacy, debate, or expression of opinion about its desirability, can never be deemed to be part of a mischievous action in this sense.

As against Mill's assertion that *all* silencing of opinion is an assumption of infallibility, some incidental points have to be conceded. In the first place no such obvious assumption is made where opinions which are admittedly true are suppressed or where opinions are suppressed without the suppressors caring whether they are true or false. Sir James Fitzjames Stephen cited for example the silencing by Henry VIII and Elizabeth of religious controversy between Catholics and Puritans for the sake of peace and order.[1] It is not, however, a matter of great difficulty to think of other arguments against suppression of admittedly true opinions, or of all opinions, on the grounds attributed to the Tudor monarchs; so perhaps these objections to Mill's argument are not fatal ones.

In defending his principle against imagined objections, however, Mill perhaps goes further than may be necessary in describing its virtues as an aid to the pursuit of truth. He begins by meeting the contention that men and governments cannot perpetually suspend judgment and are always assuming infallibility in the sense of acting on the assumption that their own judgments are right. Otherwise, it might be argued, no debatable decisions would ever be taken over the heads of minorities; no taxes would be laid and no wars fought. As against this objection Mill argues that assuming an opinion to be true when there is freedom for others to attempt to refute it is different from assuming it to be true for the purpose of forbidding anybody the right to attempt its refutation. It is only the second attitude which he wishes to outlaw as an assumption of infallibility. We may suppress polygamy because we think it wrong. We only assume our own

---

[1] *Liberty, Equality, Fraternity* (1967 edn.), p. 78.

infallibility if we forbid others to argue that it is none the less right. We have the moral title to act on our opinions precisely because we do not prohibit arguments against the rightness of our action. Liberty to contradict our opinion is 'the very condition which justifies us in assuming its truth'. Mill must surely here mean that it is a necessary condition, since it is obviously not a sufficient one. Nobody at present is prohibited from arguing that all power should be handed over to the Prime Minister, but that in itself is not 'the very condition' which justifies us in assuming the proposition to be true. Mill adds that on no other conditions could we ever have any rational assurance of being right on any question. This again is saying too much. We have at the moment rational assurance that the earth is roundish in shape from photographs produced by astronauts, and we should still have it if the Flat Earth Society were an illegal organization.

Mill's praise of his principle could perhaps be put in a more modest, more general, and more long-run manner by saying first that mistakes have been made by particular generations of men even about matters of supposed scientific or astronomical fact, and secondly, that to suppress the views of the Flat Earthers *solely* on the ground that their views were firmly and widely believed to be erroneous would be to act on an assumption at variance with the assumptions we normally make about rational inquiry and behaviour. It would amount to a claim that on some particular point argument is superfluous, whereas we normally accept the principle that decisions about what to do and what to believe should be settled by argument. This is in part the basis of Mill's distinction between 'feeling sure of a doctrine' and 'undertaking to decide that question for others without allowing them to hear what can be said on the contrary side'. To suppress an *action* we do not have to assume that it could not be right but only that it is not right or tolerable in the light of all the arguments which we have attempted to weigh rationally against each other. But to suppress an *argument* and not to allow it into the scales at all is to do something inconsistent with acting on the basis of argument—namely to assume that it could not be true. The only way in which we could know that a proposition could not be true without considering it and allowing its expression to be weighed against counter-arguments would be if we had some process which was independent of argument, namely some alternative access to truth. This thesis, it must be admitted, might not impress a rational dictator who himself acted on the basis of evidence but considered, after weighing it, that some part of it was too misleading or shocking or dangerous to be expressed or published to some or all of those under his authority. Any argument therefore about the inconsistency between the suppression of opinion and rational decision-making would have to be filled out with arguments about the equal rights of all citizens themselves to hear and determine. The right to argue and hear arguments rests at least in part on the same basis as the right to vote.

If Mill's principle is to be salvaged it will have to incorporate some rephrasing. It may be more acceptable if we say: 'All silencing of opinion on the ground of its asserted falsity amounts to an assumption of infallibility.' It may be advisable to add the proviso 'whatever those who silence opinion in fact assume', in order to meet the objection that censors of opinion may well in fact not think themselves infallible. 'A man may admit his fallibility and may yet, believing the matter to be of the utmost importance enforce his own opinion and suppress that of others, having no other ground for his action than his belief that he is very probably right and that disaster will follow if another opinion prevails.'[1] There is, however, a difference between what a man thinks or assumes and the assumptions, premises, or justifications which constitute the grounds for his action. Mill was not attempting to describe anybody's state of mind and was no doubt aware that men, rulers, or majorities may well admit and sincerely believe themselves to be fallible whilst acting on principles which involve censorship or suppression,[2] and in Mill's sense acting on an assumption of infallibility. Action on the basis of a justifiable 'belief that disaster will follow' from

[1] John Plamenatz, *The English Utilitarians* (1958), p. 127.

[2] 'Acting on a principle of censorship or suppression' might be a better way of making Mill's point than the phrase 'assuming infallibility'. It is less likely to confuse logical and psychological issues. Perhaps also it may aptly describe an element present in some forms of 'protest'.

If the notion of 'protesting' about an action or utterance implies (as distinct from 'disliking', 'contradicting', 'rejecting', or 'contesting' it) that it ought not to be permitted to happen, then a principle of suppression must be embodied in any protest which relates to expression of opinion rather than action. If this is so, a great many liberals either do not know what the word 'protest' means or they are doing what they have no business to be doing.

unrestrained speech, however, would not necessarily be outlawed by Mill's thesis. It depends what is to count as disaster. The implication of Mill's insistence that discussion of the truth or falsity of opinions must remain outside the other-regarding sphere of law and social coercion is that offence given by an opinion's alleged falsity cannot on balance be deemed to constitute disaster, damage, or harm to others. The difficulty is, of course, in providing criteria for separating this type of 'harmless' offensiveness or social consequence from other social consequences of utterances which society may properly suppress, whether it be under the rubric of libel, treachery, indecency, blackmail, intimidation, or incitement to crime or disorder.

2. SPEECH AND PUBLIC ORDER

If the freedom of thought and opinion includes, as it must, the right to express opinions, it is obvious that the necessary criteria for permissible and impermissible activity cannot rest upon any simple distinction between opinion and action. The communication of an opinion to others is as much an overt action as striking a policeman or causing a riot. Nor can it rest upon the distinction, whatever it is, between advocacy and incitement. For advocacy and incitement are not distinct activities (in the sense, for example, that advice and command are distinct activities). Mr. Justice Holmes made the point effectively in 1925 in *Gitlow* v. *New York*. There the defendant was convicted of inciting political strikes and a militant communist revolution. Holmes said that his manifesto was alleged to be more than a theory—it was an incitement. But 'every idea is an incitement. It offers itself for belief, and if believed it is acted on unless some other belief outweighs it. . . . The only difference between the expression of a belief and an incitement . . . is the specific enthusiasm for the result.'[1] The relation between belief, conduct, and incitement is not simple. Whether a belief is an incitement is not, for example, dependent upon the belief's being about matters of fact or about conduct. An assertion of alleged fact may be more of an incitement than an assertion about what ought to be done. 'The earth is flat' might not incite. 'The workers are exploited' might well do so, given the right time and place, and to a greater

[1] 268 U.S. 652 at 673 (1925).

extent than many assertions about policy (e.g. 'The constitution should be revised'). Whether an assertion 'incites' is not a matter of grammatical or logical form but of all the circumstances of time, place, and enthusiasm in which it occurs. The appropriate question is not whether there should be incitement, but what it is permissible to incite. In Britain and the United States the most obvious consequence of incitement by public speech which legislators have sought to inhibit has been violence and dis-order (amongst citizens at large or by creating disaffection or mutiny in police or armed forces).

Such disorder provides the thread (if there is a thread) which runs through the modern English cases dealing with seditious libel and unlawful assembly. The test, Coleridge J. said in *R*. v. *Aldred*,[1] is 'was the language used calculated to promote public disorder or physical force or violence in a matter of state?'

One of the difficulties of the law relating to free speech and public order in Britain is that it results from a miscellaneous and disconnected heap of decisions arising under different statutes and in different branches of the law. English judges seem indeed sometimes to have wanted to deny that any general prin-ciples were involved. Thus we have Lord Hewart in *Duncan* v. *Jones*[2] saying that the case had nothing to do with the right of public meeting—though it plainly had. Consequently we find cases (like *Duncan* v. *Jones*) about obstruction of the police, ques-tions about unlawful assembly, prosecutions under the Public Order Act, and issues arising under the Highways Acts, local Acts, and by-laws—all adding up to a complex and partly in-consistent body of law about free speech and assembly. Since 1965 we also have a new set of statutory restrictions on speech and publication in the Race Relations Act (which confusingly contains an unrelated extension and amendment of the Public Order Act dealing with signs and written representations). In the United States, by contrast, problems involving speech, whether they relate to public order, censorship, libel, police powers, or contempt, are necessarily grouped together and classified as questions about the application of the First and Fourteenth Amendment guarantees of free speech, religion, and assembly. The ideas of freedom and restraint which emerge in these dif-ferent contexts react on each other. For example the idea of

[1] (1909), 22 Cox 1.   [2] [1936] 1 K.B. 218.

'clear and present danger' has appeared as a unifying concept in cases involving libel, contempt of judicial and legislative agencies, and in public meeting and censorship cases.

In the public order field, two areas where American experience is relevant to our own, despite the different constitutional background, are perhaps those which involve the problem of the hostile audience and the problem of group libel and racialist speech.

In neither of these areas are British attitudes very clear at the moment in either a legal or a moral sense. The common law started out with what seemed at first blush a clear principle about unlawful assembly which has been complicated by subsequent judicial dicta about the preventive power of the police to forestall breaches of the peace. In *Beatty* v. *Gillbanks*[1] it was suggested that the Salvation Army could not be held to be acting unlawfully merely because they knew that their lawful assembling would cause others to commit unlawful acts. The premise of this (admittedly question-begging) principle was that the disorder which did or was likely to occur was not the natural outcome of the appellants' act. It followed that a procession of the orderly kind in question could not be said to involve the participants in *causing* an unlawful assembly. Others had caused it, not they. On the other hand, if they had behaved in an insulting or abusive way—as did the 'protestant Crusader' with his beads and crucifix in *Wise* v. *Dunning*[2] or the female defendant in *Humphries* v. *Connor*[3] whose orange lily was forcibly removed, they could have been said to have caused, or been about to cause, the resultant or likely uproar. It might well have been thought that a body of persons who were not the cause of a breach of the peace could not be obstructing the police in their duty to preserve it whilst they themselves were acting lawfully unless the duty of the police extended to removing or silencing the innocent objects of others' violent behaviour. But in prosecutions for obstructing the police something like that conclusion about the ambit of police duty seems in fact to have been drawn. In *Duncan* v. *Jones* Mrs. Duncan's meeting outside a labour exchange was not conducted in an abusive or provocative way. So on the test implied by *Beatty* v. *Gillbanks* and *Wise* v. *Dunning*

---

[1] (1882), 15 Cox 138.   [2] [1902] 1 K.B. 167.
[3] (1864), 17 Ir. C.L.R. 1.

she could not be said to have caused whatever disorder was un-lawfully initiated by others. Nevertheless, there was said in Mrs. Duncan's case to be 'a clear causal connection' between her meetings and disorderly behaviour. The test applied, however, was not really a causal test at all, but one related to the probable or likely consequences of her actions as envisaged by the police. This is not a causal test, since acts are not necessarily the causes of all their consequences. The result seems to be that the police may now be held to be acting in the course of their duty in issu-ing orders, silencing speakers, or even committing assaults, if their activities are directed to preventing the probable disorderly consequences of a meeting or procession. In principle it is pos-sible to contest the reasonableness of the police judgment[1] (though dangerous to do this by resisting them). But the courts in England do not seem over-anxious to investigate the precise extent to which the preventive action was directed towards those who are primarily responsible for causing disorder, as compared with those who are its victims. The problem arose in *Feiner* v. *New York* in 1951, where Mr. Justice Black, in a dis-senting judgment, saw a danger of censorship by a combination of threatened violence and police complacency. The police had arrested Feiner, who refused to stop speaking in the face of a hostile audience. They had not, it was admitted, first attempted to arrest or restrain those who had threatened the speaker. A man making a lawful address was not, Mr. Justice Black said, required to be silent merely because an officer directed it. Mr. Justice Black, of course, has a wide view of what constitutes lawful language which was not on this occasion shared by a majority of his colleagues. What Feiner said was, at the least, vigorous. ('Mayor O'Dwyer is a bum', 'Mayor Costello is a champagne-sipping bum', 'President Truman is a drunken bum'.) He also expressed the view that the American Legion was a Nazi Gestapo and that the Negroes should rise up in arms and fight for their rights.

---

[1] The dictum in *Piddington* v. *Bates*, [1960] 3 All E.R. 660 at 663, that 'a police officer charged with the duty of preserving the Queen's peace must be left to take such steps as, on the evidence before him, he thinks are proper', was directed to the particular question of a discretion to restrict the number of pickets and intended perhaps more to rebut the suggestion that the Trades Disputes Act gave an un-limited right to cause obstruction by picketing than to insist on a subjective police discretion in *all* matters connected with the preservation of order.

Both section 722 of the New York Penal Code[1] and the British Public Order Act of 1936 penalize the sort of inherently provocative or abusive speech which was censured in *Wise* v. *Dunning*. The Public Order Act forbids the use of 'threatening, abusive or insulting words or behaviour with intent to provoke a breach of the peace or whereby a breach of the peace is likely to be occasioned'. This statutory formulation does not concede any general preventive power in relation to breaches of the peace. It is not any words which fall under the Act's prohibitions. The words have to be used with the intention of provoking or be likely to occasion a breach of the peace. But they first of all have to be 'threatening, abusive or insulting' words. It is difficult to understand, therefore, what Lord Parker meant in *Jordan* v. *Burgoyne*[2] by saying that there was no room for any test as to whether the audience were reasonable men and that a speaker must take his audience as he finds it. That is only so (as in fact Lord Parker conceded) 'if words are used which threaten, abuse or insult'. That question is a prior one and it cannot be the case that words are threatening or abusive simply *because* they occasion or even provoke an audience of hooligans to disorder. There must be some other test of abusiveness. But in considering whether something is abusive, threatening, or insulting, its impact on some conceivable audience must be considered. There are people who might well feel threatened by anything, or who may feel insulted by anything—by the mere presence of a politician of a particular party or the appearance of the Prime Minister to read a lesson at morning service. Clearly such words could not be prosecuted as abusive under the Public Order Act even if they did occasion disorder or if disorder had been known to be their likely outcome. Mr. Harold Wilson once provoked such an outbreak; but nobody told him to take the audience as he found them and moderate his words accordingly, or that there was no room for any consideration as to whether he was using language likely to provoke ordinary reasonable men as distinct from Trotskyites, Empire Loyalists, or students.

Lord Parker did in fact suggest an objective, if unimpressive test of abusive or insulting language. To insult, he said, was 'to hit with words'. Since words differ from sticks and stones in having no literal impact, we are offered a metaphor and to say

[1] See *Feiner* v. *New York*, 340 U.S. 315 (1951).   [2] [1963] 2 Q.B. 744.

that it is an unhelpful one is perhaps being unduly compli-
mentary. We must not hit our opponents with words. Yet 'a man
is entitled to express his opinions as strongly as he likes, to criticize his opponents, to say disagreeable things about his opponents
and about their policies'. Was Jordan expressing his views
strongly? He was certainly doing that. 'More and more people',
he said,' are coming to say with us Hitler was right. They are
coming to say that our real enemies, the people we should have
fought, were not Hitler and the National Socialists of Germany
but world Jewry and its associates in this country.' Was Jordan
criticizing his opponents? He was doing that too. ('As for the red
rabble here present with us, it is not a good afternoon at all.
Some of them are looking far from wholesome. . . . Let them
howl, these multi-racial warriors of the Left. It is a sound that
comes natural to them.') Like Feiner's his speech was a mixture
of invective and opinion. It is not altogether clear whether Lord
Parker thought that the abusive and insulting parts of his
address were the 'red rabble' greetings or the criticisms of
war-time strategy. There is some suggestion that it was, at least
in part, the latter, since the Lord Chief Justice remarked that he
could not imagine any reasonable citizen not being 'provoked
beyond endurance' by being told that they were tools of the Jews
and had fought in the war on the wrong side.[1] If that is so it
suggests a threshold of intolerance in Lord Parker considerably
short of that attributed to Voltaire. It may be right of course to
suspect that the man on the Wolverhampton omnibus is not
much like Voltaire either.

There is considerable similarity between the circumstances of
Jordan's case and those in *Terminiello* v. *Chicago* in 1949. Terminiello also spoke scathingly of his opponents. He referred to
'Communist scum', to 'the 57 varieties of pinks and reds and
pastel shades' in the country, and alleged that 'all of it could be
traced back to the twelve years . . . spent under the New Deal'.
Terminiello's conviction was reversed on the ground that the
city breach of the peace ordinance under which he was charged
was unconstitutional in making it an offence to 'stir the public
to anger, invite dispute, or bring about a condition of unrest'.
Mr. Justice Douglas said: 'A function of free speech . . . is to
invite dispute. It may indeed best serve its high purpose when

[1] Ibid., at 748.

it induces a condition of unrest, creates dissatisfaction with conditions as they are and even stirs people to anger.'[1]

In Britain the position of public speakers under the Public Order Act and the Race Relations Act is now far from clear. In the first place, whether or not they use words which are threatening, abusive, or insulting, it is uncertain to what extent they may be silenced by the police in the exercise of a general preventive power to avoid prospective breaches of the peace. Secondly, there seems some possibility that objective tests related to the words used may be neglected, so that they are penalized as abusive solely because of their production, for whatever reason, of reaction or unrest. Thirdly, there may be a tendency for the courts to accept too readily the views of the police both as to the probability of disorder in particular cases and as to the nature and effect of the words used. Certainly the average English police-constable, and for that matter the average English Attorney-General, seems to have a more flexible view of what constitutes insult or abuse than does the average American Supreme Court Justice. In a prosecution in Oxford which arose from the picketing of a hairdresser's saloon by the Oxford Committee for Racial Integration, the police thought that the words 'This shop operates a colour bar' were 'insulting and likely to cause a breach of the peace'. The pickets were arrested after refusing to disperse. There was no evidence given of any imminent disorder but only of police belief that a breach of the peace might occur, and the magistrates dismissed the charges.

Further problems arise under the Race Relations Act of 1965. That Act amends the Public Order Act by including writings, signs, and other visible representations within its scope (presumably to deal with insulting banners, car-stickers, football slogans, smoke signals, and deaf and dumb language). It also creates the new offence of using, publishing, or distributing threatening, abusive, or insulting words or written matter with intent to stir up hatred on grounds of colour, race, or ethnic or national origin.

Does legislation of this kind violate the principle of freedom of speech as Mill believed in it by introducing an ideological criterion into the law in place of one related solely to the preservation of order? There seems some impression that it does, since offences do not on the face of it require any proof of the likeli-

[1] 337 U.S. 1 at 4 (1949).

hood of physical disorder. Yet how can this be so? The problem is the same as that raised by the Public Order Act and it comes back to the nature of the words used. The description of these in the Act is presumably not redundant. It is not any words at all which are proscribed. The Act does not prohibit the bringing about of feelings of racial hatred, but only the instigation of it by threatening, abusive, or insulting words.

What then is the character of such words which distinguishes them from words we must be at liberty to use if freedom of speech and opinion is to mean anything?

Some assistance might perhaps be sought at this point from American attempts to grapple with the problem of defining the limits of free expression. The description of 'fighting words' hits off rather better than the phrase used by Lord Parker ('hitting with words'), the notion that some spoken or written expressions may, by the circumstances of their utterance or delivery, be thought of as mere epithets rather than as attempts to communicate an idea. There may also be assistance in another American context—that of obscenity—where the question has been put in terms of whether allegedly obscene publications can be considered to have any redeeming social content. One might conceivably construct an analogous test by asking whether anything said or written has any redeeming 'communicative' element. The relevant distinction would be between, on the one hand, an attempt to communicate an idea—however loathsome—and, on the other hand, something that rises no higher than an invitation to fight. The application of a test of this kind to the incitement prohibitions of the British Race Relations legislation would make it clear that, on a proper construction, it is the latter and not the former that it restrains.

This is of course only a special case of the general problem of defining the social interests that may legitimately restrain the absoluteness of the right to free expression. Any attempt at such definition must necessarily take into account the continuing exploration of the issue made necessary in the United States by the requirements of the first article of the Bill of Rights.

3. THE AMERICAN DOCTRINE OF FREE SPEECH

In the United States, as in every other system of constitutional government, the protection of free speech and discussion has had to be balanced against other community interests, such as the security of the State, the maintenance of public order and decency, the protection of reputation, and the need for fair trial proceedings. All these cases involve speech, though they may involve more than speech. The more that they involve may be dubbed sedition, libel, obscenity, contempt, nuisance, or conspiracy and it may be entwined with physical consequences such as trespass, obstruction, or breach of the peace. Even those who take the view that the Bill of Rights places an absolute veto on legislative restraint of speech concede that these conflicting needs and consequences exist and have to be reconciled somehow with the free speech principle. 'Congress shall make no law . . . abridging the freedom of speech' cannot be regarded as an unambiguous, self-applicable formula, immunizing all forms of verbal activity from punishment or regulation. But what is it to 'abridge' speech? And to what activities may the concept 'speech' extend? The varying answers to this question have reflected differences in both historical and philosophical attitudes towards the Bill of Rights. At least two distinct viewpoints have existed towards the plan of the First Amendment civil liberties guarantees. On one view the freedoms of speech, assembly, press, and religion were not intended by the constitutional draftsmen to oust the right of the Federal or state legislatures to restrain or regulate speech in proper cases, and their interpretation requires a balancing on an equal footing of civil liberties against all other community needs, including the right of elected bodies to a wide measure of discretion in defining such needs and striking the balance between them. On this view the First Amendment was to secure to Americans the freedoms of Englishmen as understood by the common law. Those freedoms were not to be 'abridged' in the sense of suffering any further novel restriction, but they were to be understood as subject to the traditional restraints, such as those on libel, blasphemy, sedition, and incitement to crime. The First Amendment, Mr. Justice Holmes once said, 'while prohibiting legislation against free speech as such, cannot have been and obviously was not intended to give immunity for every possible use of language. . . . Neither Hamilton nor Madison, nor any other competent person, then or later, ever supposed that to make criminal the counselling of a murder within the jurisdiction of Congress would be an unconstitutional interference with free speech.'[1] In 1952 Mr. Justice Frankfurter and a majority of the Supreme Court pressed a similar view. The Bill of Rights, they said, was not intended to lay down any novel principles of government, but simply to embody the guarantees and immunities inherited from England. These English common law liberties had been subject to certain well-recognized exceptions which the Founding Fathers had had no intention of disregarding.[2] Nevertheless, other judges and critics have taken a quite different view on both historical and conceptual grounds of what Mr. Justice Holmes called 'free speech as such', holding that the First Amendment was intended as a radical new departure to establish a wider guarantee of freedom than had existed in England, and urging that this guarantee creates an absolute requirement of free discussion that is not to be balanced against legislative estimates of the need for regulation. They have argued further that civil liberties, including that of speech, occupy a preferred position among constitutional protections and that a special duty falls upon the judicial branch to protect such liberties against legislative invasion. The clash between these attitudes has produced a voluminous literature, from which a number of general arguments about the legitimate limits of a free speech principle, whether in America or elsewhere, may be gathered. Perhaps the easiest way to collect and examine these arguments is to consider the many ways in which attempts have been made to cut down or limit the apparent absoluteness of the requirement that speech shall be free of restraint. Since a free speech guarantee is incorporated in many constitutional instruments throughout the world, these arguments are often quite general in their application. They may take the form of saying, for example, that only 'prior restraint' of speech is to be ruled out; or that there are 'exceptions' to the free speech principle; or that the principle has to be applied with the aid of some subsidiary formula; or that free speech has to be weighed or balanced against other requirements; or that some types of speech fall outside the scope of the constitutionally guaranteed immunity in view of their content; or that speech may lose its protection

[1] *Frohwerk* v. *U.S.*, 249 U.S. 204 at 206 (1919) *per* Holmes, J.
[2] *Dennis* v. *U.S.*, 341 U.S. 494 at 524 (1951).

because of its connection with other types of activity that may properly be penalized.

4. 'ABRIDGEMENT' AS PRIOR RESTRAINT

The idea that freedom of speech and of the press exists when there is an absence of prior restraint on publication was asserted in categorical terms by Blackstone.[1] Liberty of the press is essential, Blackstone held, but it consists in laying no previous restraints on publication and not in freedom of censure for the matter published. To punish dangerous or offensive writings that on a fair and impartial trial should be adjudged pernicious was necessary, Blackstone thought, for the preservation of peace, order, good government, and religion, which were themselves the foundations of civil liberty. Two themes occur in Blackstone which have since acquired an air of familiarity. One is that punishing the public manifestation of private sentiments leaves thought itself free. The other is that the law punishes only 'licence' or the abuse of freedom and not the genuine freedom of individuals. Nothing very much needs to be said in rebuttal of either point. Nobody who has urged the necessity of the freedom of thought can have seriously meant anything by that phrase but the expression of free thought by some public manifestation. The absence of impediments to mere cognitation poses no issue for politics or public law. Nor does the notion that liberty cannot be licence offer any useful guidance. The liberty to do or forbear *is* a licence to act, and the question can only be what it is that should be licensed. There is undoubtedly some force in Blackstone's strictures on censorship—or 'the restrictive power of a licenser', whose effect is 'to subject all freedom of sentiment to the prejudices of one man and make him the arbitrary and infallible judge of all controverted points in learning, religion, and government'. But the whole problem of freedom of expression is not co-terminous with that of censorship, and the notion of censorship can sensibly be extended to embrace more than the application of a prior unprincipled restraint. What if the prior restraint be founded on some set of democratically decided principles, embodied perhaps in a statute, and not based on the whim of

[1] 4 *Commentaries* 145 (1876).

a single censor? And cannot the regular imposition of punishment, even after an impartial trial by jury, amount to censorious interference by a majority in the rights of a minority to express themselves?

Whether those who incorporated a protection for free speech, assembly, and religion in the American Bill of Rights were entirely satisfied with the ordered liberty of the common law can be argued at length. In relation to the English law of sedition, at any rate, Mr. Justice Holmes had little doubt. In *Abrams* v. *U.S.* he remarked: 'I wholly disagree with the argument of the Government that the First Amendment left the common law as to seditious libel in force. History seems to me against the notion. I had conceived that the United States through many years had shown its repentance for the Sedition Act of 1789 by repaying the fines that it imposed.'[1] Others also, whilst conceding that the American document probably intended no new departure in relation to such rights as habeas corpus, fair trials, and unreasonable searches and seizures, have agreed with Holmes's view in *Abrams* v. *U.S.* and argued that an entirely novel principle was embodied in relation to the limitation of legislative power, which radically departed from the tradition of legislative sovereignty. 'To say that the relation between the people and the legislature was now in principle as it had been before is to miss the meaning not only of the First Amendment but of the constitution as a whole.'[2] The sponsors of the First Amendment 'were well aware of the way their British cousins had been fined, whipped, pilloried, jailed, and mutilated for daring to say what they thought about their government. They saw signs of the same system developing in America, both in the attitude of some judges and in the tyrannical conduct of some colonial assemblies. They wrote an amendment designed to stop it and plainly worded to achieve that result.'[3] Wilkes and Junius, it has been suggested, were household words to the men who drafted and ratified the First Amendment. They 'intended to wipe out the common law of sedition and make further prosecutions for criticism of the government, without any incitement to law-breaking, for ever

---

[1] 250 U.S. 616 at 630 (1919).
[2] Alexander Meiklejohn, *Political Freedom* (1965), p. 102.
[3] Irving Brand, *The Bill of Rights: Its Origin and Meaning* (1965), p. 225.

impossible in the United States of America'.[1] Conceivably there may be historical grounds for doubting the accuracy of this assessment.[2] But whether history is against it or not now hardly matters since posterity has come down in its favour.

5. IMPLICIT 'EXCEPTIONS' TO AND 'ABSOLUTENESS' OF FREE SPEECH

The view that the First Amendment does not impose an 'absolute' requirement can be put by saying that there are implicit exceptions to the principle that Congress shall make no law abridging the freedom of speech. 'The most stringent protection of free speech', Mr. Justice Holmes remarked, 'would not protect a man in falsely shouting fire in a crowded theatre.'[3] One difficulty about this way of speaking is that it amounts to a variation on the Blackstone theme that liberty must not be licence and it tends to confuse assertions about the meaning of freedom of speech with assertions about justifiable prohibitions on speech or desirable exceptions to the free speech rule. Since there is no *a priori* need to assume that all freedoms are desirable freedoms, it may well be that some forms of free speech (such as the one mentioned by Holmes) are intolerable. But that can be said without suggesting that they are not genuine examples of freedom. It might be that a number of issues about free speech could be more honestly framed by asking whether freedom should in a particular case be rejected in the interest of some other value, such as security, safety, justice, or fairness, than by treating such clashing requirements as compatible with the freedom principle, or as part of its meaning when properly considered. In fact, given the existence of the First Amendment requirement, justifiable legislative regulations, restraints, or abridgements of speech cannot easily be treated as explicit and desirable exceptions to the free speech principle (since no

---

[1] Zechariah Chafee Jr., *Free Speech in the United States* (1948), p. 21.

[2] A different view is advanced by Leonard W. Levy in *Freedom of Speech and Press in Early American History* (1963), p. 248: 'We do not know what the First Amendment's freedom of speech-and-press clause meant to the men who drafted and ratified it at the time that they did so. Moreover, they themselves were at the time sharply divided and possessed no clear understanding either.'

[3] *Schenck* v. *U.S.*, 249 U.S. 47 at 51, 52 (1919).

exceptions are explicitly stated). Such restrictions, therefore, if held to be constitutional, must either be characterized as justified by unstated and implicit exceptions to the guarantee of freedom in the First Amendment, or else it has to be said that some proper restraints on freedom are part of the meaning of the guarantee or compatible with it. The assertion that the First Amendment is not an 'absolute' could be interpreted in either sense—namely, that it is not a specific unambiguous requirement, but a general principle whose meaning has to be filled in; or that it means something it does not say and allows for exceptions that it does not explicitly state. Correspondingly, the argument that the free speech guarantee is 'absolute' may be put in terms of its alleged specificity, or unambiguity, or its alleged lack of exceptions. Advocates of the absolutist thesis may therefore be found asserting that the free speech requirement of the First Amendment is without exceptions or that it makes a specific and unambiguous requirement; or, sometimes, simply that it 'means what it says'. The best-known judicial advocate of this position, Mr. Justice Black, has written: 'It is my belief that there are "absolutes" in our Bill of Rights and that they were put there on purpose by men who knew what words meant and meant their prohibitions to be absolutes.'[1] The liberal critic Alexander Meiklejohn, whose writings did much to stimulate the so-called absolutist position, wrote in similar vein:

No one who reads with care the First Amendment can fail to be startled by its absoluteness. . . . It admits of no exceptions. To say that no laws of a given type shall be made means that no laws of that type shall under any circumstances be made. That prohibition holds good in war as in peace, in danger as in security. The men who adopted the Bill of Rights were not ignorant of the necessities of war or national danger. . . . They established an absolute unqualified prohibition of the abridgement of the freedom of speech. That same requirement, for the same reason, under the same Constitution, holds good today. . . . For our day and our generation the words of the First Amendment mean literally what they say.[2]

If the absolutist position rests solely on the argument that the words used in the First Amendment have a clear, specific

---

[1] 'The Bill of Rights and the Federal Government', in *The Great Rights*, ed. Edmond Cahn (1963), p. 45. [2] *Political Freedom* (1965), p. 20.

meaning that must be literally applied, it could hardly be supported. That the constitution is 'the same constitution' and that its words 'mean what they say' are transparent and question-begging debating points. Admittedly 'no law' means 'no law'. But the phrase 'no law abridging' has no literal or obvious meaning. Nor has the term 'speech'. There are forms of communication by speech of which those who wrote the First Amendment were necessarily ignorant (for example, communication by radio, television, or sound amplification devices). And how far the notion of 'speech' may properly cover modes of communicating ideas that are not literally by word of mouth is not something that can be discovered by any conceptual or historical rule of thumb. Nevertheless, much of what proponents of the 'absolute' or 'no exception' thesis wish to say may be more plausibly maintained in terms of a series of further arguments about the balancing of the free speech guarantee against other requirements, or about the primacy or 'preferred position' of civil liberty and about the usefulness of interpretative formulae such as the 'clear and present danger' test. All of these sets of arguments overlap (and all of them have become entangled with the broader question of activist or restrained attitudes to judicial review in general). But there are some features which are peculiar to each.

6. 'BALANCING' OF SPEECH AND OTHER INTERESTS

Once it is admitted that freedom to speak may have consequences which may sometimes be legitimately penalized, it may be argued that the proper boundaries of free speech can only be discovered by a process of weighing or balancing the damage done by speech against the benefits accruing from the freedom enjoyed. Both Mr. Justice Black and Professor Meiklejohn have rejected this conclusion. All constitutional safeguards, it may be said, involve a delicate balance of conflicting interests. Fair trials have to be weighed against the releasing of guilty men. Free speech and press may endanger security or privacy. But the balancing of these interests against each other is, on the 'absolutist' view, already incorporated in the First Amendment. The Framers themselves did this balancing when they wrote the Constitution and the Bill of Rights. In particu-

lar, they did not hand over the duty of balancing entirely to
the elected representatives of the people at any particular
moment. 'There is, I am sure', Meiklejohn wrote, 'a radical
error in the theory that the task of balancing the conflicting
claims of security and freedom has been delegated to Congress.
It is the failure to recognise that the balancing in question was
carefully done when, 170 years ago, the Constitution was
adopted and quickly amended.'[1] A milder way of asserting the
point, without making too many historical assumptions, is
simply to say that the First Amendment neither leaves the
balancing of interests entirely to Congress (as if it were a sovereign
legislature) nor requires the question of competing values to
be approached *de novo*. Rather it gives a bias and emphasis to
the freedoms of speech, religion, press, and assembly, so that
legislation in restraint of them cannot be upheld, as other legislation might, merely on the ground that it has a rational basis
in legislative beliefs, or that a temporary majority believes
such restraints to be reasonable. One opponent of 'balancing'
has put the point in the following way:

It doesn't make any difference whether a law abridging the
freedom of speech has a rational basis or not, any more than it does
whether a law abolishing trial by jury in the federal courts has a
rational basis, as well it might have. . . . Most laws suppressing free
speech and all such laws which could pass Congress have a rational
basis, in the sense that some rational men may believe their enforcement would do good. The suppression of free speech seems quite
evidently rational to all but a small fraction of humanity.[2]

7. 'PREFERRED POSITION' OF SPEECH

Arguments against 'balancing' merge into what has usually
been called the doctrine of the preferred position of civil
liberties. Its first explicit expression seems to have stemmed from
some dicta, first of Mr. Justice Cardozo, and then of Mr.
Justice Stone. Stone in *U.S.* v. *Carolene Products Company*[3] spoke
in fact of a 'narrower scope for operation of the presumption of
constitutionality' and a 'more searching judicial enquiry'

[1] *Political Freedom*, p. 111.
[2] Charles L. Black Jr., *The People and the Court* (1960), p. 221.
[3] 304 U.S. 144 at 152 (1938).

where legislation appeared to curtail the civil liberties of the Bill of Rights. In cases where Congress exercised regulatory power over commerce or economic activity, it was suggested, the legislation should be upheld unless it could not be said to rest upon any rational basis within the knowledge of the legislature. Such legislation, if undesirable, could be repealed through the political processes of government. But if those processes themselves (upon whose free-working the argument for restraint and a presumption of constitutionality rested) were to be restricted by legislation, then it might (Stone suggested) be necessary to apply a different standard of scrutiny. Mr. Justice Frankfurter, who did not like the doctrine of preferred freedoms, called it a 'mischievous phrase' that had uncritically crept into some opinions of the Court.[1] The basis of the argument against it is that if legislators are to be allowed to make the primary judgments needed to reconcile individual freedom with community needs, there is no good reason to deny them the right where civil, as distinct from economic, liberties are concerned. If elected members are fit to balance individual economic freedom against the general welfare, then perhaps they are fit to balance individual civil liberty against the needs of security, secrecy, privacy, or public order. Supporters of the preferred position doctrine may deny this on a number of counts. They may rest on Stone's suggestion, or assertion, that judicial duty implies a keeping open of the channels of political communication, which are not threatened by mere commercial regulation. Or they may urge that economic freedom is only protected in the Constitution, if at all, by way of indirect inferences from the due process clause, whereas civil liberties are specifically protected in a strong, if not an unequivocal, way. On the other hand, it seems difficult to defend, *a priori*, a dual standard of judicial review. If some phraseology in a constitutional instrument is more equivocal than others, one might think the moral to be drawn would be simply that judges should get the substantive interpretation right and then apply a consistent standard to all legislative judgment where rights

---

[1] *Kovacs* v. *Cooper*, 336 U.S. 77 at 90 (1949), where Frankfurter traced the development of the preferred position doctrine. He attributed the first occurrence of the phrase to a dissenting opinion by Stone in *Jones* v. *Opelika*, 316 U.S. 584 at 600 (1942).

and legislation are alleged to clash. Even to characterize legislation as 'restricting' or trenching upon the civil liberty sphere is itself perhaps to beg a question at issue. But if one can believe, either on the basis of historical interpretation, or simple conviction, that civil liberties are more important than economic freedom, it becomes unnecessary to speak of different standards of scrutiny. 'The free speech right', it may then be argued, 'is substantively of vastly broader scope than the right to be immune from 'unreasonable' economic regulation. An elephant weighs more than a rabbit, not because he has a "preferred position" on the scale, but because his mass is greater.'[1]

8. THE 'CLEAR AND PRESENT DANGER' TEST

Arguments about 'balancing' and the 'preferred position' of civil liberty are closely connected with arguments about the application of the 'clear and present danger' test. The formula originated as an attempt to make more specific the terms of the First Amendment. What it said, in Mr. Justice Holmes's phraseology, was that in applying the guarantee of free speech, the question in every case is whether the words used are used in such circumstances and are of such a nature as to create 'a clear and present danger that they will bring about the substantive evils that Congress has a right to prevent'.[2] An obvious feature of this formula is that, on its face, it goes no way at all towards stating the circumstances under which the legislature may regulate speech. It does not even say that Congress may act to prevent *any* clear and present danger, but only that it may prevent a clear and present danger of the kind that it has a right to prevent. The kinds of danger that Congress does have a right to prevent are left entirely unclear. In fact the words 'clear' and 'present' seem simply ways of stating the obviously necessary requirement that the dangers in question must be identifiable and not remote or improbable, and they fail to say what dangers may be so identified as plausible, immediate, and serious. It might even be thought that the formula suggests the legitimacy of restraining speech whenever it is considered by the legislature to prejudice the attainment of some valid social

---

[1] Charles L. Black Jr., *The People and the Court* (1960), p. 220.
[2] *Schenck* v. *U.S.*, 249 U.S. 47 at 52 (1919).

objective[1]—a view that would give an extremely low value to free speech. A concession of a large degree of free expression obviously poses a threat to many things which the legislature has a valid claim to protect if 'the function of free speech . . . is to invite dispute' and it may 'serve its high purpose when it induces a condition of unrest, creates dissatisfaction with conditions as they are or even stirs people to anger'.[2] Those who used the clear and present danger formula could certainly not have intended it to imply that speech could be restricted whenever Congress believed it to endanger an object within the legitimate field of regulation. Holmes was clearly far from believing this. 'We should', he said, be vigilant against 'attempts to check the expression of opinions that we loathe and believe to be fraught with death, unless they so imminently threaten immediate interference with the lawful and pressing purposes of the law that an immediate check is needed to save the country.'[3] One might perhaps ask: 'To save the country from what?' But Holmes's intention was clearly that the alleged damage to social objectives must be serious and that it must be imminent in the sense of presenting 'an emergency that makes it immediately dangerous to leave the correction of evil councils to time'.[3] This point was underlined by Mr. Justice Brandeis in *Whitney* v. *California* in 1927—'No danger flowing from speech can be deemed clear and present, unless the incidence of the evil apprehended is so imminent that it may befall before there is opportunity for full discussion.'[4]

Undoubtedly, however, the clear and present danger test has at times been applied in a quite different way which is really indistinguishable from a straightforward balancing test with no presumption in favour of speech and no specification of the evils to be prevented other than that they must in legislative calculations outweigh the advantages of permitting the impugned expression. The majority view in *Dennis* v. *U.S.* provides a prime example. There, in considering whether Congress could legitimately penalize advocacy of the desirability of overthrowing government in the United States by force or

[1] See Thomas I. Emerson, *Towards a General Theory of the First Amendment* (1963), p. 51.

[2] Douglas, J. in *Terminiello* v. *Chicago*, 337 U.S. 1 at 4 (1949).

[3] *Abrams* v. *U.S.*, 250 U.S. 616 at 630 (1919).

[4] 274 U.S. 257 at 377 (1927)

violence, the Court simply set itself to consider whether 'the gravity of the evil discounted by its improbability justifies such invasion of free speech as is necessary to avoid the danger'.[1]

Perhaps because of its lack of bite in the *Dennis* case some judicial libertarians seem to have abandoned the clear and present danger test and the Court has decided a number of recent civil liberty cases without recourse to it. 'I see no place in the regime of the First Amendment', Mr. Justice Douglas has said, 'for any "clear and present danger" test whether strict or tight . . . the test was so twisted and perverted in Dennis as to make the trial of those teachers of Marxism an all-out political trial which was part and parcel of the Cold War that has eroded substantial parts of the First Amendment.'[2] Nevertheless, the clear and present danger formula, as earlier interpreted by Justices Holmes, Brandeis, and Black, is capable of placing a far-reaching restriction on what legislatures may count as serious evil. The evil must be serious and substantial and rising 'far about public inconvenience, annoyance or unrest'.[3] It must also on this view be closely related to some imminent criminal action other than speech, as was Mr. Justice Holmes's example of an attempt to create panic by shouting 'fire', or attempts to initiate or procure violence or crime.

9. THE 'ADVOCACY–INCITEMENT' DISTINCTION

The proviso 'other than speech' raises the issue of how speech acts which do constitute attempts at legitimately punishable crime may be distinguished from speech acts that deserve constitutional protection. A legislature could, of course, purport to make many kinds of speech acts into criminal offences, so that attempting to engage in them would indeed constitute (if the legislation were valid) an attempt to commit a crime. One

---

[1] 341 U.S. 494 at 510 (1951). Cf. E. S. Corwin, 'Bowing Out "Clear and Present Danger'" (in *American Constitutional History*, 1964, p. 165) and W. Mendelson, 'Clear and Present Danger from Schenck to Dennis', 52 *Col. L.R.* 313 (1952).

[2] *Brandenburg* v. *Ohio*, 395 U.S. 444 at 454 (1968).

[3] A formula from *Terminiello* v. *Chicago* repeated in *Edwards* v. *S. Carolina*, 372 U.S. 229 at 237–8 (1963). Cf. the use of the Clear and Present Danger test by Black, J. in *Bridges* v. *California*, 314 U.S. 252 (1941), where newspaper comment on the merits of a case under trial was held not to constitute such a danger and it was said that 'the substantive evil must be extremely serious and the degree of imminence extremely high before utterances can be punished'.

familiar way of setting off what is protected from what is punishable is constituted by the distinction between 'advocacy' and 'incitement'.

We have seen that Holmes found little merit in this distinction, on the ground that any effective advocacy might well act as an incitement. It could also conceivably be true that effective advocacy might 'instigate' some act of a legitimately punishable kind. Or it might 'provoke' such an act, or 'promote' it, or 'procure' it, or 'stimulate', or 'foment' it, or 'suggest' it, or 'urge it on'. To advocate, counsel, or argue for some course of action may in certain circumstances do all of these things. Perhaps for this reason a word such as 'instigate' is often ambiguous. When John Stuart Mill, for example, said that 'instigation' to tyrannicide might in a specific case be a proper subject of punishment,[1] it was not entirely clear whether he was speaking of causing or promoting the act by words or in some other way. In the context it seems clear that he was referring to the counselling or advocating of the criminal act and going on to argue that such incitement, procurement, or instigation by speech or advocacy ought in some circumstances to be permissible. An act, however, may be instigated, incited, procured, promoted, stimulated, or caused by means other than mere speech (e.g. by coercion, intimidation or direct physical assistance or participation). The relation, therefore, between counsel and advocacy on the one hand and procurement, incitement, and promotion on the other, is not simply that these terms lie along the same line and merge into each other. The latter catalogue of terms stands for activities that may have nothing to do with speech acts. Nevertheless, they may also be brought about by or (in J. L. Austin's term) be the 'perlocutionary effects' of speech-acts such as counselling, advocacy, or exhortation. What has to be devised is some test for identifying circumstances in which such perlocutionary effects of advocacy and counselling may properly be punished. One such test was offered in 1957 in *Yates* v. *U.S.*,[2] in which convictions for advocating and teaching the duty and necessity of overthrowing the government of the United States were reversed. The distinction there drawn was in terms of 'abstraction'. But in seeking to distinguish between permissible 'advocacy of abstract

[1] *On Liberty*, Everyman edn., p. 78. [2] 354 U.S. 298 (1957).

doctrine' and punishable 'advocacy of action', the judgment seemed to waver uncertainly between the notion of abstractness in the manner of teaching and abstractness in the nature of what is taught. One sense in which the manner of teaching might be abstract would be to do with its setting and circumstances, the nature of the audience, and so forth. Academic discussion in a lecture or seminar, or views propounded in a treatise or newspaper editorial, might be abstract or academic in their mode of promulgation. On the other hand, the proposals discussed or advocated might themselves be general or abstract, or they might be specific, particular, or concrete. In this sense there could be 'abstract' advocacy of a general doctrine about, say, the desirability of overthrowing governments when they become tyrannical, or abstract discussion or advocacy of the proposition that a particular government or statesman ought to be forcibly removed. To speak of drawing a line between 'abstract doctrine' and 'advocacy of action' masks this distinction and seems to suggest that doctrine can only be abstract if it is not about any particular specifically identifiable action. This in turn suggests that there are no circumstances in which the desirability of the specific act of (for example) revolution or violence or civil disobedience can be discussed or argued for, whatever the setting in which the advocacy takes place.

Similar uncertainty is to be found in English doctrine about seditious libel, where some emphasis has been placed on the circumstances in which words are used. In *King* v. *Aldred*[1] the defendant had published articles in the *Indian Sociologist* advocating the principle that political assassination was not to be counted murder, at a time when such assassinations had in fact occurred. Coleridge J., summing up to the jury, remarked that the expression of 'abstract academic opinion' was free. A man (even, presumably, a non-academic) might lawfully, he said, express his opinion on any public matter, however distasteful or repugnant to others. He might say that a despotism or a republic or no government at all is the best way of conducting human affairs. He might seek to show that rebellion, outrages, or assassinations were the inevitable outcome of the policies criticized. But he must not 'make use of language calculated to advocate or to incite others to public disorders . . . or any

[1] (1909), 22 Cox 1.

physical force or violence of any kind'. 'The test is this: was the language used calculated, or was it not, to promote public disorder or physical force or violence in a matter of State?'

There is an odd twist in Mr. Justice Coleridge's argument here. The suggestion that the expression of academic opinion is free, and that a man may lawfully state his opinion on any matter, however distasteful, seems to lead to the conclusion that even in the distasteful matter of assassination or violence he should, given the proper circumstances, be permitted to state his views. However, in relation to violence a different thesis is suggested, namely that *warnings* may be issued about its imminence—but there is no mention of the right to advocate it. Instead, it is said that to advocate physical force or violence of any kind is to publish a seditious libel. Elsewhere in the judgment, however, the terms 'incite', 'encourage', and 'promote' are used. What it amounts to is that whether advocacy has the effect of promoting or encouraging violence is a matter for the jury, which is entitled to look at all the circumstances surrounding the publication, 'because language which would be innocuous, practically speaking, if used to an assembly of professors or divines, might produce a different result if used before an excited audience of young and uneducated men' and 'there are times when a spark will explode a powder magazine'. At such times advocacy or exhortation is not divorced from, but may be a part of, a criminal act. The question becomes one of proximity, a question on which an English jury gets little help, so that freedom of discussion can be alleged to amount to the right to say whatever a jury of twelve shopkeepers thinks expedient.[1] What the shopkeepers have not got is any formula analogous to the American 'clear and present danger' test. This seems (in at least some of its formulations) a better guide to the relevant questions of degree and proximity than the debatable distinction between advocacy and incitement. Even when the Supreme Court has not specifically made use of the clear and present danger formula or rejected it, it has in recent times treated the question at issue as being the proximity of speech or advocacy to *imminent* criminal violence. In *Brandenburg* v. *Ohio*[2]

[1] A. V. Dicey, *Introduction to the Study of the Law of the Constitution* (10th edn., ed. E. C. S. Wade), p. 246.
[2] 395 U.S. 444 (1968). Cf. *Noto* v. *U.S.*, 367 U.S. 290, 297–8 (1961).

the Court reversed the conviction of a Ku Klux Klan leader convicted under a State Criminal Syndicalism statute after a meeting at which words had been spoken derogatory of Negroes and Jews and the possibility of racial vengeance discussed. To advocate the moral necessity of a resort to violence or violation of law, the Court said, is not the same as 'preparing a group for violent action and steeling it to such action'. The State Criminal Syndicalism Act failed to distinguish advocacy from incitement to *imminent* lawless action. In attempting to punish those who teach, advocate, or 'justify' the commission of violent acts without drawing this distinction, the statute impermissibly intruded on the freedoms guaranteed by the First and Fourteenth Amendments.

10. EXCLUSIONS FROM CONSTITUTIONALLY PROTECTED 'SPEECH'

Arguments for restricting certain forms of expression have sometimes taken the form of an assertion that the words in question are not 'speech', of the kind protected by the First Amendment. Thus, in *Chaplinski* v. *New Hampshire*,[1] insults or 'fighting words' were said not to be speech for constitutional purposes. In *Roth* v. *U.S.*[2] obscenity was held 'not within the area of constitutionally protected speech'; and in *Beauharnais* v. *Illinois*[3] libellous utterances were also held to be outside the protected area. If such remarks figure as arguments rather than as conclusions reached on other grounds they would obviously be question-begging. In the *Beauharnais* case the majority opinion did in fact appear to treat the assertion that libel was not a protected form of speech as a ground for declining to consider the application of the clear and present danger test, which was supposedly a test designed to help decide that very question—namely whether particular words were or were not constitutionally protected speech. Both *Roth* and *Beauharnais* cite with approval a passage in *Chaplinski* about 'certain well-defined and narrowly limited classes of speech, the prevention and punishment of which has never been thought to raise any constitutional problem'. *Chaplinski* concerned a statute which

[1] 315 U.S. 568 (1942).   [2] 354 U.S. 476 (1957).   [3] 343 U.S. 250 (1952).

(like the British Public Order Act) penalized insulting language likely to provoke violence. But there at least the conclusion reached by the Court rested not simply on an *a priori* assumption about the boundaries of 'speech' but at least in part on an independent argument. 'Fighting words', they said, are not an essential part of any communication of ideas, and are of such slight social value as a step to truth that they are easily out-balanced by the need to maintain public order. In fact *Chaplinski* bracketed with 'fighting words' the 'lewd and obscene' and 'the libellous'. Whilst there is some forc e in the view that a distinction can be drawn between the expression of an idea, however loathsome, and an invitation to fight, the distinction is not easy to apply to the case of libel and of obscenity. Very frequently in these cases speech or writing on public issues may be involved, and the social interest in peace and quiet, personal comfort, and decorum does not so obviously outweigh the value of free discussion that no test need be applied to the challenged expression beyond the observation that it is not a constitutionally protected form of speech.

Oddly, an analogous tactic for short-circuiting argument seems to be deployed by some who wish to give a wide ambit to the First Amendment and who seem to suggest that it sometimes can be determined directly without any subsidiary formula that legislation abridges speech. 'When the Supreme Court finds that a statute directly abridges speech and it is thus unconstitutional it need not mention clear and present danger.'[1] But interpretative formulas of some sort are essential to decisions about whether statutes abridge speech, since that question is not soluble by intuition. What some defenders of a wide interpretation of the First Amendment seem, however, to have done is to adopt an implicit formula that allows them to read into the First Amendment protection of 'speech' a distinction between speech on public matters and speech on private matters. By excluding the latter category from the ambit of 'speech' properly or constitutionally so called it is possible to argue for an absolutist interpretation of the speech guarantee without denying the right of legislatures to punish certain categories of speech acts whose effect is held to be connected

---

[1] M. Shapiro, *Freedom of Speech: the Supreme Court and Judicial Review* (1966), p. 123.

with essentially private matters. 'The guarantee given by the First Amendment', Professor Meiklejohn suggested, 'is assured only to speech which bears directly upon issues with which voters have to deal and only therefore to the consideration of matters of public interest. Private speech or private interest in speech, on the other hand, has no claim whatever to the protection of the First Amendment.'[1] Similarly, in his dissenting opinion in the *Yates* case, Mr. Justice Black said: 'I believe that the First Amendment forbids Congress to punish people for talking about *public* affairs, whether or not such discussion incites to action, legal or illegal.'[2]

The notion that the First Amendment gives an extensive ambit of protection to speech directed to public affairs received powerful support from the decision in *New York Times* v. *Sullivan*,[3] where (without any resort to the clear and present danger formula) the Court held that comment on the conduct of public officials enjoyed a protection defeasible only on a showing of actual malice, even where such speech contains factual errors. In public controversy, it was said, 'there are notoriously resorts to exaggeration, to vilification of men who have been or are prominent in church or state and even to false statements. . . . Erroneous statement is inevitable in free debate and . . . must be protected if the freedoms of expression are to have the breathing space they need to survive.'[4] One line of thought pursued in the *New York Times* case was the supposition that the attempt to punish criticism of government by characterizing it as libel amounts to the imposition of punishment for a form of seditious libel (as perhaps does the attempt to penalize criticism of judicial officers under the cloak of punishment for contempt). An implication of this analogy might seem to be that the protection should be an absolute rather than a qualified protection. This indeed was the view of Mr. Justice Black, though not of the majority of the Court in the *New York Times* case. But even those who wish to protect only the dissemination of innocent falsehood about public affairs may find some difficulty in discerning a clear boundary line between public and private spheres. In *Curtis Publishing Company* v. *Butts* and *Associated Press* v. *Walker*,[5] Chief Justice

---

[1] *Political Freedom*, p. 79.   [2] 354 U.S. 298 at 340 (1957).
[3] 376 U.S. 254 (1964).   [4] Ibid., at 271-3.   [5] 388 U.S. 130 (1967).

Warren found it difficult to draw a distinction between 'public officials' and 'public figures'. Increasingly, he noted, the distinctions between governmental and private sectors of policy-making have become blurred. Policy determinations are now originated through 'a complex array of boards, committees, commissions, corporations and associations, some only loosely connected with the government'. Thus 'many who do not hold office at the moment are nevertheless intimately involved in the resolution of important public questions or, by reason of their fame, shape events in areas of concern to society at large'.[1] Some rationales for exposing public officials in the traditional sense to unrestrained criticism (such as their implied assumption of the risks inherent in public office and their presumed access to facilities for counter-speech and criticism) may not apply with equal force to all who become involved in matters of public controversy, and still less to those who may be inadvertently subjected to publicity by newspapers[2] or individuals. At this point a policy of protecting individual privacy becomes difficult to reconcile with Mr. Justice Black's view that the First Amendment was intended to leave the press free from the harassment of libel judgments.[3] If that is indeed the intention of the First Amendment, there seems no reason to make the press or newspaper proprietors its exclusive beneficiaries. Newspapermen are citizens. So may not the First Amendment have been intended to free all citizens from the harassment of libel actions? That is certainly the conclusion towards which defenders of an absolute protection for free expression are pushed if it is in fact impossible to draw workable distinctions between public officials and private citizens.

11. FREE SPEECH SUBJECT TO 'RULES OF ORDER'

Professor Meiklejohn, despite his absolutism, was prepared to exclude from the concept of protected speech certain modes of its expression which could properly be described under the

---

[1] 388 U.S. 130 at 163–4.

[2] As in *Time Inc.* v. *Hill*, 385 U.S. 374 (1967).

[3] 388 U.S. 130 at 172 (1967); or as Douglas, J. (dissenting) put it in *Ginsberg* v. *U.S.*, 390 U.S. 629 at 655 (1967): 'As I read the First Amendment, it was designed to keep the State and the hands of all State officials off the printing presses of America.'

rubric of 'rules of order'. Using the analogy of the town meeting he argued that no objection could be raised to procedural restrictions on speech. The First Amendment was not, he thought, 'the guardian of unregulated talkativeness'. It does not require that on every occasion every citizen should take part in debate or that 'every individual has an inalienable right to speech whenever, wherever, however he chooses'.[1] Unrestricted speech must for example be limited in a meeting by the requirements of a moderator who calls speakers in turn. Speakers must be relevant. If they are abusive or disobey the rules they may be declared out of order, denied the floor, or thrown out of the meeting.

The application of this analogy to society at large is not without difficulty. Political argument is not umpired by any acknowledged chairman or moderator. We do not in general demand relevance (even in many legislative bodies). The concept of 'order' is itself vague and the notion of order in society at large is a difficult metaphor from which to draw practical conclusions. If 'order' means decorous procedure it merges easily into matters of substance. A society might consider itself to be preserving order by forbidding certain varieties of speech such as those held to be offensive or blasphemous. Moreover, political argument outside debating chambers is accompanied by various forms of assertion, protest, persuasion, and pressure which some like to characterize as disorderly or intimidatory and others not.

12. 'EXTENDED' OR 'SYMBOLIC' SPEECH

It is in this area that there arises the problem of fitting into a free speech philosophy the kinds of speech that are essentially accompanied by action and which have been given by American judges and critics such labels as 'speech plus', 'symbolic speech', and 'speech brigaded with action'. These concepts have to some extent sprung naturally out of a felt need to extend constitutional protection to activities such as picketing, protesting, marching, and demonstrating. All these activities are, in a sense, forms of expression closely analogous and allied to speech and petitioning. Nevertheless, they undoubtedly

[1] *Political Freedom*, pp. 26-7.

involve actions which may properly at some times and places be restrained and which potentially conflict with the legitimate demands of public order, the protection of private property, and the rights of conflicting groups. It is these cases that most clearly pull the liberal supporters of free speech in differing directions. Some Supreme Court judges have been prepared to hold, particularly in cases involving pickets and protests against racially segregated facilities and discriminatory practices, that First and Fourteenth Amendment free speech rights are not confined to verbal expression. In *Adderley* v. *Florida* Mr. Justice Douglas in a dissenting judgment urged that

the right to petition for the redress of grievances has an ancient history and is not limited to writing a letter or sending a telegram to Congressmen; it is not confined to appearing before the local city council or writing letters to the President, governor or mayor. . . . Conventional methods of petitioning may be, and often have been, shut off to large groups of our citizens. Legislators may turn deaf ears; formal complaints may be routed endlessly through a bureaucratic maze; courts may let the wheels of justice grind very slowly. Those who do not control television and radio, those who cannot afford to advertise in newspapers or circulate elaborate pamphlets may have only a more limited type of access to public officials. Their methods should not be condemned as tactics of obstruction and harassment as long as the assembly and petition are peaceable.[1]

In this case a minority of the Court, including Chief Justice Warren, would have reversed the convictions of student demonstrators charged with criminal trespass after a peaceful march to the county jail followed by a refusal to disperse. The protest had been a peaceful one, the dissenting justices thought, and what was essentially an attempt to petition for redress of grievances should not be thrown into the form of a trespass action. Otherwise states could similarly misuse breach of the peace or vagrancy statutes to prevent citizens from exercising their constitutional rights. Whether the breach of a properly drawn public order statute does constitute such a right needs of course to be argued. In a number of cases the Court has reversed convictions because state statutes dealing with breach of the peace, obstruction, or parading were unconstitutionally vague, or drawn in unduly sweeping terms, or administered

[1] 385 U.S. 39 at 49–51 (1966).

in a discriminatory fashion violating the equal protection provisions of the Fourteenth Amendment. But in *Adderley* v. *Florida* the majority of the Court saw nothing that was unconstitutionally vague in the relevant state law. Nothing in the Constitution, Mr. Justice Black suggested, prevented Florida from an even-handed enforcement of its trespass statute, and there was no evidence that the students were arrested because the police objected to the content of what was said at the demonstration. In earlier cases also, Mr. Justice Black had opposed the view that the free-speech guarantee implies an unrestricted right to march and demonstrate. In *Brown* v. *Louisiana*[1] in 1966, he suggested that the First Amendment does not guarantee a general right to use other people's or government's property as a stage for ideas. In that case the Court had, by a 5–4 majority, reversed the convictions of five Negroes who had refused to leave a public library. Mr. Justice Black thought the majority, decision dangerous if it required public officials to stand by whilst protesting groups staged sit-ins or stand-ups to dramatize their views. If one group could take over libraries for one cause, other groups might assert the right for causes which, whilst wholly legal, might not (he argued) be so appealing to the Court. *Cox* v. *Louisiana*[2] also impelled Mr. Justice Black to some remarks about a particular form of demonstration, namely the picketing of court houses. Though the Court reversed convictions for breach of the peace, obstruction, and picketing, Black would have upheld the convictions relating to the last charge. His view was that:

The streets are not now and never have been the proper place to administer justice. Use of the streets has always proved disastrous to individual liberty in the long run, whatever fleeting benefits may have appeared to have been achieved. . . . It is not a far step from what may seem the earnest, honest, patriotic, kind-spirited multitude of today to the fanatical threatening lawless mob of tomorrow.[3]

He added:

The First and Fourteenth Amendments, I think, take away from government, state and federal, all power to restrict freedom of speech, press and assembly *where people have a right to be for such*

[1] 383 U.S. 131 (1961).   [2] 379 U.S. 536 (1965).   [3] Ibid. at pp. 563-4.

purposes. This does not mean, however, that these amendments also guarantee a constitutional right to engage in the conduct of picketing or patrolling whether on publicly owned streets or privately owned property. . . . Picketing, though it may be utilised to communicate ideas, is not speech and is not of itself protected by the First Amendment.[1]

The notion that forms of expressive activity other than speaking or writing may be classified as speech for constitutional purposes raises obvious questions about the potential reach of any such category of 'symbolic' speech. Many things such as music or flags or banners obviously do have symbolic force. Flags or posters are things, not words, but they may contain or display words in written form. In the flag salute cases of the Second World War, compulsory saluting of the American flag was in effect characterized as interference with the freedom of speech and religion,[2] and in more recent times punishment for burning it has been characterized in the same way.[3] The burning of draft cards and the destroying of draft records have also been advanced as expressive and symbolic acts, but with less success.[4] The difficulty is that anything can in a sense express opinion. As the manifestos of many radical protesters indicate, the symbolical expressive aspect of even violent or disorderly action may be uppermost in the minds of the actors. They may well believe that 'when we attempt to block the Pentagon with our bodies, or interfere with an induction centre, or a napalm plant, or a campus recruiting booth, we are *saying* something very special'.[5]

---

[1] 379 U.S. 536 at 560 (1965).

[2] *West Virginia State Board of Education* v. *Barnette*, 319 U.S. 624 (1943).

[3] *Street* v. *New York*, 394 U.S. 576 (1968), a 5–4 majority of the Court expressed the view that the Constitution tolerates and protects the public expression of defiant or contemptuous opinion about the flag.

[4] In *U.S.* v. *O'Brien*, 391 U.S. 367 (1968). The Court upheld a conviction under a 1965 amendment to the 1948 Universal Military Training and Service Act for destroying a Selective Service registration certificate. They were unable to accept the view 'that an apparently limitless variety of conduct can be labelled speech whenever the person engaging in the conduct intends thereby to express an idea'. A substantial governmental interest in preventing harm to the frustrating of the Selective Service System was involved—the governmental interest here being unrelated to the suppression of ideas and the incidental restriction on the communicative aspect of the defendant's conduct being no greater than was essential to the furtherance of the governmental interest.

[5] Quoted in *Rights in Conflict: Report to the National Commission on the Causes and Prevention of Violence* (1968), p. 88 (italics added).

Couched in these terms the doctrine of symbolic speech clearly represents a conceptual blind alley. It suggests at best that opinions may be signalled, symbolized, or dramatized in other ways than by speech or writing, but it provides no guide-line to help decide which non-verbal performances are sufficiently analogous to the communication of ideas by speech or writing as to deserve the protection of free speech guarantees. The issue may perhaps have been confused by a tendency in the Supreme Court to characterize non-speech as speech so as to extend constitutional protection to forms of civil disobedience aimed at states or state officials who were themselves violating the federal constitution. These non-speech activities of the Civil Rights campaigners that involved picketing, obstruction, and various forms of rule-violation, could perhaps be better characterized as forms of self-help in asserting legitimate Fourteenth Amendment rights to equality (that were to be ultimately vindicated in law courts) rather than as the exercise, in an extended sense, of rights to free speech.

Summing up these activities, one critic has argued that 'not one of the great events in the Civil Rights movement involved Negroes in disobedience of an admittedly valid law'. They involved 'no instance in which Civil Rights demonstrators used sheer weight of numbers "non violently" to obstruct the lawful activities of others, to suppress argument, or in an attempt to impose their views upon the community by sheer harassment'.[1] That claim could not so easily be made on behalf of other groups who have tried to claim First Amendment privileges for various forms of militant activism.

Something of a watershed may be seen in the demonstrations against the war in Vietnam which occurred in 1967 and 1968. The easily crossed boundary lines between demonstrative protest and civil disorder were well illustrated by the episodes in Chicago during the 1968 Democratic Convention. These events had more than local interest since they aptly illustrated the manner in which twentieth-century demonstrations can easily evolve into riots when direct action provokes counter-violence. The disorders arose from the confrontation of a considerable body of protesters with police and National Guardsmen attempting to enforce city ordinances and to prevent marches to, and

---

[1] Archibald Cox, *The Warren Court* (1968), p. 113.

incursions into, the Convention amphitheatre and the Hilton Hotel. The numbers were large—possibly 10,000 protesters on one side and the Chicago police force and 6,000 National Guardsmen on the other. In addition, the Federal authorities assembled as a reserve a further 6,000 regular troops armed with rifles, flame-throwers, and bazookas. The police, besides being armed with their normal weapons, carried and made free use of 'mace', a form of tear-gas. There resulted what the report prepared for the National Commission on the Causes and Prevention of Violence called 'a police riot' directed against, amongst others, demonstrators, bystanders, residents, and television reporters. On two nights during the week there seemed to be indiscriminate police beatings accompanied by threats and obscenities and an absence of effective supervision or discipline.

It may well be wondered how violence reached this pitch. The protesters who came to Chicago in 1968 were a heterogeneous collection of the extreme and the moderate. Most of them probably did not want or intend violence, but many of them expected it after the disorders that had accompanied the anti-war protest march to the Pentagon in 1967. Some of them were McCarthy supporters, Civil Rights workers, and pacifists. Others were anti-war activists and political militants of various kinds with varying degrees of revolutionary inclination. (Prominent figures at this end of the spectrum were the Youth International Party—the Hippies—dedicated to peace in Vietnam, legalization of marijuana, the abolition of money, theatre in the streets, copulation in public, and an alternative society.)

The protesters had a number of immediate and practical wants. One was for the suspension of prosecutions for drug offences during the Convention period. The Chicago authorities were apprehensive and had some cause to be. Reports of intended violence, some absurd and impractical, some less so, were spread by word of mouth and underground newspapers. The Walker Report mentioned proposals to dynamite natural gas lines, dump hallucinatory drugs in the City water system, to take over petrol stations, flood sewers with gasoline, and bombard the Convention amphitheatre from several miles distance with mortars. Intelligence information supplied to the City from Federal governmental agencies reported plans for the assassination of political figures, including the presidential candidates, and the possibility that apartments near the Convention hall might be rented for use as sniping posts.

The demonstrators' foremost requirement was for a permit to allow a large open space, Lincoln Park, to be used as an all-night dormitory. This permit was refused, and litigation to compel the City to grant it was unsuccessful. The District Court's opinion was that such a use of the park was in violation of City ordinances and 'it would be a novel interpretation to hold that the First and Fourteenth Amendments require a municipal government to provide a public park as sleeping accommodation for persons desiring to visit the City'.[1]

When the demonstrators assembled by daylight in the park they made it clear that they were not going to accept this ruling or obey the City ordinances and the police were left in the end with no option but to obey their instructions and enforce the closing and clearing of Lincoln Park at the announced time of 11.00 p.m. It does not appear from the Report, which shows no inclination to favour the police, that they attempted to do this with undue force or at this stage initiated the violence which resulted. The attempt to close the park was met with obstruction, assaults, stone-throwing, and obscene taunts and, having been forced out of the park, a number of demonstrators went off to attack bars and shop windows in the City. The subsequent police violence was a response, and finally an uncontrolled one, to violent tactics by the frustrated marchers, which at various stages encompassed bombardment of the police lines with sticks, bottles, cement blocks, containers filled with human faeces and urine, and a variety of Krafft-Ebingesque epithets.

The Walker Report concludes that 'the right to dissent from national policy is fundamental' but 'the expression of that right has become one of the most serious problems in contemporary democratic government'. What happened in Chicago was an extreme version of a type of disturbance that is becoming commonplace in Western democracies. It undoubtedly involved an abuse of any reasonable right to action by the police, who went far beyond what was necessary to secure public safety. On the other hand, the police were not faced by

[1] *Rights in Conflict*, p. 5.

dissenters exercising civil rights in a traditional manner but by large numbers of people expecting a violent confrontation and driven to extreme measures by a mixture of idealism and political fervour. They were there on their own terms and nobody else's, determined to march, perform, sleep, and demonstrate as and when they wished. Some here and elsewhere were prepared to argue in favour of 'constructive vandalism' and to believe that in a capitalist society the only way for minority groups to secure the attention of the press and public is by violent manifestations. It seems plain enough that there is little possibility of accommodation between this thesis and the belief of more orthodox liberal democrats that liberty is not the right to throw urine at the police, nor the freedom of assembly the right of mobs, however virtuous, to occupy the streets or to break up conventions or political meetings on the ground that wicked or unjust sentiments are being expressed at them. A striking feature of some current radical political theory, however, is that it treats toleration of opinion as something to be extended selectively to opinions of a respectable political colour,[1] and sees little value in public order or in freedom of expression as it has existed in Anglo-American society.

[1] The clearest expression of a view of this kind is in Herbert Marcuse's essay 'Repressive Tolerance' (in *A Critique of Pure Tolerance*, essays by R. P. Wolff, Barrington Moore Jr., and H. Marcuse, 1969, pp. 81 and 88). 'Tolerance cannot be indiscriminate and equal with respect to the contents of expression, neither in word nor in deed; it cannot protect false words and wrong deeds which demonstrate that they contradict and counteract the possibilities of liberation . . . certain things cannot be said, certain ideas cannot be expressed, certain policies cannot be proposed, certain behaviour cannot be permitted without making tolerance an instrument for the continuation of servitude.'

THE RIGHT TO DISOBEY THE LAW.
CIVIL DISOBEDIENCE

Questions about the right to disobey the law are questions about the relationships between legal, moral, and political obligation. It is worth noticing, to begin with, that there are some uncertainties about the meaning of the first and last of these terms.

1. 'LEGAL', 'POLITICAL', AND 'MORAL' OBLIGATION

Looking first at the phrase 'political obligation', we can see that it might be used to refer to such duties as were prescribed by some system of political behaviour stemming from an acknowledged source of political authority. On the other hand, its more familiar use has undoubtedly been to describe a range of traditional problems about the origin, justification, and limits of the *moral* obligation to render obedience to *political* authorities. In a similar way the phrases 'legal obligation' or 'the obligation to obey the law' might signify either the particular form of non-moral obligatoriness—whatever that may be—of legal rules, or it might be used to refer to the *moral* obligation to comply with particular rules of law or to acknowledge the authority of a legal system. There is on the face of it no very good reason for confusing these two senses of legal obligation, but perhaps some temptation to ambiguity lurks in the notions of 'the binding force' and the 'validity' of law. Hans Kelsen, for example, begins an essay entitled 'Why should the law be obeyed?' with the potentially confusing question: 'What is the reason for the validity of the law?'[1] The validity or the binding force of a legal norm, he remarks, is simply its existence. What exists, however, is not merely an act of legislation or certain words in a prescriptive form but a 'specific significance' which those words have when

[1] *What is Justice* (1957), p. 257.

promulgated in proper form as part of an effective system
of legal norms. 'That a norm possesses validity', Kelsen writes,
'means that individuals *ought to behave* as the norm stipulates.'
The construction to be given to this is presumably not: 'When
a norm is valid, it follows that individuals morally ought to
behave as it stipulates', but something like: 'The intended sense
of a valid norm is that individuals ought to behave as the norm
stipulates.' This stipulated conduct might be called, Kelsen
seems to suggest, the subjective meaning[1] of the norm. One
thing that remains puzzling is what is to be understood by what
Kelsen calls the 'legitimization' of this intended or 'subjective
meaning' of legal norms as their 'objective significance'?—
a process which is brought about (Kelsen adds) by the acceptance of the basic proposition that the provisions of the legal
order laid down by the historically first constitution-makers are
binding. There seem to be at least two possible processes involving so-called subjective/objective phenomena or types of
'bindingness' which might be in question here. One might be
that a certain form of words whose mere grammatical sense is
prescriptive of what individuals ought to do becomes, if part
of an effective system of norms, what individuals legally ought
to do. Another possible interpretation is that the presupposition that we have a moral obligation to obey validly made laws
may convert what a legal norm *says* that individuals ought
(legally) to do into what they really, or morally, or finally ought
to do.

It is not obvious which, if either, of these things Kelsen
means, because it is unclear from at least some of his discussions
of the 'binding force' of law what it is that he holds to be involved in accepting, or postulating, or presupposing the bindingness of a norm or system of norms. On the face of it it would
seem that the 'objective significance' of the statement that individuals 'ought to behave as the norm stipulates' could, even
for those who accept the legitimacy, validity, or binding force
of a particular legal system still collide with an equally objective sense in which they might hold that they ought not to

---

[1] *What is Justice*, p. 262. At p. 257 Kelsen writes: 'The subjective meaning of the
acts by which the norms . . . of positive law are created is necessarily that these
prescriptions ought to be obeyed. . . . Why is their *subjective* meaning considered to
be their *objective* meaning as well?' 'The commands of a robber', he adds, 'have subjective meaning as norms but they lack normative meaning.'

behave in conformity with any of the rules of that system or with some particular rule. Yet Kelsen has denied the possibility of any collision of legal and moral obligations in the 'same system of cognition' or the same 'sphere of the ought'.[1] This might perhaps be taken to mean simply that there is no contradiction between the assertion that we ought legally to behave in a certain way and the assertion that we ought morally to behave in a different way. This would not prevent us from wanting to say that there could be a 'collision' of legal and moral duties. In the *General Theory*, however, Kelsen does seem to deny the propriety of this expression. 'What is ordinarily called "A collision of duties"' is, he says, 'an event which does not occur in the normative sphere.'[2] He appears to treat the notion of a collision of legal and moral duties either as a 'competition of two different motives, of two psychological impulses pushing in different directions', or as a contrast between a statement of legal obligation and a statement that such a psychological feeling or impulse (towards disobedience) exists. Thus 'the statement that an individual has the positive legal duty to obey the mobilization order of the head of State does not contradict the statement that the same individual, for moral reasons, *considers himself bound* to do the contrary'.[2] Strictly speaking the contrast stated here is neither between two contrary impulses—to act and not to act; nor between a legal obligation to act and an impulse not to act; but between a legal obligation to act and a feeling or belief that a conflicting rule or obligation not to act exists. This situation cannot on Kelsen's view embody a genuine contradiction or conflict when rightly analysed, because 'a system of norms can only be valid if all other systems of norms with the same sphere of validity have been excluded'. In stating what is legally required, a jurist 'must disregard the moral aspect' and 'no moralist would think of letting considerations of positive law interfere with the validity of norms which he has recognised from his point of view'.[3] Perhaps this is only one way of saying that we should distinguish legal and moral judgments by segregating them in

---

[1] *General Theory of Law and State* (1961), p. 409. For criticism on this point see H. L. A. Hart, 'Kelsen Visited' (1963), *U.C.L.A. Law Review*, pp. 709 and 722 ff.

[2] *General Theory*, p. 409.

[3] Ibid., p. 410.

different 'realms of cognition' or 'spheres of oughtness', or that
we cannot make both a legal and a moral judgment at the same
moment in time. But it portrays the making of either sort of
judgment as if it consisted in momentarily postulating the non-
existence or rejection of all other systems of rules bearing on
the same action. In this framework one can only picture the
rejection or qualification of a legal obligation by imagining
oneself to be, for the moment at least, exclusively or solely a
moralist, or an anarchist, or a religious believer, and not at all
a subject of law. For the purpose of discussing the conflict of
obligations arising from morally justifiable disobedience or
limited obedience to law (and especially to particular laws
within a morally acceptable system of law) this is a clumsy
framework and possibly a misleading one—in part because it
risks a serious mis-description of the recognition and deference
to valid law which enters into the application of moral rules
themselves when they deal with legal obligations and their
limits. Such application is not one in which 'considerations of
positive law' are simply rejected, disregarded, or consigned to
non-existence by moralists. It is at least more evocatively pictured by thinking in terms of a conflict between legal and moral
obligations, each of which is recognized as exercising some
compulsion on the agent and as stating competing claims which
have to be balanced.

2. GENERAL QUESTIONS ABOUT THE OBLIGATION TO OBEY LAW

When asked in a sufficiently general way, the question why
law should be obeyed and what the limits of such obedience are,
is a question about the foundations of political authority. Since
a system of political authority is most clearly identified by its
legal system, the range of questions which can be grouped under
the head of legal obligation in this sense is more or less co-exten-
sive with the queries traditionally discussed under the heading
of political obligation: 'Why and to what extent ought men
to obey their rulers and the law?'[1]

It is not too much to say that political theorists have lately
become rather shy of this question, or at least reluctant to

[1] J. P. Plamenatz, *Consent, Freedom and Political Obligation*, 2nd edn. (1968),
pp. 164–5.

generalize. Some, indeed, have suggested that no one could
sensibly or even meaningfully ask for any general justification
of obedience to law, but only for answers to questions about
duties to obey particular rulers, governments, or legal systems.
This seems unduly modest and also a little odd, since it cannot
be a necessary fact that there are any such duties or obligations
as are involved in participating in a political system. An anarchist could meaningfully deny the existence of all of them. So is
it really the case that it only 'makes sense to ask "Why should
I obey the Conscription Act" or "Why should I oppose the
present German Government?"',[1] and that these are the only
possible types of question to be posed about political or legal
obligation? It might perhaps be plausible to argue that no
single criterion can be specified which will provide a good
reason for obeying any conceivable kind of law. Even that
seems to be a matter to be tested rather than something to
dogmatize about. It might conceivably be that when we look
at our reasons for approving of and obeying this and that
ruler, and this and that system of law, we find that they all
have some single element in common. Even if no single element
appears, systems of law must have some things in common beyond the fact that they are German or British or existing in
the twentieth century. The relevant things they have in common
will no doubt be that they do or do not protect certain interests;
that they rest or do not rest upon coercion or upon consent in
various senses; that they embody certain electoral and constitutional procedures. As criteria for testing the deserts of
political societies, some of these criteria may conflict (the consent criterion, for example, perhaps conflicts with the protection of interests criterion). But the moral of that would seem
to be that we should argue out which we hold to be the most
important, or whether some criteria are vital in some circumstances and others in others. Having done that, we ought to be
in a position to generalize, at least to the extent of saying that
systems of government which perform such and such functions
merit allegiance. We may never agree about it, but it surely is
not 'stretching language beyond the bounds of significance'[2]

---

[1] Margaret Macdonald. 'The Language of Political Theory', in *Logic and Language*, ed. A. G. N. Flew (1951), p. 183.
[2] Ibid., p. 184.

to try. 'Why, in general, ought one to obey laws?' perhaps ought not to be confused with 'What single general criterion will always decide whether a law ought to be obeyed?'

A related tactic also aimed at dismissing the need for any general justification for obedience to law, government, or political authority is to suggest that the notion of allegiance is 'analytically connected with the concept of political society and with the idea of authority'.[1] 'Why ought we to obey government?' may then be said to be a pointless query, since to refer to something as 'the Government' is a way of saying that it has authority. To hold that someone has authority just is to say, amongst other things, that he or they ought to be obeyed. So to ask why we ought to obey government is 'rather like asking "Why ought we to do what we ought to do?"'.[2]

But perhaps these tactics dispose of matters too quickly. Of course the question 'Why should we obey those authoritative agencies who are entitled to our obedience?' is otiose. But the notion of 'authority' which, it is alleged, is entailed in the idea of government is itself imprecise. One sense of 'authority' is connected with the idea of legitimacy of origin or title. Rulers or governmental agencies or law-makers may possess authority in this sense. But whether and under what conditions those who possess authority (and analytically a title to obedience), in the sense of having legitimacy of origin, may be held to have lost their title to obedience is a question which remains open to argument.

Again, the notion of accepting or consenting to the exercise of authority has no single or simple meaning. It obviously is not to be understood in terms of acknowledging a simple right to issue orders or to require unqualified obedience. It is in fact a commonplace that the acceptance of authority commits nobody to unlimited obedience. Not even Hobbes believed that it did. Generalizations of several kinds therefore seem possible. They may be about the sorts of governmental agencies which ought in general to be accorded authority and obedience; and they may be intended to specify under what conditions and with what exceptions obedience may legitimately be limited or withheld. This second question as to the 'limits' of obedience raises

[1] Thomas MacPherson, *Political Obligation* (1967), p. 65.
[2] Ibid., p. 60.

a number of distinct issues besides the traditional one about the conditions under which law-makers lose their legitimacy or general title to obedience.

3. 'LIMITS' OF OBLIGATION

Three such questions are:

1. Under what conditions (if any) may obedience be withheld from particular laws validly made by law-makers who have not lost their general legitimacy or title to obedience?
2. What duty (if any) exists to continue, in certain circumstances, to give obedience to the laws of legislators who have lost their title to obedience?
3. What duties exist where the validity of laws or the authority of law-makers is legally or constitutionally doubtful?

None of these three questions has until very recently been discussed in much detail by political or legal theorists.

An important consequential problem about the limits of obligation and obedience is that the notion of 'rejecting', or 'withdrawing obedience' to, laws, which occurs as an element in each of the three questions, is itself a vague idea which may cover a range of activities. The withdrawal or cessation of obedience which is described by traditional social-contract theorists is usually an all-or-nothing affair. Abuse and forfeiture of authority leads to what may be described as 'an appeal to heaven' or in extreme cases, such as Hobbes's, a relapse into a state of nature or war. In either case governmental failure or excess brings about a replacement of the offending sovereign organ, and there is no place for either a manual of tactics or a moral assessment of the various intermediate courses of action which may face citizens between the extremes of courteous agitation and armed rebellion. Nor is there anything much to be gathered about the degrees of toleration to be extended to validly made but unwise, bad, unprincipled, or ridiculous laws. This last question introduces an obvious complication into the discussion of 'limits of obligation'. In one sense the limits of obligation might be stated by specifying the things, or kinds of things, which ought not to be imposed on citizens as obligations. Nevertheless, there may be things which, on any theory, it is improper to impose but which, if imposed, ought not necessarily to be resisted. In a liberal society, for example, censorship of the press, or an inequitable conscription law, might be held to be things which ought not to be imposed, but their actual imposition by law may not automatically invest citizens with a good moral title to resist their application. That, of course, would be true in certain senses of 'resist' and untrue in others. Anyone who dislikes a law is entitled lawfully to resist its making and to continue to resist its application afterwards by agitation of certain kinds within the existing law. Such a person might be said to reject or not to accept the law, or alternatively the term 'rejection' might be reserved for the point at which disobedience to, or non-compliance with, the law takes place. This stage may be preceded by legal advocacy of non-compliance and possibly illegal incitement to non-compliance. It may be succeeded in the scale of disobedience by passive or non-violent resistance to enforcement, violent resistance to enforcement, obstruction or organized disobedience to other unrelated legislative or administrative measures, and, at the extreme end of the scale, by sabotage and revolutionary attempts to supplant and replace the existing governmental authority. Some of these activities might be described as 'protest', and others as 'civil disobedience', and others still as 'rebellion'. Two morally significant points on this scale are: first, where 'protest' and 'non-acquiescence' merge into 'non-compliance' and illegality; and, secondly, where illegality is accompanied by violence. It may not always, incidentally, be possible, ahead of time, to classify any particular activity as being on one side or the other of these borderlines. The first borderline—between legality and illegality—is vague, because some parts of the law of public order are unclear, and even more so in jurisdictions where questions of the constitutionality of the laws themselves may be in dispute. The second borderline is unclear because violence has degrees and the concept of violence has imprecise boundaries. Physical harm to persons is one obvious form of violence, but there may be other forms of coercion or pressure (intimidation, victimization, boycott, and non-physical damage to persons or property) which might or might not be characterized as in some sense violent or aggressive.

4. MEANING OF 'CIVIL DISOBEDIENCE'

Both violence and the question of legality affect the way in which we apply concepts such as 'direct action' and 'civil disobedience'. The adjective 'direct' is presumably intended to point a contrast with action that is protracted, normal, and legitimate. 'Direct' action, though it may not involve physical damage to persons or property (as a refusal to pay income tax, for example, would not) is nevertheless coercive. It is intended on a large or small scale as a threat or weapon invoked to short-circuit normal processes of argument, negotiation, or legislation. Not all forms of direct action, however, need necessarily be thought of as 'civil disobedience'. A distinction may be made between actions which violate what are admitted to be valid laws and actions which, though involving conflict with civil authorities, are undertaken to vindicate legal or constitutional rights against persons or agencies who are (or are alleged to be) improperly and illegally denying them and infringing the laws. This distinction is clearest where direct action takes place in the context of a federal system or where there are constitu-tional limitations on the kinds of laws which legislators can constitutionally make, as in the United States, where such action has been directed against state officials failing to comply with federal constitutional requirements or, for that matter, against federal law which is, or may turn out to be, unconsti-tutional. Some have wished to say that in these circumstances 'such action involves no civil disobedience—no violation of law in the ultimate sense—because the only orders that are violated are nullities' and 'to talk about this kind of assertion of con-stitutional rights as civil disobedience is extremely dangerous because it lumps lawful with lawless conduct and gives the erroneous impression that both are permissible if only one is sympathetic enough to the demonstrators' "objectives"'.[1] It may, of course, be that in appropriate circumstances both are morally permissible, or that neither is. There may also be some-thing to be said for confining the term 'civil disobedience' to action directed against laws conceded to be valid. This ter-minology does, however, involve some difficulties. It implies that

[1] Archibald Cox, 'Direct Action, Civil Disobedience and the Constitution', in Cox, Howe, and Wiggins, *Civil Rights, the Constitution and the Courts* (1967), p. 9.

it will frequently not be possible to know whether or not 'civil disobedience' is occurring, since it may be unclear whether the activities or laws which are the subject of protest are or are not nullities, and it may be a matter of years before appellate courts have settled this constitutional issue. Moreover, there is the difficulty of assessing the relevance of a sincerely held but erroneous belief by those engaging in direct action that the objects of that action are illegal activities. Ought we to narrow the definition of civil disobedience to exclude from it not only those attempting to vindicate law but also those whose action is mistakenly based on the belief that they are vindicating law rather than violating it? Is there an important moral gulf to be found dividing those who turn out to be right on this issue from those who guess wrong? Will it be any more difficult to make moral judgments about civil disobedience if we do spread the notion of civil disobedience to cover all those who engage in direct action against asserted official authority, whatever the status of that authority is, or ultimately turns out to be? The phrase may perhaps do better service as a convenient shorthand for distinguishing between the differing tactics adopted in political agitation than as an aid to the making of moral distinctions between worthy and less worthy forms of protest.

5. THE OBLIGATION TO OBEY: ARGUMENTS FROM DEMOCRACY AND CONSTITUTIONALISM

Traditional reflections on the limits of obedience, whether written from a natural law or a utilitarian point of view, suffer from several deficiencies. First, they are cast primarily in terms of the justification of rebellion or replacement of intolerable governments. Secondly, they do not contain much discussion of borderline cases. Thirdly, when they exemplify governmental defects, these may often be described in general terms such as 'despotism' or 'slavery'.

In the *Principles of Political Obligation*, for example, T. H. Green discussed disobedience to law as raising 'two questions . . . which the good citizen should set himself in anticipation of a *possible rebellion*'.[1] John Austin also concluded that although obedience to an established government was normally enjoined

---

[1] *Lectures on the Principles of Political Obligation* (1895), p. 120.

by the Deity (via the principles of utility) disobedience might be useful if it replaced a bad government with a good one. The members of a political society must measure 'the mischief wrought by the actual government' against 'the *chance of getting a better* by resorting to resistance',[1] throwing into the scales the extensive, but possibly passing, evil of the transitional anarchy. Green, on the other hand, seemed to doubt whether anybody is ever likely to make an accurate and impersonal calculation of this kind at a time when resistance to government is in anticipation. The effort to make it, he thought, would probably paralyse the citizen's power of action. In the aftermath of revolutions we can say whether revolutionaries were vindicated by the result, but we cannot tell whether they were doing their duty in acting as they did. For Green a right to resistance can only exist when resistance is justified by the common good, and if that condition is fulfilled there is, for him, a *duty* to resist. Leaving aside situations in which sovereignty is disputed, the duty to resist and replace legitimate authority may be dictated by the common good, Green suggests, in three circumstances. The first is when government is so conducted that there are no legal means of obtaining the repeal of a law (a bad law presumably). The second circumstance is where the political system is so permeated by 'private interests' that there has ceased to be any common interest in maintaining it. The third case is where the authority from which an objectionable command proceeds is so clearly separable from that on which the maintenance of social order and the fabric of settled rights depends that it can be resisted without serious detriment to this order and fabric. The third is an interesting category, but Green unfortunately tells us nothing about it. It is not clear whether, like the first two cases, it is related to the problem of rebellion, or to particular laws. Does it envisage resistance to a *particular* act of authority that is separable from the *general* authority of the law-makers? Or does it refer to the possibility of a successful rebellion or *coup*, in which one government is replaced by another without endangering the fabric of law and order? If it is the second, we learn from Green that we are unlikely to know for sure when action of this kind is a duty in time to act on the knowledge. But all Green's categories remain unexemplified.

[1] *The Province of Jurisprudence Determined*, ed. H. L. A. Hart (1954), p. 54.

How objectionable must laws be and what forms of objectionableness must they embody to endanger the common good and precipitate an exception to Green's rule that 'the common good must suffer more from resistance to a law . . . than from the individual's conformity to a particular law or ordinance that is bad until its repeal can be obtained'?[1]

Apart from Green, English-speaking political theorists have had little to say about the conditions for disobeying law, most of them going no further than advising citizens to weigh the relative advantages of rebellion and anarchy. In the United States Henry Thoreau's essay of 1849 on *Civil Disobedience* did at least embody some more specific assertions.

> Unjust laws exist. [he wrote] Shall we be content to obey them or shall we endeavour to amend them and obey them until we have succeeded, or shall we transgress them at once. . . . Those who call themselves Abolitionists should . . . not wait until they constitute a majority of one before they suffer the right to prevail through them. I think that it is enough if they have God on their side without waiting for that other one. Moreover any man more right than his neighbour constitutes a majority of one already.[2]

Why, he asks, has any man a conscience? 'The only obligation which I have a right to assume is to do at any time what I think right.' As a recipe for the careful citizen Thoreau's formula suffers from certain limitations. It paints a simplified picture of a realm of 'expediency' which is to be the province of government and a realm of 'conscience' which is to be left for the individual. Unhappily the history of public affairs suggests that not much hope exists of sorting social decisions into two such heaps. Men have been found to have conscientious reservations about the propriety or impropriety of almost any course of action. Moreover, conscientious judgment must in any social unit find room for at least some actions and decisions which are acceptable to the agent though thought by him to be wrong. Given, therefore, that the idea of political society involves a partial surrender of judgment and a willingness to see individual inclinations and even moral instincts overruled, the question becomes one of stating the grounds against

---

[1] Green, *Principles of Political Obligation*, p. 11.
[2] Reprinted in A. T. Mason, *Free Government in the Making* (1965), p. 488.

disobedience to valid laws without overstating them. The arguments for Green's 'normal rule', as of the Benthamite maxim 'censure freely, obey promptly', have usually turned upon several loosely related ideas which emphasize majority decision, constitutionality, and consent. These may be identified as arguments about the rule of law, the availability of legal opportunities for the repeal of law, and the presuppositions of the democratic process.

6. THE RULE OF LAW

Citation of the need to maintain the rule of law as an argument against civil disobedience sometimes takes the form of putting into opposition the rule of law and anarchy, or the rejection of all ordered society. It seemingly contrasts unconditional obedience with an unlimited right to subject rules of law to individual judgment. This may lead to remarks such as: 'No one is entitled to take the law into his own hands.' Those who say this seriously must, however, be speaking in an abbreviated way about a particular context (such as, say, present western democratic society) in which it is held that there is no moral right, generally speaking, to disobey the law. So an American critic of direct action may conclude that 'representative government affords the opportunity to secure redress of grievances and the constitution secures enormously wide opportunities to speak, publicize, persuade, and demonstrate, without undermining the force of law. Possibly there are a few rare occasions on which the goal would be so important and so plainly right as to outweigh the price which a challenge to the rule of law exacts from the community. I know of none today.'[1] The 'few rare occasions' suggest that the existence of free speech and representative government may not be the only conditions which govern the possibility of justifiable disobedience to law. It seems, in fact, that the 'rule of law' argument goes no further than establishing the existence in democratically and constitutionally organized societies of a prima facie obligation to obey the law. This may be to say either that (1) it is generally right to obey the law, but in some cases the illegality of a course of conduct may justifiably be regarded as irrelevant, or (2) that

[1] Cox, op. cit., p. 29.

illegality of conduct, though never irrelevant, may sometimes
be overridden by other considerations.[1] The second formulation
seems better, given the assumptions made about law in Western
Europe and the United States.

7. 'CONSENT' TO GOVERNMENT

Like the rule of law argument, various assertions about consent and participation in democratic decision procedures serve
to elaborate the prima facie obligation to obedience, but they
do little to fix its limits. In its simplest form what might be
called the 'democratic process' argument suggests that those
who voluntarily take part in free elections consent to the results
of the electoral and legislative process and cannot 'pick and
choose' which laws they wish to obey. 'Picking and choosing'
of course introduces an air of whim and personal preference and
may be alleged to misrepresent what is involved in conscientious
disobedience on stated grounds. But one might rephrase the
point and say that even carefully reasoned selectivity in matters
of obedience is inconsistent with the implicit consent to subsequent laws given by those who take part in voting.

What is the force of this? In the first place, it cannot be
accepted that there is any simple, agreed relationship between
voting and consent to laws, whether consent is regarded as
actual, tacit, implicit, indirect, or imaginary. Secondly, even
amongst those who believe that consent in some sense can be
inferred from participation in elections there is room for argument about what is consented to.

The phrase 'government by consent' may indeed be used
acceptably without any reference to whether any particular
person has voted at all. There is, in one sense, government by
consent when governments are subject to removal. Many people
take no part in politics and do not vote at elections. Nevertheless, if they could do so and the elections are free they are being
governed by consent. Is the case stronger where people do vote?
'When you vote for a person or a party that wins an election,'
Professor Plamenatz has written, 'you directly consent to his or
to their authority. Even if you dislike the system and wish to

---

[1] This point is made by Richard Wasserstrom in his article, 'The Obligation to
Obey the Law' (1963), *U.C.L.A. Law Review* 780.

change it, you put yourself by your vote under an obligation
to obey whatever government comes legally to power under
the system and this can properly be called giving consent. For
the purpose of an election is to give authority to the people who
win it and if you vote, knowing what you are doing and without
being compelled to do it, you voluntarily take part in the process which gives authority to those people.'[1] To wonder how
far these conclusions are true is to see how indefinite a notion
'consent' is. Does it describe what we do in some way? Can it be
imputed to us or inferred from our actions without our being
aware of it? It is plain enough that many people who take part
in elections may not accept the implications or have, in fact,
any such state of mind as might be inferred from the paragraph
quoted. They may not intend and, on one view, do not consent
to obey. In some voting systems they may be voting in order
to bring the system into disrepute or voting without knowing
who will hold legislative authority as the result of their participation in the election. We may of course hold that certain
psychological attitudes or purposes which people actually have
are improper or indefensible. But this is to treat consent in a
more stipulative sense. 'When you vote, you consent . . .' perhaps is not intended as any form of description of the voters'
minds or of any attitude that they may in fact have, but is something that may rightly be imputed to them when the implications of their conduct are rightly understood—even if not by
them. But however consent is taken, it might be maintained
that the connection between participating in voting procedures
and accepting the results of an election is at least looser than that
between voluntary participation in, and the obligations of, say,
games, bargains, or promises. The kind of political and electoral activity open to, or thrust upon, citizens is not equally a
matter of free choice, and there is no equally well-defined
agreement about the aim or end product of political machinery.
Professor Plamenatz, though he wishes to infer consent from
participation in voting, does not suggest that prior consent
authorizes any governmental action at all without limitation.[2]
Elected governments may betray their election promises, or
acquire oppressive habits, or perhaps interfere with the working

[1] Plamenatz, *Man and Society* (1963), vol. 1, p. 239.
[2] Ibid., p. 240. Cf. *Consent, Freedom and Political Obligation*, p. 172.

of the system by which they were elected. An unstated number of reservations therefore may be understood to be incorporated in the consent to be governed which is given by exercising the right to vote.

Here the differences between different political systems may be relevant. In the United Kingdom, where majority rule is not legally restrained by the provision of a Bill of Rights, there is nothing to guarantee that laws will be just. There may be a general presumption that they will be. But it is a textbook commonplace that the presumption is theoretically capable of breaking down, and that what makes unlimited legislative power morally tolerable to minorities and the citizens in general is the permanent possibility of an extra-legal check to the legal sovereign. The idea of popular resistance as a remote but exist-ent possibility is implicitly written into the political and con-stitutional system. But even when a political system incorporates a Bill of Rights in an attempt to guarantee the compliance of majority action with justice, it is always conceivable that the guarantees may be circumvented or abused, or that they may not extend to all possible areas of injustice. So even here the possibility of resistance to unjust laws might be said to be implicit in the system, and in participating in such a system nobody can be said to have consented to exclude the possibility of disobedience or to have agreed to accept the requirements of any conceivable legislative act or judicial decision.

8. THE 'AVAILABILITY OF REPEAL' ARGUMENT

What of the third set of arguments which turn upon the availability or non-availability of procedures for amending allegedly objectionable laws? Green's discussion in his *Lectures on the Principles of Political Obligation* implies that if such pro-cedures exist, obedience is the only justifiable course until repeal can be secured. But is it the case either that disobedience to a law can always be justified if there is no legal avenue for its repeal or that disobedience will never be justified if there are such avenues? The mere non-existence of a method of repealing a law whose effect, on balance, was entirely beneficial, would obviously not, in itself, entitle anybody to disobey it. Is it any clearer that the existence of an amendment procedure must conclusively rule out disobedience? The existence of a means for securing alteration in the law is a matter of degree. Repeal may be easy, or difficult, or well-nigh impossible. And are we thinking here of legal forms or political possibilities? Suppose that repeal is in practice impossible because there is an insufficiently large majority to pursue the amendment procedure to a conclusion. Such procedures, whether they embody special majorities, joint sessions, or referenda are pieces of constitutional machinery just as are votes by simple majorities, and the same doubts and questions may be raised about them as about the democratic process and 'consent to government' argument. They are conceivably compatible with a high degree of injustice and they may be used to introduce oppressive legal measures as well as to guard against them.

If anything is to be made of the 'availability of repeal' argument, it must at least be widened to include other aspects of the democratic process such as the existence of free speech, a free press, and the right of public meeting, protest, and agitation. All of this may be unavailing in the absence of public opinion and a political community likely to use such channels effectively. But to feed all this into 'the availability of a method of repeal' is to make it very unclear what has to be missing before resort to unlawful disobedience is justified, and what lines can be drawn between the absence of the means of securing repeal, and the absence of inclination or willingness on the part of the majority to permit repeal. There are many laws whose repeal is a practical impossibility because (apart from anything else) they ought not to be repealed.

9. CIVIL DISOBEDIENCE TO VALID LAWS

Given, then, that one has, in general, consented to the authority of the lawgiver, that one accepts the case for maintaining the rule of law, and that political processes of one kind or another offer a possibility that change may sooner or later be brought about without illegality, it seems possible, nevertheless, to conclude that in some circumstances it will still be justifiable to step over the line which divides argument, protest, and agitation from direct and disobedient action. How is the calculation to be made?

Extreme cases present no difficulty. We can in general identify the fundamental principles of western democratic society (freedom, equality, due process, and so forth) and say that laws which invade these principles may deserve disobedience depending upon the degree of iniquity, the spread or frequency of such laws, and the possibilities of alternative remedies to unlawful action. Problematic cases will obviously arise when these considerations conflict—where, for example, a law is highly iniquitous but uncharacteristic of the general body of laws and there has been no attempt to interfere with the normal channels of communications or free speech. Again, a law might not be excessively iniquitous, but one of a body or series of objectionable laws, some of which constituted interferences with the rule of law, the electoral process, or civil liberties.

There might be imagined here an analogy between the citizen's problem of striking a balance before rejecting the moral authority of a law and the problem of balancing which faces constitutional courts before striking down as invalid an act of the legislature. In neither case does it seem possible to formulate any recipe or rule of thumb for performing the calculation. In each case toleration of democratically derived legislative decisions has to be weighed against an individual evaluation of fundamental principles. In the citizen's case a parallel thesis could be constructed to the doctrine that some principles connected with the free working of the political process deserve a 'preferred position'. Doubtful or unwise legislation of many kinds may be enforced or obeyed since it remains possible for errors to be corrected by further democratic argument. But if the civil liberties of speech, assembly, and franchise on which that argument depends are themselves undermined, the basis for tolerance or restraint in the face of legislative or majority judgment is weakened This test or principle is not of course self-applying, since it may be a matter of dispute between the proponents and opponents of a law whether it does in fact invade the area of civil liberty. For those who think that it does, there are further difficulties of weighting and definition. Even in the free speech and civil liberties area, there will be restraints and regulations of behaviour which cannot be counted as invasions or infringements of the relevant freedoms. And even if they can, there are different degrees of infringement or invasion. In one sense a principle is invaded if it is overturned, as the principle of a free press might be entirely subverted by a system of press censorship. But a particular act, not obviously in itself of any great moment, may also be said to invade a principle. The prohibition of the publication of 'pirate' radio programme details in the Marine Broadcasting (Offences) Act, for example, or the proposal to prohibit the publication of opinion polls immediately before general elections, both invade the principle of freedom of speech, without putting freedom of speech in England in jeopardy.

One factor which must be weighed, even where free speech and civil liberties exist, is the relation between the seriousness of the moral objection and the possible speed of the remedy. There is no guarantee that individuals may not be brought face to face with some single requirement which will exact from them what they take to be morally repugnant conduct before there is any question of securing repeal of the law. Objections in the United States to military service in Vietnam might fall into this category. There is also the possibility that moral revulsion may result from governmental action in the executive or foreign sphere, which may take place suddenly and where no question of repeal of legislation can arise. Englishmen involved in the invasion of Egypt in 1956 or Russians ordered into Czechoslovakia in 1968 might well, if convinced that they were engaged in crimes against international morality, remain unconsoled by the thought that they might later return to use their votes or their voices to bring about a change of government or political leadership.

Another element which must enter into the calculations of those who contemplate disobedience to law or to legitimate orders is the immediate and less immediate effect upon society of their unlawful activity. Here they have to meet the argument that their conscientious disobedience, if their example were to be generally followed, would be subversive of law and order. A necessary distinction arises here between the proposition that the concession of a moral right to disobey law on conscientious grounds provides good reasons for less deserving claimants to conscientious scruples to follow suit, and the argument that disobedience in fact causes or stimulates others to similar lawless activity. Some American critics, for example, have attacked

direct action in defence of civil rights by suggesting that the
claims which underlie it provide equally good grounds for
direct action to suppress civil rights. Thus, it may be argued
that those who have violated the law in defence of the rights of
Negroes should consider whether they are asserting a principle
different from that of Governors Barnett and Wallace who
defied Federal court orders to admit Negroes to public schools,
thus exercising out of sincere conviction a right of protest
through non-violent civil disobedience against what they regarded as the immoral fiat of Federal judicial officials.[1] If, it may
be felt, I claim a moral entitlement to break the law when
conscience dictates law-breaking to me, must not the same
principle entitle anyone else who is equally sincere to do the
same when conscience suggests law-breaking to him? In reply
to this it may perhaps be said that whilst what it is right for
me to do must in the same circumstances be right for others too,
'the same circumstances' cannot simply be 'thinking it right to
break the law'. That might be so if sincerity were all that is
required by those who break the law with justification. But
sincere law-breakers may be ill informed, shortsighted, super-
stitious, or stupid, and, whilst their sincerity may in various
degrees excuse them, it does not compel us to approve of what
they do. So we certainly need not endorse the principle that
anyone who breaks the law from sincere conviction is entitled
to do so. There would undoubtedly be some danger to the rule
of law in that proposition.

The argument that a justifiable example of law-breaking may
in fact stimulate others to follow it is, however, a different
matter. There is a possibility that breaking a law for good
reasons may cause other laws to be broken for bad reasons, and
there is some evidence that some who engage in civil disobedience do not care very much if this happens. Those who are
trying to save the world, or their souls, or to bring about a
fundamental re-structuring of human relationships, may under-
standably be reluctant to worry about the secondary effects of
their example on the incidence of, say, shop-lifting or tax-
evasion. At what points, if any, emulation of lawless action
occurs is a question for sociology. But recent history does suggest

---

[1] See Cox, op. cit., p. 14. Cf. Wasserstrom, op. cit., on 'generalization' arguments against disobedience.

that imitation of direct action techniques may spread from one section of the population to another, from one country to another, and from conceivably deserving issues to possibly less deserving ones. (Nuclear protest, race relations, colonial and foreign policy, university administration, and organized sport.)

In calculating the morality and expediency of direct, disobedient, or violent action, it is necessary to consider what the results of such action have been in the past. It is undeniable that illegal action has sometimes righted wrongs and procured useful changes in the law which would not otherwise have occurred when they did. Possible examples are the voting rights of women, the industrial rights of trade unionists, and the civil rights of American Negroes. But none of these cases is a simple and straightforward case of direct illegal action in a democratic society to force the alteration of valid but unjust laws. The legal rights of trade unionists were unclear. The rights of black Americans have been legally clear and the direct action taken to promote them has at least in part been aimed at invalid laws or illegal administrative action. In the case of the suffragettes it might be said that they were shut out from the political process and had no direct way of acting upon it in a normal way. Examples of straightforward civil disobedience which is admitted to have produced substantial and beneficial results are not particularly easy to assemble, and the full future consequences of recent exercises in direct action are as yet unknown and incalculable.

Disagreements about civil disobedience today are likely to arise not so much from uncertainty about the conditions which would justify it if they were present, but much more from differences of opinion as to whether conditions are or are not present. Thus both A and B may agree that the availability of democratic electoral arrangements, and the existence of free speech, constitute good reasons for excluding direct action. But they may have such divergent views of the nature of society that they are unable to agree whether society possesses these characteristics or not. For this there may be both ideological and psychological reasons. At times of political tension a minority with strong views is peculiarly tempted to cast its disagreement with others into the form of an assertion that there are defects in the political process which are preventing their

P

views from being effectively put to the electorate and that suppression of opinion is being practised. Thus one of the most important conditions for direct action is for them fulfilled. Assertions of this kind were sometimes made by exponents of unilateral nuclear disarmament in the 1950s.[1] Essential facts and arguments, it may be said, are being withheld by those in control of the mass media and by the leadership of the major political parties. Free speech and free choice are therefore an illusion. It is not easy to make effective political propaganda with the slogan that the people are wrong although no one is deluding them.

Suggestions of this kind may be reinforced by some current political theory whose exponents insist that freedom of speech, or indeed freedom of any kind, cannot exist in any advanced industrial society. This being so, traditional forms of protest are pointless. The system simply absorbs and tolerates them, whilst the manipulated masses are unlikely to respond, being in their unawakened state oblivious to the direction in which freedom is to be found. The institutions of capitalist society (or possibly any existing society) may be characterized as coercive —as a form of institutionalized violence against the individual. Consequently those who advocate or use violence against them are not initiating violence but responding to it. Thus violence is given special senses which are difficult to measure or to quantify and in which the breaking of heads by policemen and the raising of taxes by governments fall into the same category.

Social democrats and liberals who characterize society and the idea of violence differently are not, it is clear, going to have much success in debating the morality of civil disobedience with post-Marxian revolutionaries. From their liberal viewpoint the problem is one of measuring and minimizing violence whilst preserving the possibility of some degree of defiance or disobedience to the law when this appears to be morally required. Their excursions into illegality must be adjudged in relation to the prospective evil and to the short- and long-term damage to the continued observance of laws which they themselves wish to be obeyed. Several different forms of their dilemma may be presented to them. They may themselves

---

[1] For some examples see L. J. Macfarlane, 'Disobedience and the Bomb' (1966), *Political Quarterly* 366.

decide to disobey a law and accept the legal penalties. Or they may couple individual refusal of a legal obligation with active counselling or incitement of others to disobey. The first is of course a form of submission to the law rather than a rejection of its general authority. But this choice only presents itself where law imposes an unwelcome obligation. If the law is morally objectionable to the individual not because it imposes an obligation but because it permits what he deems morally impermissible, he can neither break the law himself nor provoke others to break it. If urging others not to take advantage of the law is ineffective and the issue is of sufficient moral importance he can only make his protest by breaking other obligation-imposing laws in an attempt to enforce repeal of the disputed provision.

10. OBLIGATION IN CONDITIONS OF UNCERTAIN OR DISPUTED VALIDITY

In many cases at the present time the distinction between disobeying unjust but valid laws and disobeying what is alleged not to be law at all may be less clear-cut than is suggested by those who see a patent moral distinction between 'lawful' and 'lawless' civil disobedience. In a society which recognizes—as most do—constitutional restrictions of legislative power, any law which is bad enough to deserve disobedience will be arguably in breach of one or other of the basic rights or freedoms. Those who disobey can at least assert that they are acting not against, but in defence of, the law, and if their instincts are sound they may often eventually be acknowledged to be right. The war which is resisted may turn out to have been improperly declared; the draft law may be a violation of equal treatment provisions; punishment for alleged offences of incitement, or obstruction of administrative measures, may be infringements of the freedoms of speech and assembly. In a society without justiciable guarantees of this kind, similar forms of resistance to authority would have to be posited on the determination to make the law what it ought to be. Though such action stands no chance of ultimate legal vindication by any domestic tribunal, it might be claimed that its illegality results from local constitutional defects and that resistance is in no way hostile to the rule of law but is undertaken in deference to legal standards which ought to be incorporated in all legal systems.

Where disobedience is contemplated in pursuance of asserted legal rights, problems arise, both for the individual and society, both as to what is expedient and as to what is right. Direct assertion and exercise of a legal right where the issue is disputed may be more prudent in some fields than in others. In the field of public order, for example, it may not always be expedient forcibly to resist what are believed to be illegal measures such as arrest, or to resist the police in the exercise of an asserted right of public meeting. In other spheres there may be fewer disadvantages involved in a direct exercise of the right, say, of free speech or of franchise, even in the face of official attempts to deny or obstruct the exercise of such rights. Where the issues are genuinely in doubt, and violence or loss of life might result from the assertion of rights, the vindication of such rights by legal process where possible is an obvious alternative, to be rejected to the extent that the evil suffered is great and the prospects of legal or political redress remote or non-existent.

For society, dealing with a dissident but conscientious minority, there also exists a problem of expediency. Whilst it would be absurd to create a legal privilege to violate any law in order to contest its constitutionality, it does not follow that all such violations should be prosecuted or severely punished if prosecuted to conviction.[1] The areas in which a case for tolerance can be made are not difficult to identify. They are obviously those military and medical spheres in which men are involved in others' lives and deaths. Provided that the tolerance extended is a regulated one (which may entail imposing alternative duties or obligations which do not violate conscience) it is unlikely that a liberal society will suffer serious damage from the admission of a principle of conscientious dissent, even if some citizens escape entirely from what others believe to be their legal and moral obligations.

Two conclusions do not, however, follow from this concession. The principle of tolerance for conscientious dissent cannot here, any more than with dissent from admittedly valid laws, be a general one. It is surely saying too much to urge that 'we should

---

[1] Cf. Ronald Dworkin, 'On not Prosecuting Civil Disobedience', *New York Review of Books*, 6 June 1968; and 'Taking Rights Seriously', ibid. 17 Dec. 1970.

defend the social and moral right to disobey a law that one sincerely believes will be held unconstitutional, even though he turns out to be wrong' in order to 'conform the law to the demands of conscience'.[1] Outside a narrow, if vaguely delimited sphere, we do not need to concede any immunity from the normal forms of prosecution and penalty. We do not strive to find alternative forms of social service for those who conscientiously object to the imposition of income-tax or to the filling of census forms, or to the acquisition of their property by public authorities, however sincere their belief that the State's demands are invalid or unconstitutional. A legal system which permitted unlimited exemptions from commonly imposed obligations, turning simply on the sincerity of the dissenters' belief, would not be inconceivable, but it would be one which neglected the task of protecting the rights of the majority of citizens.

A second conclusion equally does not follow from the admission of a limited policy of tolerance to dissenters. Those who dissent need not be conceded any immunity from the consequences of breaching other laws which they may infringe in the course of propagating their opinions about law or morality. A man who burns a draft card or stops traffic may properly be made to suffer the usual penalties for obstruction or damage to government property whatever sincerely held legal or philosophical principles have motivated his action. Public order in general is patently not one of the spheres in which minority disobedience based on sincere conviction is respected. Those whose scruples drive them to violent protest will in all likelihood believe and say either that law and order are secondary to the need to establish the truth of their beliefs or that the law and order in question is corrupt and worthless, being that of a repressive and immoral establishment. If they are right about this it will be wrong to punish them; if not, not.

An extreme condition of uncertainty about obligation occurs when there is doubt not about the validity of particular laws but about the legitimacy of the law-making authority and therefore about all the laws. The occurrence of revolutions, *coups d'état*, military government, and experiments in autochthonous constitution-making expose the difficulty most clearly. If those who seize power are, *ex hypothesi*, not in a position to make valid

[1] Cox, op. cit., p. 27.

law there can be no question of any obedience to law. But there obviously remains a serious issue, sooner or later, about obedience to the commands or alleged laws of those newly in control of the machinery of legislation and administration. May one here argue that in this situation all obligation is dissolved? It would have to be from some such view that one could draw the inference that 'any man in Rhodesia after the Unilateral Declaration of Independence was morally entitled to disobey the enactments of the illegal regime, as any man in Britain would have been had Parliament not been dissolved in October 1964'.[1] On the other hand, some political theorists (in disputing the ideas of consent or social contract as foundations of obedience to government) have claimed that the right to obedience is earned by the protection of rights. Thus 'where government protects men's rights they ought to obey it whether or not they have consented to do so'[2]—and whether or not, presumably (if protection of rights is a necessary and sufficient condition for obedience), the governors are in possession of any legitimate title to exercise legislative power. The difficulty about the notion of 'protecting rights' is to know what it includes. It is possible to envisage a bloodless revolution in which law and order (in a sense) and the safety of the inhabitants continue to be secured. But many illegal seizures of authority do not proceed with such smoothness. There may be some rights which are not in fact threatened, but the question could in many cases be raised whether a group of politicians or soldiers who have ignored the principle of legality to the extent of usurping the authority of the legitimate law-maker can ever properly be described as 'protecting rights', particularly if they subsequently take steps that appear to threaten civil liberties. What then is the citizen's obligation at the point at which major illegality occurs? Suppose that the United Kingdom Parliament were not in fact to be dissolved within the five-year limit set by the Parliament Acts. Suppose that no enabling amendments were passed, that existing members of Parliament and ministers decided not to submit themselves to re-election and that the police and armed services continued to obey orders. Would Englishmen be morally entitled to refuse to pay income-tax, decline mili-

[1] J. R. Lucas, *The Principles of Politics* (1966), p. 332.
[2] John Plamenatz, *Man and Society*, vol. 1, p. 224.

tary service, or disregard any future amendments to the Road
Traffic Acts? Would they be entitled to set up barricades and
embark on insurrectionary activities in an attempt to compel
the holding of a General Election and a return to legality?

Fortunately this example, besides being happily remote from
reality, is lacking in hypothetical factual background. We do not
know why the supposed illegal behaviour has taken place and
we do not know whether anyone has tried to contest the questions at issue or subsequent alleged acts of legislation in the
courts, or if this has happened and judicial declarations have
been ignored. The attitude of the judges, though it cannot be
morally conclusive, is an important element in the citizen's calculations.

For the citizen, and for foreign observers, moral judgment in
actual revolutionary situations is complicated by the fact that
theoretically distinct situations may be difficult to separate.
T. H. Green, for example, saw some importance attaching to
the question whether there was a genuine competition between
contesting Sovereigns or some alternative determinate authority.
But this question is likely to be obscured by revolutionary assertions of the existence of geographically distinct governments in
exile or embryo. Factual questions about the control exercised
over territory are confused when a part of what is at issue is
what the sovereign territorial unit is in cases where schism takes
place. (Is the relevant territory Britain plus Rhodesia or simply
Rhodesia?) Again, no agreement may be possible about whether
the citizen is confronting a situation in which revolution is
complete, or in which the constitutionality of government action
is merely doubtful. For Green, when sovereignty was in abeyance because of competing sovereign claims, there was nothing
amounting to a right on either side of the conflict and the citizen
had no rule of right to guide him. (He had, we gather, to hope
that the goodness of his character would propel him in the right
direction.) But whether, for example, the sovereignty of the
United Kingdom Parliament was in abeyance in Rhodesia in
1967 was, as we have seen, not simply a question of fact and
by no means a question of simple fact.

Judgment in the Rhodesian situation involved assessment of
the future course of British policy and a calculation about the
effects of domestic and foreign economic activity. But suppose

these doubts to be cleared up and a revolutionary regime to be in effective control of the territory, unthreatened by external intervention and retaining the allegiance of the civil and military forces. What then is the obligation of the citizen? We have seen that courts might in a legal emergency see a distinction between the edicts of illegitimate authorities regulating the ordinary affairs of life, and edicts essentially connected with the imposition or prolongation of the usurper's alleged authority.[1] But this principle seems as difficult to apply with any rigour as a guide to moral obligation as it does when it is considered as a criterion of legal validity, and for similar reasons. Many of the rules and incidents of ordinary life assume a different character altogether when enacted and enforced by a usurper. Almost everything that he or they do that protects or maintains the revolutionary order is connected with the maintenance of its authority against the legitimate ruler. Even to have life go on in a normal fashion is an important element in the consolidation of a usurper's position. In maintaining law and order, and even the regularity of private transactions, the citizen is assisting the regime to establish its claim to effective control. How far is it morally right or obligatory to give such aid? May it not be better to obey where necessary, to disobey where possible, and to overthrow when reasonable? The answer must platitudinously depend upon the conduct of the regime and of the legitimate authorities. It may in some circumstances be a moral duty to obey all the edicts of the new regime, even those designed to preserve its illegitimate authority. Revolutions are not identical in character and the conduct of revolutionaries has not been the same in, say, the American colonies, Russia, Spain, Pakistan, Greece, Nigeria, and Rhodesia. Reflection on the existence of governments established by legal and political revolutions, however, may mask the elementary truth that they earn their moral title to obedience by acting justly and not by longevity. Tyrannies, however firmly entrenched, deserve to be overthrown. We need not infer that any particular person or government has a duty to overthrow them. The maxim *Fiat justitia, ruat coelum* is, as David Hume said, evidently false; and perhaps more evidently so in our time than in his.

---

[1] See above, chap. 3, pp. 67–9.

BIBLIOGRAPHY

THE LAW AND THE CONSTITUTION

JOHN AUSTIN, *The Province of Jurisprudence Determined*, ed. H. L. A. Hart (1954), Lecture VI, pp. 257–68.

F. W. MAITLAND, *The Constitutional History of England* (1909), pp. 526–39.

A. V. DICEY, *Introduction to the Study of the Law of the Constitution*, 10th edn., pp. 1–38, 417–73, and Introduction by E. C. S. Wade, sections 2 and 5.

SIR IVOR JENNINGS, *The Law and the Constitution*, 5th edn., chaps. ii and iii.

K. C. WHEARE, *Modern Constitutions*, 2nd edn. (1966), chaps. 1 and 3.

J. D. B. MITCHELL, *Constitutional Law*, 2nd edn. (1968), chaps. 1–3.

S. A. DE SMITH, *The Lawyers and the Constitution: an Inaugural Lecture* (1960).

A. L. GOODHART, 'An Apology for Jurisprudence' in *Interpretations of Modern Legal Philosophers*, ed. P. Sayre (1947).

—— book review, 75 *Law Quarterly Rev.* 112.

O. HOOD PHILLIPS, *Constitutional and Administrative Law*, 4th edn. (1967), chap. 4.

—— 'Constitutional Conventions: Dicey's Predecessors', 29 *Modern Law Rev.* 137.

—— 'Constitutional Conventions: a Conventional Reply', *Journal of the Society of Public Teachers of Law* (1964–5), N.S. vii, p. 60.

THE STATE, THE CROWN, AND THE EXECUTIVE

F. W. MAITLAND, 'The Crown as Corporation', 17 *Law Quarterly Rev.* 131 (1901).

—— *The Constitutional History of England* (1909), pp. 387–447.

H. C. DOWDALL, 'The Word "State"', 39 *Law Quarterly Rev.* 98 (1923).

W. W. WILLOUGHBY, *The Fundamental Concepts of Public Law* (1924), chaps. iv, v, and xxv.

W. W. BUCKLAND, *Some Reflections on Jurisprudence* (1945), chap. vii.

HANS KELSEN, *General Theory of Law and State* (1945), part 2.

KENNETH C. COLE, 'The Theory of the State as a Sovereign Juristic Person' (1948), *American Political Science Review* 16.

D. M. WALKER, 'The Legal Theory of the State', 65 *Juridical Rev.* 255 (1955).

DONALD THOMPSON, 'The Committee of 100 and the Official Secrets Act' (1963), *Public Law* 201.

J. D. B. MITCHELL, *Constitutional Law*, 2nd edn. (1968), chaps. 9 and 17.

W. FRIEDMANN, 'The Shield of the Crown', 23 *Australian Law Journal* 275 (1950).

—— *Law and Social Change in Contemporary Britain* (1951), Chap. 12.

LOUIS L. JAFFE, 'Suits against Governments and Officers: Sovereign Immunity', 77 *Harvard Law Review* 1, 209 (1963).

LEGISLATIVE POWER AND SOVEREIGNTY

SIR FREDERICK POLLOCK: 'Sovereignty and Legislation', *History of the Science of Politics* (1918), p. 98.

W. W. WILLOUGHBY, *The Fundamental Concepts of Public Law* (1924), chaps. vii and ix.

A. V. DICEY, *Introduction to the Study of the Law of the Constitution*, 10th edn., part I.

SIR I. JENNINGS, *The Law and the Constitution*, 5th edn., chap. iv.

D. V. COWEN, 'Legislature and Judiciary', 15 *Modern Law Rev.* 282 and 15 *Modern Law Rev.* 273.

H. W. R. WADE, 'The Legal Basis of Sovereignty' (1955), *Cambridge Law Journal* 172.

R. F. V. HEUSTON, *Essays in Constitutional Law*, 2nd edn. (1964), chap. 1.

J. D. B. MITCHELL, *Constitutional Law*, 2nd edn., chap. 4.

G. MARSHALL, *Parliamentary Sovereignty and the Commonwealth* (1957).

G. SAWER, *Modern Federalism* (1968), chap. vii.

W. J. STANKIEWICZ (ed.), *In Defence of Sovereignty* (1968).

H. L. A. HART, *The Concept of Law* (1961), chaps. iv and vi.

—— 'Bentham on Sovereignty' (1967), *Irish Jurist* 327.

—— 'Self-referring Laws', *Festskrift till Karl Olivecrona* (1964), p. 307.

ALF ROSS, 'On Self-reference and a Puzzle in Constitutional Law', *Mind* (1969), p. 1.

S. A. DE SMITH, 'Constitutional Lawyers in Revolutionary Situations', 7 *University of Western Ontario Law Rev.* 93 (1968).

A. M. HONORÉ: 'Reflections on Revolutions' (1967), *Irish Jurist* 268.

J. RAZ, *The Concept of a Legal System* (1970), chaps. 1–2.

JUDGES AND LEGISLATORS

OLIVER WENDELL HOLMES, 'The Theory of Legal Interpretation', 12 *Harvard Law Review*, 417 (1899).

MAX RADIN, 'Statutory Interpretation', 43 *Harvard Law Rev.* 863 (1930).

FELIX FRANKFURTER, 'Some Reflections on the Reading of Statutes', 47 *Columbia Law Rev.* 527 (1947).

Committee on Ministers' Powers, Cmd. 4060 (1932), Annex V.

RUPERT CROSS, *Precedent in English law* (1968), chap. v.

J. L. MONTROSE, 'Judicial Implementation of Legislative Policy', 3 *University of Queensland Law Journal* 139 (1957).

—— 'The Treatment of Statutes by Lord Denning', 1 *University of Malaya Law Rev.* 87 (1959).

GERALD C. MACCALLUM, JR., 'Legislative Intent' (1966), 75 *Yale Law Journal* 754 (also in R. S. Summers, *Essays in Legal Philosophy* (1968)).

Report of the Law Commission and the Scottish Law Commission on the Interpretation of Statutes, H.C. 256 (1969).

LOUIS L. JAFFE, *English and American Judges as Lawmakers* (1970).

THE SEPARATION OF POWERS

M. J. C. VILE, *Constitutionalism and the Separation of Powers* (1967).

W. B. GWYN, *The Meaning of the Separation of Powers* (Tulane Studies in Political Science, 1965).

MALCOLM P. SHARP, 'The Classical American Doctrine of the Separation of Powers', 2 *Univ. of Chicago Law Rev.* 385 (1935).

JAMES B. THAYER, 'Origin and Scope of the American Doctrine of Constitutional Law', 7 *Harv. L. Rev.* 129 (1893).

E. S. CORWIN, 'The Higher Law Background of American Constitutional Law', 42 *Harv. L. Rev.* 149, 365 (1928, 1929).

—— 'The Basic Doctrine of American Constitutional Law', in *American Constitutional History: Essays*, ed. Mason and Garvey (1964).

ALAN F. WESTIN, Introduction and Bibliography to Charles A. Beard, *The Supreme Court and the constitution* (1962 edn.).

C. J. POST, *The Supreme Court and Political Questions*, Johns Hopkins Studies in Historical and Political Science (1936).

Louis L. Jaffe, 'Delegation of the Legislative Power' (1947), 47 *Columbia Law Reveiw* 359.

G. Sawer, 'The Separation of Powers in Australian Federalism', 35 *Australian Law Journal*, 177 (1961).

J. M. Finnis, 'Separation of Powers in the Australian Constitution' (1968), 3 *Adelaide Law Review* 154.

S. A. de Smith, 'The Separation of Powers in New Dress', 12 *McGill Law Journal* 491.

CIVIL RIGHTS

H. J. Laski, *A grammar of politics* (5th edn. 1948), chap. 3.

Sir I. Jennings, *The Law and the Constitution* (5th edn.), chap. viii (Fundamental Rights).

K. C. Wheare, *Modern Constitutions* (2nd edn. 1966), chap. 3.

S. A. de Smith, *The New Commonwealth and its Constitutions* (1964), chap. 5.

—— 'Constitutional Guarantees' 1966–7, *McGill Law Journal* 491.

D. V. Cowen, *The Foundations of Freedom* (1961), chaps. 6 and 7

H. Street, *Freedom, the Individual and the Law* (2nd edn. 1967).

E. S. Corwin, *The Constitution and What it Means Today* (12th edn.), pp. 188–240.

Charles L. Black, Jr., *The People and the Court* (1960).

International Commission of Jurists, *The Rule of Law and Human Rights: Principles and Definitions* (1966).

D. D. Raphael (ed.), *Political Theory and the Rights of Man* (1967).

EQUALITY UNDER THE LAW

J. Fitzjames Stephen, *Liberty, Equality, Fraternity*, 2nd edn. (1874), chap. v.

J. R. Pennock and J. W. Chapman (eds.); *Nomos IX, Equality* (Yearbook of the American Society for Political and Legal Philosophy, 1967).

B. Barry, *Political Argument* (1965), chaps. vii and ix.

B. Williams, 'The Idea of Equality', in Laslett and Runciman (eds.), *Philosophy, Politics and Society*, 2nd series (1962).

D. D. Raphael, 'Equality and Equity', *Philosophy*, vol. xxi, p. 1 (1966).

—— *Problems of Political Philosophy* (1970), chap. 7.

W. VON LEYDEN: 'On Justifying Inequality' (1963), *Political Studies* 56.

S. M. HUANG-THIO, 'Equal Protection and Rational Classification' (1963), *Public Law*, 412.

E. S. CORWIN: *The Constitution of the United States of America: Analysis and Interpretation*, 1964 edn., pp. 1073–1329.

H. WECHSLER: 'Towards Neutral Principles of Constitutional Law', 73 *Harvard L. Rev.* 1 (1959).

CHARLES L. BLACK JR., 'State Action, Equal Protection and California's Proposition 14', 18 *Harvard L. Rev.* 69 (1960).

CARL A. AUERBACH, 'The Re-apportionment Cases: One Person, One Vote—One Vote, one Value' (1964), *Supreme Court Review* 1.

A. COX, *The Warren Court* (1967), chaps. 2, 3, and 6.

FREEDOM OF SPEECH AND ASSEMBLY

J. S. MILL, *On Liberty*, chap. ii.

J. FITZJAMES STEPHEN, *Liberty, Equality, Fraternity*, 2nd edn. (1874), chap. ii.

WALTER BAGEHOT, 'The Metaphysical Basis of Toleration', *Literary Studies*, vol. iii (1913).

WILMORE KENDALL, 'The Open Society and its Fallacies' (1960), *American Political Science Rev.* 972.

J. R. LUCAS, *Principles of Politics* (1966), ss. 68–70.

H. J. McCLOSKEY, D. H. MONRO, 'Liberty of Expression: its Grounds and Limits' (1970), *Inquiry* 219, 238.

J. D. B. MITCHELL, *Constitutional Law*, 2nd edn., chap. 18.

IAN BROWNLIE, *The Law relating to Public Order* (1968).

T. C. DAINTITH, 'Disobeying a Policeman—A Fresh Look at *Duncan* v. *Jones*' (1966), *Public Law* 248.

DAVID WILLIAMS, 'Threats, Abuse, Insults' (1967), *Criminal Law Review* 385.

—— *Keeping the Peace* (1967).

—— 'Protest and Public Order' (1970), *Cambridge Law Journal* 96.

—— 'Racial Incitement and Public Order' (1966), *Criminal Law Review* 320.

ANTHONY DICKEY, 'Prosecution under the Race Relations Act 1965 S. 6 (Incitement to Racial Hatred)' (1968), *Criminal Law Review* 589.

ZECHARIAH CHAFEE, *Free Speech in the United States* (1948).

LEONARD W. LEVY, *Freedom of Speech and Press in Early American History: Legacy of Suppression* (1963).

WALLACE MENDELSON, *Justices Black and Frankfurter, Conflict in the Court* (1961).

RONALD GOLDFARB, *The Contempt Power* (1967).

ALEXANDER MEICKLEJOHN, *Political Freedom: The Constitutional Powers of the People* (1965).

THOMAS I. EMERSON, *Toward a General Theory of the First Amendment* (1963).

MARTIN SHAPIRO, *Freedom of Speech: the Supreme Court and Judicial Review* (1966).

EDMOND CAHN, 'Justice Black and First Amendment "Absolutes": A Public Interview', 37 *New York Univ. Law Rev.* 549 (1962).

F. R. STRONG, 'Fifty Years of Clear and Present Danger, from Schenck to Brandenburg—and Beyond' (1969), *Supreme Court Review* 41.

HARRY KALVEN, JR., 'The New York Times Case: a Note on the Central Meaning of the First Amendment' (1964), *Supreme Court Review* 191.

—— *The Negro and the First Amendment* (1965).

C. PETER MAGRATH, 'The Obscenity Laws: Grapes of Roth' (1966), *Supreme Court Review* 7.

HARRY KALVEN, JR., 'The Reasonable Man and The First Amendment: Hill, Butts and Walker' (1967), *Supreme Court Review* 267.

DEAN ALFANGE, JR., 'Free Speech and Symbolic Conduct: The Draft Card Burning Case' (1968), *Supreme Court Review* 1.

THE RIGHT TO DISOBEY THE LAW: CIVIL DISOBEDIENCE

T. H. GREEN, *Principles of Political Obligation* (1895), pp. 110–19.

J. R. LUCAS, *Principles of Politics* (1966), ss. 72–3.

R. WASSERSTROM, 'The Obligation to Obey the Law', *Essays in Legal Philosophy*, ed. R. S. Summers (1968).

A. H. CAMPBELL, 'Obligation and Obedience to Law' (*Proc. of the British Acad.*, vol. 51, p. 237 (1956).

L. J. MACFARLANE, 'Justifying Civil Disobedience', 79 *Ethics* 24 (1968).

—— 'Disobedience and the Bomb' (1966), *Political Quarterly* 366.

STUART M. BROWN, JR., 'Civil Disobedience' (1961), *Journal of Philosophy* 676.

H. A. BEDAU (ed.), *Civil Disobedience: Theory and Practice* (1969).

RONALD DWORKIN, 'Taking Rights Seriously', *New York Review of Books*, 17 December 1970, p. 23.

A. COX, 'Direct Action, Civil Disobedience and the Constitution', Cox, Howe, and Wiggins, *Civil Rights, the Constitution and the Courts* (1967).

I. M. HEYMAN, 'Civil Rights, 1964 Term: Responses to Direct Action', (1965), *Supreme Court Review*, 159.

HOWARD ZIM, *Disobedience and Democracy: Nine Fallacies on Law and Order* (1968).

HERBERT MARCUSE, 'Ethics and Revolution', *Ethics and Society*, ed. R. T. de George (1968).

PAUL F. POWER, 'On Civil Disobedience in Recent American Political Thought' (1970), *American Pol. Sci. Rev.* 35.

GERALD C. MCCALLUM, JR., 'Some Truths and Untruths about Civil Disobedience' (in *Nomos XII, Political and Legal Obligation*, ed. J. Roland Pennock and John W. Chapman (1970).

TABLE OF CASES

LIST OF STATUTES

INDEX

Advocacy, and incitement, 160, 179-83

Allegiance, alleged gaseous character of, 20

Anson, Sir William, 17, 32

'Arbitrariness', senses of, 143

Aristotle, distinction of governmental functions by, 101

Atkin, Lord, and liberal interpretation, 82

Attainder, Bills of, 118, 123, 137

Austin, John:
on constitutional law, 3-5, 6-7
on sovereignty, 35, 37, 38, 39, 44, 126
on disobedience to law, 204-5

Australia, doubtfully autochthonous condition of, 58

Autochthony, 57-64, 219

Bentham, Jeremy:
and divisibility of sovereignty, 36
on judicial function, 87-8
on English liberties, 130
and rights, 128

Bills of Rights, 125-35
Canadian, 126, 127

Black, Charles L., Jr., 175, 177

Black, J.:
on equal protection, 150
on free speech, 163, 173, 174, 179, 185, 186, 189

Blackstone, William, 15, 16, 17, 21, 43-4, 87, 101
'honied Mansfieldism' of, 104
on attainder, 123
on liberty of the press, 170

Bramwell, Lord, 77, 82

Bryce, Lord, on sovereignty, 40

Burlamaqui, J.J. 16

Byles, J., on repair of legislative omissions, 83

Cabinet, 11, 12

Campbell, Enid, 51

Censorship, principle of, 159

Ceylon:
sovereignty in, 53-7
autochthony of, 62

Churchill, Sir Winston, on Statute of Westminster, 76

Civil Disobedience, 195-222

Civil Rights:
objections to formalization of, 125-6
contrasted with economic rights, 134
freedom of speech, 154-94
equality, 135, 136-53
privacy, 146-53

'Clear and Present Danger', 162, 177-9

Coke, C.J., 19
uncompromising ambiguity of, 43

Cole, G. D. H., 13

Coleridge, J., on seditious libel, 181-2

Colonial constitutions, comparability to Dog Acts, 56

Commonwealth, 20
autochthony in, 57-64

Consent, and civil disobedience, 208-10

Constitutional Law, nature of, 3-12

Convention, contrast of with laws, 7-12

Cook, Bishop of Rochester's, boiling of, 138

Cooley, Thomas, 48, 114

Corwin, E. S., 100, 104, 179

Cowen, D. V., 43

Crown:
and King, 17
demise of, 19
and Statute of Westminster, 1931, 19
allegiance to, 19-20
and Commonwealth, 20
privilege, 21, 39
immunities, 21-4, 40
and Public, 24-7
Law Officers of, 26
and interests of State, 30

Curtiss, Charles P., on abuse of legislative history, 93

Davis, K. C., 34

De Gaulle, amendment of French Constitution by, 48

'Delegatus non potest delegare',
dubious truth of, 113-14
inapplicability of to colonial legislatures, 116